Dear Kristin

You can bake and cook
with some patience and
determination!

Good luck and best wishes

Nancy
J

Sizzle AND Drizzle

Sizzle AND Drizzle

Tips for a modern day
home-maker

Nancy Birtwhistle

DAISA & CO
PUBLISHING

Sizzle & Drizzle – Tips for a modern day home-maker published in 2019

Written by Nancy Birtwhistle

A CIP catalogue record for this book is available from the British Library.

Hardback ISBN 978-1-9162023-6-8

Book typeset by:
DAISA & CO PUBLISHING
Barton upon Humber
North Lincolnshire
United Kingdom
DN18 5JR
www.daisapublishing.com

Printed in England

Daisa & Co Publishing is committed to a sustainable future for our business, our readers and our planet. This book is made from paper certified by the Forestry Stewardship Council (FSC), an organisation dedicated to promoting responsible management of forest resources.

This book is dedicated to my Grandparents, though long since passed - they may be watching.

They had patience, skills and an unconditional love. Without their nurturing, teaching and encouragement this book would not exist.

Foreword

Nancy first leapt out of the TV and into my heart when I saw her slay the competition on The Great British Bake Off.

Long before I was on Queer Eye, I was cheering on Nancy as she breezily knew when to employ the use of a microwave to her Bake Off Championship. And so when I later became friends with her through Instagram, I was ecstatic.

Since then, Nancy has been one of my most gratifying Instagram friendships. From baking, to gardening, to organization, resourcefulness, and just her incredible energy, I look forward to seeing what Nancy is up to everyday. She creates art out of everything in her life, and takes so much joy in the process.

I can't wait to have this book, and I know that all of us who read it will become smarter and more clever when it comes to caring for ourselves, our families, and our homes.

Keep slaying, Nancy!

-Jonathan Van Ness
Author 'Over the Top'
Grooming Consultant 'Queer Eye' on Netflix
'Getting Curious' - Apple Podcast with JVN

My Favourite Quote...

"It cannot be denied that an improved system of practical domestic cookery, and a better knowledge of its first principles, are still much needed in this country; where, from ignorance, or from mismanagement in their preparation, the daily waste of excellent provisions almost exceeds belief."

Modern Cookery by Eliza Acton – 1860

Contents

A Letter from Nancy...

I wonder why I wasn't given the name Prudence?

I cannot remember how or when cooking and home-making became part of my being. Making my own, growing my own, making do and mend and generally using every last scrap from the fridge and cupboards. Part for certain, in my younger life, was due to money pressures but also I felt a responsibility against unnecessary waste.

My Grandmother was a huge influence – she had lived through two world wars and during those times people learnt resilience, prudence, self-sufficiency and pride. She taught me to sew, knit, cook and bake and as she described it 'keeping house'. My grandad on the other hand taught me how to grow food, when to sow, identifying problems and when to harvest and how to preserve everything to make sure there were enough provisions to carry us through the winter.

Now in my sixties I consider I have a wealth of experience and knowledge which needs to be shared. I decided to embrace social media as a platform to communicate with this modern age. It took a little time to find my way around but soon I started to gather a 'following' when I announced I would share a hint, tip, 'how to' video or free recipe every day – for a whole year. The first year then became a second and together we have shared problems and solutions, recipes and tips ever since.

The response has been tremendous and here I am almost three years on still visiting thousands of followers' screens every morning. The best of my daily posts are contained within these pages along with links to the videos which have become an integral part of the success of my work.

I have included around 100 recipes with a whole section of 'free from' recipes containing gluten free, fat free, low sugar, dairy free, vegetarian and vegan options. You will also find a section devoted to eco friendly natural cleaning solutions and alternatives to single use plastic.

I feel passionate about my little hints and tips which make such a difference in the kitchen and around the home – these nuggets of knowledge have proved to be super popular amongst followers and I have weaved them throughout this book where appropriate.

Last, but no means least is my life changer!

How many times have you picked up a recipe only to find you don't have the right size tin? The recipe says 9 inch but you have 8 inch and 10 inch – does it matter? YES IT DOES.

No stress though because I have included a table which will calculate for you how you need to adjust your ingredients to achieve the perfect bake in the tin that you own.

I thank each and every one of you for inspiring me to write this book and for keeping me energised and happy!

Now... Let me show you!

Love,

Nancy

Getting Started

Essential Equipment

Whether I am gardening, sewing, knitting, drawing, cooking or baking it is essential I have the right tools for the job.

When it comes to kitchen equipment the number of tools, tins, pans, appliances, gadgets and general clutter are too many to mention and I feel so many of them are unnecessary.

In this book I will keep equipment to a minimum and those items I recommend will be used over and over again.

SAUCEPANS, CASSEROLE PANS AND FRYING PANS

There is an enormous range to suit every kind of kitchen and hob. My only advice is to choose the best you can afford.

Non-stick saucepans are fantastic as long as metal utensils are not used with them which can scratch and eventually damage the non-stick coating.

Glazed cast iron casserole pans are my favourites as they can be used on the hob and then transferred to the oven for long slow cooking.

They can be expensive and heavy but investing in a large casserole will last you a lifetime and can be used for so many recipes.

When choosing a frying pan I select one, which again, I can use on the hob but then can be transferred to the oven if necessary – you will be choosing one with a metal handle rather than plastic.

The advantages of this type of frying pan are many, one being that it is perfect for frying a full English breakfast on the hob but then, on another occasion can be filled with apples and pastry, popped into the oven and double up as a baking dish to produce my delicious Apple Tarte Tatin!

MIXERS

Tabletop mixers have a place in many kitchens and as they can be purchased in a variety of colours have become part of the modern kitchen's look and décor.

They are expensive and for that reason I refer to their use rarely. I use mine for bread making, but for most cakes I use a handheld electric whisk.

The exception to this is when I am making a large wedding cake or my Christmas cake when I use my tabletop mixer.

Handheld whisks can be purchased for as little as £10 and make cake making so much quicker and easier than by hand.

A food processor – now that's a different story.

I always make pastry in mine and I wouldn't be without it. Like everything – top of the range models are expensive but I a good one will last you years. I have a good quality basic model and it has served me for 30 years. It is still going strong so find no reason to change it.

It's worth saving up for one or better still put one on your Christmas list.

A food processor will carry out a whole range of tasks efficiently – blending, chopping, grating, whisking, slicing.

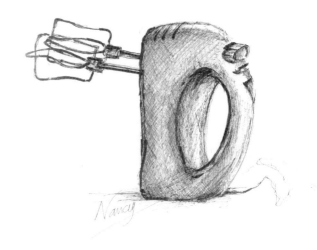

BAKING TINS

Tins can be expensive and even though I have a huge collection which have been bought over the years yet I still seem to stick to my favourites of a regular size.

How many times have you picked up a recipe book, looked at a photograph of a cake, dessert or pastry you want to make but you don't have the right size of tin?

You go out and buy the tin, make the cake (which by the way doesn't look at all like the one in the fancy studio photograph) – you then never use that tin again.

This will not be the case with my recipes because for each one, where practicable my "recipe reckoner" will calculate for you the revised quantities to fit the tins that you already have.

For sandwich cakes I prefer tins with a loose bottom for easy release. For deeper celebration cakes I use a loosed bottom tin with a spring surround.

Do invest in a couple of 1 lb loaf tins – I use them a lot. They are used for bread of course but my Lemon Drizzle Cakes, Malt Loaf, Brioche and Summer Pudding Terrine will be made in these tins.

Deep 12-hole muffin tins will be used regularly throughout this book. You will see that I use these tins for buns and muffins and supporting paper cases for small cakes.

Equally I find them ideal for shaping and baking deep filled pies. My mince pies, pork pies, deep filled cherry and apple pies will all be baked in a deep muffin tin.

Biscuits and scones are baked on flat metal baking sheets. Buy two if you can afford it but one good one is better than two cheap ones.

I have made this mistake then when the sheet goes into the oven it bends and buckles and so do your bakes. Buy one good one and when a recipe calls for a second one turn a roasting tin upside down and bake on the underside.

Essential Bits and Bobs

WEIGHING SCALES

For years I used my Grandmother's Balance Scales and I still treasure them, but they are now a kitchen ornament and souvenir rather than a trusted piece of kit.

Please invest in a set of digital weighing scales – they simplify and speed up your baking preparations.

I routinely place my mixing bowl on the scales, zero its weight, weigh in my butter, zero its weight then add the sugar and so on. You can see that using this method you will save on using extra bowls.

I realise my readers from the US are fond of measures and I have included a conversion chart if that is your preferred system. I strongly recommend that because baking is "exact" in its nature then the digital weighing scales are a must.

MEASURING SPOONS

These are used in most recipes and their measurements are not to be confused with tableware. Teaspoons for example come in all sorts of shapes and sizes whereas a proper measuring spoon will give you the exact 5g / 5ml amount – essential when working with flavourings, spices and extracts.

CUTTERS

There are so many on the market but to start with and for recipes in this book all you will need is a pack of double-sided pastry cutters in metal or plastic.

They come in various sizes – one side fluted and the other side plain. Used for biscuits, scones and tarts they are an essential but inexpensive piece of kit.

BOWLS AND JUGS

Bowls and measuring jugs are used throughout this book. I tend to use Pyrex glass or glazed earthenware jugs rather than metal simply because I can pop them into the microwave when necessary. A small, medium and large mixing bowl should be added to your kitchen collection.

SPOONS AND SPATULAS

Can you believe my favourite spatula is a plastic one I received as a free gift with a magazine? It is small and handy, gets into every nook and cranny and I love it.

Even though I have a full set of different sizes I always reach for the little one. Similarly, a spoon – a metal one is my favourite and will always be used for folding in the flour when cake making.

Don't be tempted on a "full range" of anything.

Choose something that you like and stick to it. A bench scraper is handy when bread making or in fact if you have made a mess on the worktop and need to clean it down quickly.

I have a metal one and a plastic one – I tend to reach for my plastic one for all sorts of jobs including smoothing buttercream.

I include a small angled palette knife here too – great for spreading and smoothing.

WOODEN UTENSILS

My rolling pin must be 40 years old. It is shiny, well used and rarely gets a wash. After use I wipe it with a damp cloth if necessary.

Wooden spoons are great for non-stick pans as they will not damage any non-stick coatings. Always wash wooden spoons by hand – a dishwasher will shorten their life dramatically.

SIEVE

If you don't already have a sieve and wonder which sort to buy – invest in a metal one. I have both plastic and metal; they both work well but of course boiling liquids are best passed through a metal sieve rather than a plastic alternative.

A FEW REUSABLES!

If you haven't yet tried reusable baking parchment I urge you to invest in a sheet or two.

I bake biscuits, flapjack and scones on it, roast potatoes on it, line baking tins with it then a simple wash between uses and it will keep going for years.

My sheets are several years old now – very well used, dark in colour but still going strong. No more scrubbing off baked on deposits.

I used to be a real fan of disposable piping bags but in my drive to reduce the amount of single use plastic I now only use reusable washable ones.

Going back to the old ways

really! I have a selection – a huge one for meringue and smaller ones for royal icing and buttercreams.

There are hundreds of piping nozzles but to start with a plain and star nozzle (plastic or metal) will be all that is required.

Hang onto single use shower caps and use as bowl covers in place of cling film. Particularly good when bread rising – the shower cap actually does a better job than cling film as it provides some expansion space which of course cling film doesn't.

Thought I would just mention a temperature probe. I have one and use it rarely but there are a few recipes in this book where monitoring temperature is essential.

I use it so infrequently I remove the battery before popping it back in my drawer so that it always has life!

Cake Tin Calculators

RECIPE ROUND TINS CALCULATORS...

Recipe Round Tin	Round		Square	
6 inch / 15 cm	7	1.4	6	1.3
	8	1.8	7	1.7
	9	2.2	8	2.3
	10	2.7	9	2.8
	11	3.3	10	3.5
	12	3.8	11	4.2
			12	5.1

Recipe Round Tin	Round		Square	
7 inch / 18 cm	6	0.7	6	0.9
			7	1.3
	8	1.3	8	1.7
	9	1.7	9	2.1
	10	2.0	10	2.6
	11	2.5	11	3.1
	12	2.9	12	3.8

Recipe Round Tin	Round		Square	
8 inch / 20cm	6	0.6	6	0.7
	7	0.8	7	1.0
			8	1.3
	9	1.3	9	1.6
	10	1.5	10	2.0
	11	1.9	11	2.4
	12	2.2	12	2.9

Recipe Round Tin	Round		Square	
9 inch / 23cm	6	0.4	6	0.6
	7	0.6	7	0.8
	8	0.8	8	1.0
			9	1.3
	10	1.2	10	1.6
	11	1.5	11	1.9
	12	1.8	12	2.3

Cake Tin Calculator

RECIPE SQUARE TINS CALCULATORS...

Recipe Square Tin	Round		Square	
6 inch / 15 cm	6	0.8		
	7	1.1	7	1.4
	8	1.4	8	1.8
	9	1.8	9	2.3
	10	2.2	10	2.8
	11	2.6	11	3.4
	12	3.1	12	4.0

Recipe Square Tin	Round		Square	
7 inch / 18 cm	6	0.6	6	0.7
	7	0.8		
	8	1.0	8	1.3
	9	1.3	9	1.7
	10	1.6	10	2.0
	11	1.9	11	2.5
	12	2.3	12	2.9

Recipe Square Tin	Round		Square	
8 inch / 20ccm	6	0.4	6	0.6
	7	0.6	7	0.8
	8	0.8		
	9	1.0	9	1.3
	10	1.2	10	1.6
	11	1.5	11	1.9
	12	1.8	12	2.3

Recipe Square Tin	Round		Square	
9 inch / 23cm	6	0.4	6	0.4
	7	0.5	7	0.6
	8	0.6	8	0.8
	9	0.8		
	10	1.0	10	1.2
	11	1.2	11	1.5
	12	1.4	12	1.8

This table looks complicated at first glance but once you get your head around it you will discover it is a fantastic "ready reckoner" when you want to adapt your favourite recipe to fit a different sized tin.

I have tried to simplify it but then find it just becomes more complicated to explain. Instead I will describe a few scenarios to help you navigate the rows and columns.

THE RECIPE I AM USING IS FOR AN 8 INCH (20CM) ROUND TIN BUT THE TIN I HAVE MEASURES 9 INCHES (23CM).

Go to the table and on the left hand side find the 8 inch round (20cm) section. This represents the recipe you have then go right and under the Round Tin column find your 9 inch (23cm) and you will see the recipe needs to be multiplied by 1.3 in order to achieve a cake of the same height.

E.g.: Your recipe states 180g soft margarine or butter etc.
Multiply 180 x 1.3 = 234g soft margarine or butter needed.

What to do about eggs. If the recipe states 3 eggs.
Multiply 3 x 1.3 = 3.9 eggs (round up to 4 eggs)

Let Me Show You...
Watch My 'Ready Reckoner' Video
SCAN HERE

THE RECIPE I AM USING IS FOR A 6INCH (15CM) ROUND TIN BUT MY TIN IS 8 INCHES (20CM) AND IS SQUARE.

Go to the table and on the left hand side find the 6 inch (15cm) section. This represents the recipe you have then go over to the second right column headed Square Tin and find your 8 inch (20cm) and you will see the recipe needs to be multiplied by 2.2 in order to achieve a finished cake of the same height.

E.g.: Your recipe states 125g soft margarine or butter
Multiply 125 x 2.2 = 275g soft margarine or butter will be needed.

What to do about the eggs. The recipe states 2 eggs.
2 x 2.2 = 4.4 eggs (use 4 eggs plus 1 tbsp milk)

THE RECIPE I AM USING IS FOR A 9INCH (23CM) ROUND TIN BUT MY TIN IS ONLY 7 INCHES (18CM) ALTHOUGH IT IS ROUND.

Go to the table and on the left hand side find the 9 inch (23cm) section.
This represents the recipe you have then go across to the right and find the 7 inch column and you will see the recipe needs to be reduced to 0.6 to achieve the same height to the sponge.

E.g.: Your recipe states 250g soft butter or margarine.
Multiply 250 x 0.6 = 150g butter or margarine needed.

What to do about eggs. If the recipe states 5 eggs.
Multiply 4 x 0.6 = 2.4 eggs (use 4 eggs plus 1 tbsp milk)

When calculating eggs – if your calculations come out at more than 0.5 add another egg. If your calculations are less than 0.5 then add 1 tbsp milk.

When calculating baking times you will find that for sponge cakes the baking time will be approximately the same because the finished sponge is the same height. If your recipe states that your 8 inch cake needs to bake for 20-25 minutes you will find that your adjusted cake – if adjusted to be smaller will be nearer the 20 minutes and if larger may need up to 25 minutes. Either way baking times are not substantially different.

Always check that your sponge is just leaving the sides of the tin, is well risen, springy to the touch in the centre and golden in colour, unless it is chocolate of course.

When it comes to rich fruit cakes – again the baking times are not vastly different. If you follow my Christmas cake recipe you will see that a 9 inch cake bakes for a long 10 hours. I made a smaller 7 inch cake and baked it for just one hour less.

Happy Baking!

Ingredients

You will come across many recipes especially online that will encourage you to use a certain brand of butter, sugar, flour or flavouring. Remember these are probably sponsored sites and the recipe writer will have been paid to promote that particular product.

I would suggest you buy the best you can afford. If you are new to baking are you really going to want to spend your money on 'top end' ingredients when you are experimenting for the first time? I certainly didn't.

BUTTER OR MARGARINE?

There are many out there that would never use soft margarine in cake making. In fact I recall Week 1 in that famous Bake Off tent…

Our Showstopper Challenge was to make 36 mini cakes. Our recipes had been submitted in advance and our ingredients were put out before us on our bench. I looked around the 12 benches and everyone apart from me had requested butter for their cakes. I was the only person with soft margarine. My confidence was wobbling but then I reminded myself that the cakes I was about to make were good – and they were very good as it turned out.

Star Baker was awarded!

Soft margarine creams easily, is less likely to curdle and produces a light sponge. If you choose to use butter, and that is absolutely fine then do make sure it is at room temperature before you start to cream.

If you decide to use butter and I have read so many recipes – some suggest salted and some non-salted.

For me it makes absolutely no difference whatsoever. I buy salted butter, rarely unsalted because the butter I buy is used at the table as well as in baking. There will be chefs who totally disagree with me but I have yet to be convinced.

Nancy's Top Tip

How to get cold butter up to room temperature

It has probably happened to us all. You find yourself in need of room temperature butter but you have forgotten to lift it out of the fridge or maybe your kitchen is as cold as the fridge. Whether you need soft butter for baking, cooking or simply for spreading on bread here is a simple and effective way to soften your butter in a matter of minutes.

Firstly, take a microwave proof bowl or glass that is large enough to cover the butter you need to soften. Rinse the glass or bowl under cold water, don't dry it. Pop the wet glass or bowl into the microwave and heat for one minute on full power. Take the hot bowl from the microwave (use a cloth to protect the hands) then invert it over your piece of cold butter. Leave it for 5 minutes then remove the bowl and your butter will be soft enough to use without any oiliness or melting.

SUGAR

When I was first married I only ever had granulated sugar in the cupboard. Caster sugar was more expensive.

Granulated sugar, whilst being great sprinkled over cornflakes or used to sweeten tea or coffee is course in texture and slow to dissolve when creamed with butter or margarine for a cake. Caster sugar has finer grains and will combine readily with the fat.

Nancy's Top Tip

How to make caster sugar from granulated sugar

If you have run out of caster sugar or indeed bake infrequently and have only granulated sugar you can grind your granulated sugar in a food processor. Simply pop the granulated sugar in the bowl of your machine with the blade attachment attached then blitz for 2-3 minutes. Your sugar will grind down to fine crystals - perfect for baking!

Rich fruit cakes and many dark moist cakes such as gingerbread are better made with brown sugar.

Brown sugar, light, dark, muscovado etc. have a soft texture but once the packet is opened, if not sealed really well afterwards will suffer as the humidity gets to it.

The next time you reach for your packet of dark brown sugar instead of being soft and flowing it will have formed into a brick. The sugar can be rescued but remember next time to put your bag of opened brown sugar into an airtight container to keep it soft and usable.

Nancy's Top Tip

What to do when brown sugar becomes one large lump

Your solid brick of brown sugar can be rescued. Place the required amount for your recipe in a non-metallic bowl. Take a sheet of kitchen paper and dampen with cold water from the tap. Fold the kitchen paper and lay over the sugar in the bowl. Pop into the microwave oven for about 1 minute (for 150g sugar).. Take the bowl from the microwave and you will see the sugar has softened and is good to use.

More sugar will need a longer time but increase just a few seconds at a time. You don't want your sugar to melt.

EGGS

Where would we be without eggs?

Many of my readers will know I keep chickens and have done now for some 15 years. It is a delight to collect eggs each day. Obviously having my own chickens means I have no "use by" dates on my eggs. I write the date on the shell in pencil every day and I have calculated that my eggs remain good for about six weeks not fridged. Supermarket and bought eggs will have a date stamped onto them so the user is well aware of the shelf life. If you are given eggs or, even for me, I find a random egg or have omitted to write the date – how do I know it is good to eat ? All eggs referred to in this book's recipes are large eggs.

Nancy's Top Tips

How to know if eggs are fresh

Take a large jug or bowl of cold water. A fresh egg will sink to the bottom and lay on its side.
An egg that is old but still good to eat will still sink to the bottom but will stand up. A bad egg or an egg not fit to eat will float and is best thrown away. Older eggs (the ones that sit upright but still sink) are perfect for hard boiling because the shells come away much easier.

♥

TIP: Retrieving eggshells from a mixture

Ever dropped a shard of eggshell into your mixing bowl? Try as you might it will refuse to be caught. It will slide off a spoon, will slither away from your finger and will run away from you however you might try to remove it.
Take one of the eggshell halves and take it to that slippery character and without any effort whatsoever you will see it gently swim into that empty shell.
Amazing really – but it works!

FLOUR

I buy self-raising flour for cake making and again there are many brands on the market so buy the flour you can afford. Even though self-raising flour these days is supposed to not require sifting I still do it as a matter of course – just habit I suppose. I believe a lighter, more airy sponge is the result.

Let Me Show You...
Watch My 'Fresh Eggs' Video
SCAN HERE

I will explain how I mix a sponge and the mixing is all important. I rarely use additional raising agent partly because I can taste it – a kind of bitter after taste yet I see many recipes using self-raising flour plus baking powder.

It really is not necessary if the mixing is right.

Nancy's Top Tip

Making Self Raising Flour

If you are out of self raising flour you can make your own but don't be tempted to just make sufficient for your recipe. Make a batch of 500g because then you will know the amount of baking powder added is just right. Take 500g plain flour (or all-purpose flour) and add 15g baking powder (often a sachet weight). Sift the two together, give a really good stir then transfer to a jar and use as necessary.

Let Me Show You...
Watch My 'Brown Flour' Video
SCAN HERE

Cooking Conversion Chart

WEIGHT

IMPERIAL	METRIC
1/2 oz	15 g
1 oz	29 g
2 oz	57 g
3 oz	85 g
4 oz	113 g
5 oz	141 g
6 oz	170 g
8 oz	227 g
10 oz	283 g
12 oz	340 g
13 oz	369 g
14 oz	397 g
15 oz	425 g
1 lb	453 g

TEMPERATURE

FAHRENHEIT	CELSIUS
100 °F	37 °C
150 °F	65 °C
200 °F	93 °C
250 °F	121 °C
300 °F	150 °C
325 °F	160 °C
350 °F	180 °C
375 °F	190 °C
400 °F	200 °C
425 °F	220 °C
450 °F	230 °C
500 °F	260 °C
525 °F	274 °C
550 °F	288 °C

MEASUREMENT

CUP	OUNCES	MILLILETERS	TABLESPOONS
8 cup	65 oz	1895 ml	128
6 cup	48 oz	1420 ml	96
5 cup	40 oz	1180 ml	80
4 cup	32 oz	960 ml	64
2 cup	16 oz	480 ml	32
1 cup	8 oz	240 ml	16
3/4 cup	6 oz	177 ml	12
2/3 cup	5 oz	158 ml	11
1/2 cup	4 oz	118 ml	8
3/8 cup	3 oz	90 ml	6
1/3 cup	2.5 oz	79 ml	5.5
1/4 cup	2 oz	59 ml	4
1/8 cup	1 oz	30 ml	3
1/16 cup	1/2 oz	15 ml	1

Biscuits & Scones

Biscuits

A clue to the origin of the "biscuit" is probably in the word which is French for twice cooked; "bi" meaning two and the verb "cuir" to cook. As far back as the 12th Century reference is made to bread being baked for a second time to dry it out completely.
Fast forward to the 21st Century and there are so many biscuits available to buy in the shops that you may question why there is the need to make them.

The recipes I have chosen are my favourites. Biscuits are great to make with children and if you are feeling particularly patient they can decorate them for Christmas or Easter. Biscuits have a longer shelf life than cake or pastry and make excellent gifts. A few spiced shortbread biscuits beautifully wrapped will delight the most difficult person to buy for.

I routinely reduce the sugar in my baking and biscuits are no exception. As a general rule biscuit dough needs to be on the dry side. The piece of dough may crack a little at the edges when rolling but when cut out it should hold together nicely. A dry but firm dough will bake well, have a good texture and will not spread during baking. If you have made biscuits in the past and taken time to cut out a number of interesting shapes only to find they have spread and become totally unrecognisable in the oven then the dough has been too wet.

When your dough is mixed, rolled out, shapes cut and spread onto a baking sheet pop them into the fridge. To firm up whilst your oven comes to temperature.

Nancy's Top Tip
Rolling out biscuit dough

I always mix a biscuit dough by hand because I find a machine overmixes and the biscuits can then be hard. I routinely roll out the dough between two sheets of plastic (that I use again and again – washing between each use) and in that way no extra flour is needed for rolling, the dough doesn't stick to the surface when rolling out and the biscuit 'project' can easily be popped into the fridge for a few minutes to firm up before cutting out.

Nancy's Top Tip

Create an additional baking sheet

Biscuits are usually baked on a flat baking sheet and
although you may have one or two – a batch of biscuits
may call for more. Create an additional baking sheet by
simply turning a large roasting tin upside down then grease
the base or alternatively lay over a piece of reusable baking
parchment. Spread your cut out biscuits on this newly
created flat surface and bake as normal.

Lemon Shortbread Biscuits

MAKES 40-50 BISCUITS DEPENDING CUTTER SIZE

Delicious any time of the year but a favourite in our family at Easter time. Easy to make and serve plain or why not use the left over egg white and half a lemon to make a royal icing and release your piping skills!

Ingredients

FOR THE BISCUITS:

- 200g plain flour
- 80g icing sugar sifted
- 140g butter (at room temperature)
- finely grated zest of 1 lemon
- ½ tsp Sicilian lemon extract
- 1 egg yolk
- 1 tbsp lemon juice

FOR THE ICING:

- 1 egg white
- 1 tbsp lemon juice
- 200g sifted icing sugar
- food colouring gel (optional)

USE: ONE OR TWO BAKING SHEETS LIGHTLY GREASED OR LINED WITH BAKING PARCHMENT.
PREHEAT THE OVEN TO: 175°C (FAN)

Nancy's Top Tip

Don't put biscuits and cake in the same tin.
Biscuits will keep well in a tin but beware – do not be tempted to put cake in the same tin at the same time. The moisture from your cake will make your biscuits go soft.

Method

1. In a roomy mixing bowl place the flour, lemon zest and sugar then rub in the butter until the mixture resembles fine breadcrumbs. Adding the lemon zest at the outset releases lemon flavour as the zests are rubbed together with the flour. I prefer to do the rubbing in by hand as I believe the final biscuit is much lighter than from a mix made in a machine.

2. Add the lemon juice and extract to the egg yolk, give a quick stir then pour into the mix. Stir the egg into the crumbs with a metal knife then bring the mixture together using the hands. The dough will readily form into a ball.

3. I then prefer to place the dough between two sheets of plastic and roll out into a circle about the thickness of a £1 coin. Transfer the dough into the fridge and leave for a minimum of 20 minutes.

4. Take from the fridge and cut out the biscuit shapes and transfer to two baking sheets and I like to line my sheets with reusable baking parchment. When all the dough has been used, after rolling and re-rolling the trimmings – pop the baking sheets into the fridge and leave to chill until the oven comes up to temperature.

5. Heat the oven to 175 degrees (fan) then I bake just one tray at a time. Bake for just 8-10 minutes until the biscuits are set with just the slightest hint of colour

6. Remove from the oven and lay the tray on a cooling rack. Allow the biscuits to cool before removing them from the tray – they may break otherwise. If you decide to ice your biscuits then make a royal icing as follows...

TO MAKE THE ICING...

1. In a small bowl beat the egg white until frothy then start to add the sifted icing sugar and whisk well between each addition. You need a consistency of soft peaks.

2. Add lemon juice if the icing is too thick. Whisk well for about 5 minutes so that you have a smooth shiny icing.

3. When the biscuits have cooled completely then decorate as you wish.

4. These biscuits will keep well in an airtight tin for at least a week.

Let Me Show You...
Watch My 'Recipe' Video
SCAN HERE

Spiced Christmas Shortbreads

MAKES 100 SMALL BISCUITS

Easy, quick, inexpensive, delicious and make excellent little gifts.

Ingredients

- 110g butter at room temperature
- 50g caster sugar
- 175g plain flour
- 50g semolina

- 50g chopped nuts lightly toasted
- 1 tsp ground cinnamon
- little milk to bind
- icing sugar to dust

USE: ONE OR TWO BAKING SHEETS LINED WITH BAKING PARCHMENT.
PREHEAT THE OVEN TO: 150°C (FAN)

Nancy's Top Tip
Store either in a tin or parcel up into little airtight gift bags. These shortbreads will keep easily for two weeks.

Method

1. Blitz the nuts and spice in a food processor until you have a fairly fine crumb. Do not overdo it or else the nuts will turn pasty and glue like.

2. Cream together the butter and sugar until light and fluffy. Work in the flour and semolina and then add the nut crumb. Bring the mixture together into a ball using the hands. The dough should be quite dry and then your biscuits will not spread in the oven. If you find it really difficult to knead the dough into a ball then add a couple of tablespoons of milk to bind.

3. Between two sheets of plastic (freezer bags are fine for this – cut to two single sheets) – roll out the dough to the thickness of a £1 coin then slide onto a baking sheet and chill for half an hour.

4. Take from the fridge, peel one sheet of the plastic away then cut out the shapes

5. Place the biscuits onto the already chilled baking sheet which has been either lightly greased or lined with baking parchment.

6. Chill the cut out dough until the oven has reached its temperature – 150 degrees then bake them for 25-30 minutes until pale coloured.

7. Allow to cool on the tray then carefully remove onto a cooling rack and sprinkle with icing sugar.

Let Me Show You...
Watch My 'Recipe' Video
SCAN HERE

Vanilla Shortbread Biscuits

MAKES 20-22 BISCUITS

These little shortbread biscuits - easy, inexpensive and tasty especially if you take the time to dip or drizzle with a little chocolate.

Ingredients

- 100g plain flour
- 40g icing sugar
- 70g butter cut into dice at room temperature
- 1/2 tsp vanilla extract
- 1 egg yolk

FOR DECORATION:
- (optional) 50g dark chocolate

USE: ONE OR TWO BAKING SHEETS LINED WITH BAKING PARCHMENT.
PREHEAT THE OVEN TO: 180°C (FAN)

Method

1. In a medium mixing bowl place the flour, sugar and butter and rub in with the finger tips until the mixture resembles breadcrumbs

2. Add the vanilla extract to the egg yolk, give a stir then add to the biscuit dough. Stir everything together with a knife then bring the mixture to a ball using the hands .

3. Place the dough between two sheets of plastic, roll out to about the thickness of a £1 coin then chill in the fridge for 20 minutes.

4. Once chilled - peel away one sheet of the plastic then cut out biscuit shapes - I used a 5cm cutter. Re-roll the trimmings. Place the cut outs on a lightly greased baking sheet or one lined with baking parchment.

5. Pop the biscuit shapes back into the fridge until the oven comes to temperature.

6. Preheat the oven to 180 degrees (fan). Slide the baking sheet into the oven and bake the biscuits for 8-10 minutes until just starting to colour.

7. Remove from the oven and allow the biscuits to cool.

8. If you want to dip the biscuits in chocolate then melt the chocolate in the microwave in 30second bursts, stirring between each blast. The chocolate doesn't want to be too runny or too thick. A temperature of 35 degrees is just about right. Allow to set on tin foil.

9. These biscuits will keep in a tin for at least a week.

Let Me Show You...
Watch My 'Recipe' Video
SCAN HERE

Flapjack

MAKES 16 PIECES

This is an inexpensive family favourite. These little bars will keep for up to two weeks in a tin but in my house they don't last that long. Great for kids when they come in from school, a packed lunch treat and great with a cuppa in the afternoon.

Ingredients

FOR CHERRY & COCONUT FLAPJACKS:

- 100g margarine or butter
- 3 tbsp golden syrup
- 90g granulated sugar
- 160g porridge oats
- 40g desiccated coconut
- ½ tsp almond extract
- 20 glace cherries chopped (I use morello glace cherries which are darker and packed with flavour)

FOR TROPICAL FLAPJACKS:

- 100g margarine or butter
- 3 tbsp golden syrup
- 90g granulated sugar
- 160g porridge oats
- 40g desiccated coconut
- 20g dried mango chopped into pieces with scissors (about currant size)
- zest and juice of 1 lime
- a generous grating of nutmeg – about 1 tsp

USE: AN OBLONG TIN ABOUT 4CM DEEP- MINE MEASURES 26CM X 18CM. I FIND A PIECE OF REUSABLE BAKING PARCHMENT THE VERY BEST FOR LINING THE TIN AS FLAPJACK CAN BE A REAL PROBLEM IF IT STICKS. IT CAN BE WASHED AND USED AGAIN AND AGAIN.

PREHEAT THE OVEN TO: 180°C (FAN)

Method

1. In a medium saucepan melt the margarine/butter and golden syrup.

2. Take it off the heat then stir in the sugar then the coconut and finally the oats and cherries. Mix well so that all the dry ingredients have absorbed moisture.

3. Transfer to the prepared tin and smooth with the back of a spoon or an angled palette knife.

4. Bake in the oven for 20 minutes until golden brown. Leave for 5 minutes then whilst still warm and with a sharp knife or pizza cutter score 16 pieces.

5. Leave to cool completely then remove from the tin, peel off the parchment and cut along the scored lines to achieve neat even pieces.

Let Me Show You...
Watch My 'Recipe' Video
SCAN HERE

Brandy Snaps

MAKES 20 PIECES

Easier to make than you think, not expensive and can be eaten by young and old alike as a biscuit or filled with raspberries and cream for a retro dessert.

Ingredients

- 60g butter
- 60g dark brown sugar
- 60g golden syrup
- 60g plain flour
- 1/2 tsp ground ginger

USE: TWO BAKING SHEETS LINED WITH BAKING PARCHMENT
PREHEAT THE OVEN TO: 190°C (FAN)

Nancy's Top Tips

TIP: My Brandy Snaps break when I try to mould them
If the brandy snaps cool and become brittle before you
have time to mould them pop back into the oven for one
minute and they will soften again.

TIP: I don't have this many baking sheets
If you find yourself short of a baking sheet simply flip
over a large roasting tin and use the base. Cover with a
piece of baking parchment and bake your brandy snaps
in the usual way.

Method

1. Simply place the butter, sugar and syrup in a saucepan and stir over a fairly low heat until the butter melts and the sugar dissolves. Don't allow the mixture to boil.

2. Take the pan off the heat then stir in sifted flour and ginger. Bring everything together using a wooden spoon then transfer to a bowl and cool. Transfer then to the fridge for about half an hour.

3. When ready to bake your biscuits preheat the oven to 190 degrees c (fan) and have two baking sheets lined with reusable baking parchment.

4. Take the chilled paste and cut even sized pieces. I prefer to weigh mine and then you have identical sizes for your brandy snaps and identical baking times. My pieces weighed 12g each.

5. Roll each piece into a ball and space five on each baking sheet.

6. Bake one sheet at a time and they take only 4-5 minutes. The brandy snaps are baked when the mixture has spread, is a dark golden brown, bubbling and looking like little lace doilies. Take the baked brandy snaps from the oven and leave for 2-3 minutes or until cool enough to handle but still warm to the touch and pliable.

7. Place the textured side to the outside and wrap around the handle of a metal kitchen utensil or suitable mould. You can mould them around the bottom of a pudding basin if you want to make little baskets. Leave until completely cool then take away the mould support.

8. Repeat with the other trays until you have your 20 brandy snaps.

If you want to fill with cream and raspberries do this just before serving otherwise your brand snaps will loose their crispness.

Let Me Show You...
Watch My 'Recipe' Video
SCAN HERE

Rose & Chocolate Macarons

MAKES 50-60 SHELLS

Once you have mastered the magic of macaron making you will have a friend for life. Naturally gluten free, they keep well, make marvellous gifts and whilst perfect on their own can also enhance a celebration cake or dessert.

Ingredients

- 100g ground almonds
- 100g icing sugar
- 40ml water
- 100g caster sugar
- 2 x 40g egg whites. (3 egg whites approx.

FOR ROSE & CHOCOLATE:

- 1/2 tsp rose water
- pink food colour gel
- for filling and decoration
- 100g double cream
- 100g plain chocolate
- 30g plain chocolate melted for decorating (optional)

FOR LEMON:

- 1/4 tsp lemon extract
- yellow food colour gel

FOR FILLING AND DECORATION:

- 100g white chocolate
- 50g lemon curd

FOR MOCHA:

- 3tsp instant espresso powder
- 1 tsp coffee extract
- for filling and decoration
- 100g double cream
- 100g plain chocolate

USE: TWO BAKING SHEETS LINED WITH REUSABLE BAKING PARCHMENT
PREHEAT THE OVEN TO: 125 °C (NON-FAN)

Method

1. Put the ground almonds and icing sugar together in a food processor and blitz. I do this to break down any lumps in the almonds and icing sugar - your finished macarons should be smooth and shiny. Take from the machine and sieve into a bowl.

2. Add 1 x 40g of egg white and stir until everything comes together.

3. Add the rose water and food colour or colour and flavour of choice. The colour needs to be quite deep as it will be made paler when the meringue is added - so don't be afraid to go dark.

4. Set this bowl aside and move on to making the meringue. In a saucepan dissolve the caster sugar in the water and once the mixture is clear increase the heat, bring to the boil, don't stir but allow the temperature to reach 119 degrees centigrade.

5. Whilst the syrup is heating, whisk the other 40g egg white to the soft peak stage then when the sugar has reached its temperature pour it into the beaten whites in a slow steady stream with the whisk still going all the time. Continue whisking until the mixture has cooled and when you pop a finger in it feels neither warm or cold.

6. Using a spatula incorporate about a third of the meringue into the almond paste (to loosen it) then gently incorporate the rest. This is by far the most important step - fold gently and thoroughly to make sure all the colour is evenly spread but don't beat so quickly or fiercely that the mixture becomes quite thin and runny. If this happens you may as well start again

7. The mixture needs to be quite thick. Place the mix into an icing bag fitted with a plain nozzle then take your parchment lined trays and pipe even rounds, each about the size of a 2p piece. You may want to mark circles on your parchment as a guide. The macaron mix as it is piped will leave a little nipple or point as your icing nozzle is lifted away. This is exactly right because when you look again you will see the circle has settled, the nipple has disappeared and the finish is smooth and shiny. The macarons now

need to dry for 30 minutes. If the environment is humid I find placing them in the oven with just the fan on works quite well.

8. After 30 minutes test to check whether your macarons have skinned over. Gently touch and if the mixture doesn't stick to your finger you are ready to bake. If the mix is still sticky leave for 15-20 minutes longer.

9. Preheat the oven to 125 degrees (non fan). Bake in the oven for 18-24 minutes and I bake each tray separately.

10. Take out of the oven and put the baking tray onto a dampened cloth on your work surface then the shells will be easier to remove. If your macarons crack on the top then your oven is too hot - drop the temperature a little. The perfect macaron shell is smooth on the surface, has a little ruffle skirt around the bottom and a solid smooth base.

TO MAKE THE FILLING...

1. In a small saucepan bring the double cream to the boil then pour over the chocolate which has been broken into small pieces in a heat proof bowl.

2. Stir well until the chocolate melts, allow it to cool and thicken then place into a piping bag. The ganache needs to have cooled to the consistency of buttercream before filling your shells.

3. Once filled you may want to decorate with a little melted chocolate piped over some or all of your shells.

4. If you decide on the lemon filling simply melt the white chocolate in a small bowl in the microwave in 15 second bursts then once melted stir through the lemon curd. Leave the mixture to go completely cold and thick then fill the shells as above.

Let Me Show You...
Watch My 'Recipe' Video
SCAN HERE

Baby Biscotti

CHERRY, CHOCOLATE & ALMOND (FAT FREE)

MAKES 30 PIECES

These crunchy, twice baked Italian biscuits are delicious. I often make several batches at Christmas time, wrap them in cellophane bags and give them as gifts. They keep for 2-3 weeks in a tin.

Ingredients

- 1 egg
- 75g caster sugar
- 125g plain flour
- ½ tsp baking powder
- 1 tsp almond extract
- 75g flaked almonds lightly toasted and roughly chopped
- 50g French morello flavour glace cherries, washed, dried and quartered
- 50g dark chocolate roughly chopped or choc chips

USE: ONE BAKING SHEETS LINED WITH REUSABLE BAKING PARCHMENT
PREHEAT THE OVEN TO: 180 °C (FAN)

Method

1. Preheat the oven to 180 degrees.

2. Start by whisking the egg and sugar in a mixing bowl until thick and creamy and when you take the whisk from the mixture it leaves a trail. This is commonly known as the ribbon stage.

3. Sieve into this mix the flour and baking powder - fold in briefly then add the cherries, nuts and chocolate.

4. You will have a ball of fairly sticky dough but turn this onto a floured surface, don't be tempted to knead the dough. Simply form into ball and then divide into two. Shape each half into a sausage shape about 25cm long and about 5cm wide.

5. Transfer to the baking sheet then pop into the oven and bake for 16-18 minutes. The bake will be lightly coloured and slightly risen and firm to the touch.

6. Take from the oven and leave for five minutes then I use a serrated bread knife to cut the bake into slices about 1cm thick.

7. Place the slices back onto the baking sheet and pop them into the oven and bake for 4 minutes, take them out, turn them over and pop back again for a further 3 minutes.

8. Cool on a baking sheet.

Let Me Show You...
Watch My 'Recipe' Video
SCAN HERE

Nutty Cookies

HOBNOBS

MAKES 18-20

If you like Hob Nobs then you will love these. My recipe is a cross between a biscuit and a cookie – being crunchy on the outside but then squidgy on the inside. This recipe will make 18-20 biscuits but I often double up and bake on four baking sheets. If you have a food processor you may like to blitz your porridge oats with the toasted nuts – I think the biscuit is better.

Ingredients

- 75g plain flour
- pinch salt
- ¼ tsp bicarbonate of soda
- 90g butter
- ½ tsp ground cinnamon
- 60g dark brown sugar
- 40g granulated sugar

- 1 egg
- ½ tsp vanilla extract
- 125g porridge oats or medium oatmeal
- 60g mixed chopped nuts – toasted to golden brown to improve the flavour

USE: A BAKING SHEET LINED WITH REUSABLE BAKING PARCHMENT OR NON STICK PAPER
PREHEAT THE OVEN TO: 190 °C (FAN)

Nancy's Top Tip

For uniform shaped and sized biscuits chill the mixture first then form the dough into balls with the hands. It will be much easier to work with and then you can weigh each ball. Each piece of dough will need to weigh 25g. Space evenly on the baking sheet then press down gently with a cold hand or the back of a spoon.

If you don't have a baking sheet, turn a roasting tin upside down and bake on the underside. Obviously you will need to cover with baking parchment first. Try adding 20g plain chocolate chips to the mixture for delicious twist.

Method

1. In a small bowl mix together the salt, bicarbonate of soda and plain flour. Set aside.

2. In a small frying pan dry roast the chopped nuts. To do this - heat the pan then add the nuts, swirling them around so that they toast evenly. Once they are a golden brown colour turn them out onto a cold plate. In the same frying pan melt the butter then continue to cook until the butter starts to colour but don't allow it to burn. Immediately the colour becomes golden and smells nutty pour it into a clean heatproof bowl, capturing all the cooked solids from the butter – that's where the flavour is.

3. Add the cinnamon, sugars and oil to the butter and mix well.

4. Add the vanilla and the egg followed by the flour, oats and nuts.

5. Divide the mixture into 18 – take a large spoonful of mixture and form into a ball with the hands then place onto the baking sheet. They do spread during baking so I allow nine per baking sheet. I then use a damp cold hand to flatten each ball of dough. Each disc needs to be about 5 cm in diameter.

6. Pop the tray into the fridge and leave until you have heated your oven to 190 degrees. Bake for 8-10 minutes until the biscuits are a deep golden brown around the edges .

7. Take out of the oven and leave to cool slightly then transfer to a cooling tray.

8. These cookies will keep for up to a week in an airtight tin.

Let Me Show You...
Watch My 'Recipe' Video
SCAN HERE

Rye and Fennel Thins

MAKES 36-40

These little oatcakes – short and light - with a hint of fennel are truly delicious and you may remember seeing a version of these on Bake Off! I have a friend, a real cheese addict who always raves over the flavour pairing of this biscuit with her favourite cheese.

Ingredients

- 2 heaped teaspoons of fennel seeds crushed with pestle and mortar or blitzed in a coffee grinder.
- 60g oatbran
- 140g rye flour
- 140g plain flour
- 15g caster sugar

- 1.5 tsp baking powder
- 3/4 tsp sea salt
- 1 tsp celery salt
- 1/2 tsp chilli powder
- 160g butter – room temperature
- milk to bind 75ml
- large plastic freezer bag

USE: THREE BAKING SHEETS LINED WITH REUSABLE BAKING PARCHMENT
PREHEAT THE OVEN TO: 190 °C (FAN)

Nancy's Top Tip
*Roll the biscuit dough between two sheets of plastic.
I split the side and bottom of two freezer bags and roll the dough without the need for extra flour, without sticking to the work surface and it slides into the fridge to chill easily. Take out of the fridge when ready to cut out your biscuits, peel off the top layer of plastic (it doesn't stick to the dough) – cut out and place your biscuit shapes onto a greased baking sheet.*

Method

1. In a large mixing bowl mix together all dry ingredients then rub in the butter until the mixture resembles breadcrumbs then bind together with the milk to make a fairly stiff dough.

2. Roll the dough to a thickness of 3mm (1/8 inch) and using a 6cm plain cutter, cut out 40 rounds and place on three baking sheets. You will have to re-roll the trimmings to get the 40 biscuits. I prick each biscuit with a fork or skewer.

3. Refrigerate for 15 minutes or so until the oven reaches a temperature of 190 degrees.

4. Cook each tray of biscuits separately for 8-10 minutes until the edges are just beginning to brown.

5. Remove from the oven and place on cooling tray.

6. Store in a tin.

 Let Me Show You...
Watch My 'Recipe' Video
SCAN HERE

Lemon & Caraway Scones

MAKES 6

A well made scone is light, springy and delicious. They are best served fresh and eaten the same day. The recipe below therefore is for just six scones – you need to eat them all in one sitting.
This recipe is low in fat and sugar so don't be afraid to apply plenty of clotted cream and jam!

These scones are sublime – flavoured conservatively with lemon and caraway seed. My inspiration for this recipe came from the lemon and caraway seed cake my grandmother used to make and then when jam and cream are added – this is Cream Tea at its very best.

Ingredients

- 225g self raising flour
- 45g salted butter
- 35g caster sugar
- zest and juice of 1 lemon
- 130ml whole milk
- 1 tsp caraway seeds
- ½ tsp vanilla extract

USE: A BAKING SHEET LINED WITH REUSABLE BAKING PARCHMENT
PREHEAT THE OVEN TO: 225 °C (FAN)

Nancy's Top Tip
I always make scones by hand and the secret of success with scone baking is to not have the mix too dry, try not to over handle plus you need a very hot oven.

Method

1. Firstly, in a dry frying pan toast the seeds gently for a minute or two just to release the nutty, fragrant flavours contained within. Don't burn them or they will be bitter.

2. In a medium mixing bowl grate the zest from the lemon.

3. Place the milk in a small jug or glass then squeeze the lemon juice into it (the lemon should yield about 20ml) and set aside to thicken and curdle.

4. Place the self raising flour into the bowl containing the zest then add the softened butter and using your finger tips rub the mix together until it resembles breadcrumbs

5. Stir in the sugar and toasted seeds. Add the vanilla extract to the milk mixture then add sufficient to bind the dough together. I use a knife initially then my hands. The dough needs to be just sticky, not too wet that you can't handle it and not too dry that it crumbles and doesn't hold together.

6. Turn out onto a lightly floured worktop then smooth out using a rolling pin or simply the palm of your hand. The dough needs to be quite thick – about 1.5cm.

7. Using a 7cm cutter dipped in flour to prevent the dough sticking, cut out six scones. When cutting out scones don't be tempted to twist your cutter. A simple straight up and down will give you an even rise. You will need to reuse the trimmings.

8. Place your scones on a baking sheet lined with non stick parchment then pop them into the fridge.

9. Heat your oven to 225 degrees and when your oven has reached its temperature take your scones from the fridge and if you have any milk mix left, give them a little brush just on the tops. Avoid letting any run down the sides as this will impede the rising.

10. Pop straight into the hot oven and bake for 10-12 minutes until well risen and golden. Do not overbake – the base of your scone should be golden brown not dark brown or black!

11. Cool on wire trays and serve the same day.

Cherry Bakewell Scones
WITH HOMEMADE CLOTTED CREAM

MAKES 8

One of the quickest bakes and one of the most delicious. I am always playing around with flavours and ingredients and decided that these Cherry Bakewell scones will be perfect with a spread of Black Cherry Jam and a blob of home made clotted cream!

CLOTTED CREAM...
Cream Tea – fresh scones, clotted cream and strawberry jam! If clotted cream is not available where you live – it is possible to make your own.

Ingredients

FOR THE SCONE:

- 225 self raising flour sifted with 1 tsp baking powder
- 50g salted butter at room temperature
- 35g caster sugar
- 50g French morello glace cherries

- 1 egg beaten with 6 tbsp left over clotted cream liquid (or milk)
- 1 tsp almond extract

FOR THE CLOTTED CREAM:

- 300ml double cream

USE: A BAKING SHEET LINED WITH BAKING PARCHMENT FOR THE SCONES AND A MEDIUM GRATIN DISH FOR THE CLOTTED CREAM.
PREHEAT THE OVEN TO: 220 °C (FAN)

Nancy's Top Tip
Clean cut your Scones
For a clean cut to your scones, dip your cutter in flour in between each scone and don't twist the cutter – just straight down and straight back up. You will get a better rise.

Method

1. Start by prepping the cherries. Rinse the cherries in cold water to remove the sticky glaze, dry them then chop them small (about the size of a raisin). Pop the cherries into a small bowl then add 1 tbsp of the flour to be used to make the scones.

2. Toss them around to allow them all to take a coating of flour. Set aside. This prevents the cherries sticking together in the mix and allows them to be evenly distributed.

3. In a roomy mixing bowl place the flour and baking powder then rub in the soft butter until the mixture resembles fine breadcrumbs. Add then the sugar and prepped cherries and stir everything through with a knife.

4. In a small jug mix together the egg, clotted cream bi-product and almond extract. Pour the liquid into the dry mix and start to bring the mixture together to a fairly sticky dough. Finish with the hands. You will not need all of the liquid – keep some back to brush the tops of your scones.

5. A scone dough does not like to be handled so don't over knead

6. Roll out to about 2.5cm thick then using a 5cm cutter cut out your scones and place on a baking sheet. Re-roll the trimmings as necessary.

7. Pop the tray of scones into the fridge until your oven comes up to a temperature of 220 degrees (fan).

8. Take from the fridge, brush the tops with the egg mix left over then bake for 10-12 minutes until well risen and golden.

TO MAKE THE CLOTTED CREAM...

1. If you decide to make your own clotted cream you will need to start the day before

2. Simply pour the cream into a shallow oven proof dish and pop into the oven at 50 degrees (non-fan) for 12 hours. I cooked mine overnight.

3. The next morning, take from the oven, allow to cool uncovered at room temperature then when cool cover and pop into the fridge for at least six hours.

4. Take from the fridge and you will find that the cream has formed a very thick skin. Carefully peel off this skin and transfer to a clean bowl. Keep the residual thin liquid as this will be used to make the scones.

5. Using a fork beat your very thick skin so that everything is well combined then cover and fridge until ready to use. Will keep 1 week in the fridge.

Let Me Show You...
Watch My 'Recipe' Video
SCAN HERE

Apple & Cinnamon Scones

MAKES 8

I love these little scones and like any scone, they can be made in a jiffy. My addition of apple and cinnamon gives a very interesting twist. They can be topped with butter and jam of course but I also enjoy them with a slice of cheese.

Ingredients

- 225g self raising flour sifted
- 1 tsp baking powder
- 50g salted butter at room temperature and cut into dice
- 35g caster sugar
- 25g dried apple chopped into pieces the size of a currant then tossed in ½ tsp ground cinnamon

- 1 egg beaten with 3 tbsp milk
- 3 tbsp plain yoghurt

USE: A BAKING SHEET LINED WITH REUSABLE BAKING PARCHMENT.

PREHEAT THE OVEN TO: 220 °C (FAN)

Nancy's Top Tip

Flour the cutter between each scone then they will release easily.

Method

1. Sift the flour into a bowl with the baking powder. Rub in the butter until the mixture is crumbly then stir in with a knife the sugar and dried apple.

2. Stir in the yoghurt then add sufficient egg and milk mix to form a reasonably wet dough. The dough needs to be more sticky than pastry but not so sticky that you need lots of flour to work with it!

3. Handle this dough as little as possible – roll it out to about 1.5cm thick then cut out 8 scones with 5cm cutter – reshaping the trimmings as necessary.

4. Transfer the scones to the baking sheet then brush the tops with a little left over egg and milk mix.

5. Bake at 220 degrees for 10-12 minutes until well risen and golden.

    BEST EATEN THE SAME DAY...

Let Me Show You...
Watch My 'Recipe' Video
SCAN HERE

Cheese Scones

MAKES 6

There are times when a slice of cake just will not do and a savoury bite is required in order to satisfy my cravings. This little cheese scone is packed full of flavour and I have added caraway seed which lifts the deliciousness!

Ingredients

- 125g self raising flour
- 25g rye flour (if you don't have this use all self raising)
- ½ tsp baking powder
- ¼ tsp salt
- 25g butter at room temperature

- 75g finely grated strong cheddar cheese
- 1 tsp caraway seeds (optional)
- 1 egg
- 1 tsp mustard
- 2-3 tbsp whole milk

USE: A BAKING SHEET LINED WITH REUSABLE BAKING PARCHMENT
PREHEAT THE OVEN TO: 210 ºC (FAN)

Nancy's Top Tip

How to preserve your grated cheese

If you buy bags of ready grated cheese, once opened if not used within a specified time it will go mouldy in its plastic bag. Once you've opened your cheese, use what you need for your recipe, reseal the bag then pop it into the freezer. Future times then that you need grated cheese simply take from the freezer, use what you need then pop back into the freezer. The cheese is free flowing and thaws very quickly and will last easily three months.

Method

1. In a roomy mixing bowl sift together the flours, baking powder and salt then add the butter and rub in by hand until the mixture resembles fine breadcrumbs. Add most of the cheese (keep 1 large tablespoon back to sprinkle over the scones before baking) and the seeds and stir to combine using a knife.

2. Make a well in the centre then in a cup or small jug mix together the egg, milk and mustard then pour this into the well in the mixture. Bring together using the knife then use the hand to form the dough into a soft, fairly moist ball.

3. Transfer to a lightly floured surface and roll lightly to a thickness of 2cm. Use a 6 cm cutter and cut out six scones, re-rolling and cutting until the dough is used.

4. Transfer to a baking sheet then top off with a little milk and the remainder of the grated cheese.

5. Bake for 15-18 minutes until the scones are risen, dark golden and smelling amazing!

BEST EATEN THE SAME DAY...

Let Me Show You...
Watch My 'Recipe' Video
SCAN HERE

Bread

Bread

"NANCY, REMEMBER YOU NEED A LIGHT HAND FOR PASTRY YET A HEAVY HAND FOR BREAD" - *My Nan's words still echo in my ears.*

Homemade bread gives such pleasure to the senses! The smell of bread straight out of the oven is probably one of the most comforting aromas in the kitchen, not to mention the taste and feel of a soft fresh loaf. Interestingly, whenever the grandchildren visit they always ask me for bread rather than cake or sweets.

When I was a child many people made their own bread and there were most certainly many independent bakers in most towns who served the population with fresh bread every day. This is still very much the case in France where their daily baguette is actually subsidised and "price fixed" by the government so that it is still available to everyone.

Bread making first became "automated" back in the 1960s and scientists discovered a new way of producing our daily loaf which became known as The Chorleywood method. We are all too familiar with the white sliced loaf. This new bread replaced the home baking in many homes because it was softer, it was cheaper, it was uniform in size and lasted twice as long as home made bread. It was a new innovation and Britain's bread was the cheapest in the world. Unfortunately, this put many small bakeries out of business as large factories popped up churning out the nation's bread at a fast, cheap, uniform pace.

My own thoughts here, which I cannot prove by the way, are that due to the high amount of yeast used plus enzymes and chemicals speed up the making of 'factory made loaves.'

There are more people nowadays unable to digest bread and have changed to a gluten free diet. Also a third of the bread bought in Britain is thrown away.

FLOUR

My bread recipes will call for Strong White Flour – but what does strong mean? The strength is not referring to the flavour or smell – it is the amount of protein (gluten) that it contains. This will depend on the variety of wheat and the climate in which it was grown. Wheats grown in extreme climates like Canada produce strong wheats which are higher in gluten content which means the dough will expand and stretch better – perfect for bread making.

YEAST

The wonder of yeast !!! – it is mysterious and magical, natural and for me the one living thing above any other that contains the most enthusiasm!

Yeast is available in three forms. It can be bought fresh, dried and granular or powdered in handy 7g sachets or small tins. Powdered is the most convenient to use, is sprinkled straight onto the flour and is always referred to in my recipes but if you do happen to get hold of fresh yeast then simply double up the yeast quantity quoted in the recipe.

Fresh yeast should be moist and firm with a pleasant smell. If it is dry and crumbly with an acidic unpleasant aroma then it is probably stale and will not do its work. Fresh yeast will keep in the fridge for about a week but if you do buy fresh yeast it is better to weigh it into portions (about 20g) then wrap and freeze. It will keep up to three months.

LIQUID

Water is the most common liquid used in basic bread making but when making enriched dough a mixture of egg, milk and water is used. Many recipes call for tepid or warm water but if making bread in a machine I use room temperature water as I find the machine's work and agitation warms things up perfectly. When Bread making by hand I use warm water. Half water and half milk will give a softer loaf.

SALT

Salt is required in bread for taste but salt and yeast are arch enemies. Sprinkle salt directly onto the yeast and you could kill it. Measure salt carefully and I always add it after all other ingredients.

SUGAR

Not essential as an ingredient but a tbsp honey, brown sugar (for wholemeal bread) or white sugar can add flavour and keeping quality to your loaf.

FAT

I often add a tbsp of oil, particularly sesame oil to my bread for extra flavour. Fat helps the bread keep fresh for longer but too much again will retard the yeast.

DOUGH ENHANCERS

POTATO STARCH

Yeast and potato starch are great pals and I routinely add 1 tbsp potato starch (I bought a bag online) with my yeast when making bread. The potato starch helps the yeast to grow. Potato starch creates an outer casing to the gluten bubble preventing it from popping easily. I read in an old cookery book that women used to save their potato boiling water for bread making for this very reason. I save potato water from time to time, it does make a difference to your finished loaf. Remember not to salt the water.

GROUND GINGER

Yeast loves ginger and $\frac{1}{4}$ tsp ground ginger added to your bread flour during mixing will enhance your dough, giving the yeast a boost and because you have used such a small amount there is no taste.

MILK POWDER

When making an enhanced dough for hot cross buns, Chelsea buns and croissants milk, eggs and sugar are added. When you make your routine loaf of bread try adding 1 tbsp dry milk powder to the flour. The dry milk produces a softer loaf, helps the crust to brown and adds taste.

I started making bread regularly about 20 years ago when I bought a bread making machine. I thought it was fantastic. I put all the ingredients in the pan, switched it on and in five hours I had a loaf. I was unsure of the process that was going on but knew I was in control of every ingredient. After a number of years the machine got tired, the paddle stopped working and the loaves being produced were unrisen. I had a dilemma – do I buy another machine or do I learn to make bread myself?

I have made many hard brick like loaves, edible the day of baking but even the chickens ran away when I threw chunks for them the next day. Bread for me was the most difficult baking discipline to get right and it was because I didn't understand the importance of kneading, the right amount of liquid to use and the difference between under and over proving.

HOW A LOAF OF BREAD IS MADE?

I have given exact mixing instructions with each recipe because sometimes proving times are different but I thought I would just write a paragraph here to cover those elements I used to get wrong.

Nancy's Top Tip
Make your dough easier to handle

Spray a little oil on your hands and rub them together as you would with hand cream. Your dough will not stick to your hands.

KNEADING

Once the bread ingredients have come together into a shaggy dough the kneading starts. Many recipes will suggest kneading for about ten minutes until the dough is smooth. That for me is always an understatement. I do not think it is possible to over knead by hand and ten minutes for someone new to baking seems an awful long time. Pushing and pulling this sticky mess seems not really worth the effort and the temptation always is to add more flour. My advice is to keep it going, refrain from more flour and eventually that dough will start to leave you alone. It will become as smooth and soft as the finest cotton pillow. My mistake was to cut short this process, add more flour to help make it workable – the dough still rose but the finished bread was hard.

If you have a table top mixer fitted with a dough hook then this process is super easy. If your dough has formed a ball and is simply moving around the bowl in a solid lump then add more water. The dough hook needs to be pulling and stretching at that dough, flexing at that gluten. The dough needs to be thick and sticky and then after around 10 minutes in the machine will turn to a stretchy, soft smooth mass.

RISING

Kneading either by hand or machine is done and you have achieved a beautifully smooth, soft dough. This dough now needs a warm place to rise. The top of a radiator is too hot. Some ovens have a bread proving setting which is probably around 26 degrees centigrade (about 80 Fahrenheit) but if like me you don't have that facility then turn just the oven light on in your electric oven. This generates just enough heat to rise your dough perfectly. Grease your bowl with a spray of oil otherwise the dough will stick then add the dough and cover with a shower cap (I have been using the same shower cap for around six months now and it is still going strong). I stopped using cling film on 1 January 2019!

Many recipes will suggest leaving your dough for about an hour or until doubled in size. The time taken to rise will depend on temperature and humidity but an hour to an hour and a half is just right.

Nancy's Top Tip
Slow Down your Bread making

Perhaps you have mixed your dough then something happens and you need to go out and will not be around in the next hour or so to tend to your precious dough. The dough can be slowed down by popping it into the fridge. You can go out for several hours and your dough will come to no harm. Dough can even be mixed the night before and popped into the fridge overnight then continue the next morning.

Once your dough has risen almost to the top of your bowl then it is time to "knock it back". I always consider this a fairly harsh term but it is necessary to ensure your finished loaf has an even rise (no huge air bubbles inside). I treat my risen dough with respect and carefully ease it out of the greased bowl onto a lightly floured surface. I then proceed to push out any bubbles of gas by folding it in on itself over and over again, tightening the dough as I go. The dough returns almost to its pre-risen size, begins to feel tight and firm rather than laying flat and limp as it did when it came out of the bowl.

You can now decide how your dough will be shaped. It can be transferred to tins (greased or brushed with my lining paste), shaped into a bloomer, formed into rolls or a plait or placed into a ridged bread basket – the possibilities are endless.

Nancy's Top Tip
Making a shiny glaze on a loaf

I have childhood memories of a huge cone shaped earthenware glazed bowl which sat by the fire containing the bread dough. It was covered in a damp tea towel (no plastic or cling film then) undergoing its first rise. My grandmother would then shape it into two x 1 lb loaf tins which would prove, bake and then be glazed using simply a saved butter paper.

Make enough for 2 loaves...

I carry on this family tradition and regularly bake a tinned loaf. My second loaf, rather than bake it now - I pop into the freezer un-proved so that I always have a loaf handy. When wanting a loaf, I take my frozen dough, in its tin, pop it into the oven with just the light (I cover the frozen dough with a shower cap) and following a long five hour thaw and prove remove the shower cap, preheat the oven and then bake for 25 minutes.

Your dough now needs to prove and many recipes will state 30 minutes – some just say until the dough has risen. I have spent so many years perfecting proving and 30 minutes I consider is never long enough. Placing your shaped loaf In the oven with just the light on will generate sufficient heat (creates a temperature of 25 °C to perfectly rise your dough taking 50 minutes exactly. How do you know whether your loaf is under-proved, over-proved or just right ? If the weather or your kitchen are warm then you can prove your bread at room temperature but it will need to be covered so that it doesn't dry out. A shower cap can be used again and again and is perfect for covering your dough. Alternatively, a slightly damp piece of muslin will work perfectly. If doing the second prove in the oven which is closed to the air then covering your dough is not essential.

An under proved loaf will burst its crust during baking – it will taste fine but the shape will be affected. A previously perfectly looking bloomer could come out of the oven bearing a crack at one side showing escaped baked dough or a loaf baked in a tin will have its roof blown off to one side and dislodged as dough has tried to escape from the side.

An over-proved loaf will not rise during its baking. Instead of being soft and pillowed it will be quite hard and exactly the same size as it was when it went into the oven. The yeast had done its work before it went into the oven and had nothing left to give.

After the second prove - if you press your dough and your finger leaves a mark and the dough looks deflated, a little like a balloon that is starting to lose its air – it is probably over proved and rather than bake it and risk failure reshape it again and wait for it to rise up once more. Your finished bread will not be as fine as if this had not happened but you will have a risen loaf.

The perfect proved dough will, after 50 minutes feel firm yet soft to the touch. The dough will still be smooth and have some resistance when you press it gently with the finger. I like to spray over with a fine water spray then straight into a very hot oven 220 °C . If you are baking a bloomer then a dusting of bread flour after the water spray followed by a quick slash with a very sharp knife will result in a beautiful artisan looking finished bake.

It is better to over bake than under bake bread. My recipes give baking times and once out of the oven make sure to place your bread on a cooling rack. Leaving bread to cool in a tin or on a flat surface will result in steam getting trapped and the base will become wet and soggy. A rub over your new bread whilst still hot with a butter paper will leave a long lasting shiny glaze.

Let Me Show You...
Watch My 'Bread Finish' Video
SCAN HERE

Nancy's Top Tip

Increasing the humidity in your oven when making bread

Bread loves a steamy environment and results in a better rise during baking and many modern ovens even have steam injection for this very reason. If like me you have an old oven or an Aga then you can still inject steam. If your oven is electric have a small tin at the bottom of the oven (mine is a miniature loaf tin) and this preheats with the oven. At the point I put the bread in to bake I drop an ice cube into that tiny tin. The loaf then benefits from steam. If you bake with an Aga then as the bread slides onto the base of the top oven throw an ice cube to the back of the oven at the same time.

Here are your favourite bread recipes...

Let Me Show You...
Watch My 'Bread Enhancer' Video
SCAN HERE

Soft White Bread

MAKES 1 BLOOMER OR 3 x 1lb TIN LOAVES

Ingredients

- 500g strong white flour
- 7g dried yeast
- 7g salt
- 15g soft butter or lard
- 150ml milk
- 150-170ml water

PREHEAT THE OVEN TO: 220 °C (FAN)

Method

1. If you are mixing your dough by hand place the flour, salt, yeast and fat in a roomy mixing bowl then add the milk and 130ml of the water and mix to a rough dough. The dough will be quite dry so add the rest of the water little by little until you achieve a sticky stretchy dough. Knead the dough for at least ten minutes until it becomes stretchy, smooth and non sticky.

2. I mix my bread in a table top mixer fitted with a dough hook - I usually place the yeast into the bottom of the bowl then add the flour, salt, fat and finally the milk and water.

3. Add 280ml of the liquid then mix long enough for the dough to form a ball. This takes about 5-6 minutes on the lowest speed.

1. Add the rest of the liquid a little at a time. The dough ball will bang around in the mixer in the newly added liquid which makes a much better job of mixing than adding all the liquid at the start.

2. Continue to knead the bread dough, increasing the speed slightly and mix until the dough leaves the sides of the bowl, the bowl is clean and the dough smooth and stretchy – avoid adding extra flour. This mixing will take about 10 minutes.

3. Kneading by hand will take at least ten to fifteen minutes. I use spray oil to grease a glass bowl – transfer the dough and cover with a shower cap which I use over and over again.

4. Leave in a warm place until doubled in size. This usually takes an hour.

5. When the dough has risen turn out onto a lightly floured surface, knock back gently, eliminating any air bubbles then shape into a bloomer and transfer to a lightly greased baking sheet.

6. Leave to prove for 50 minutes until the loaf has doubled in size. Spray over with a fine mist of cold water and a dusting of flour, neatly slash with a sharp knife or blade then bake at 220 degrees for 30 minutes until dark golden brown.

7. Transfer to a cooling rack and leave to cool completely before slicing.

Let Me Show You...
Watch My 'Recipe' Video
SCAN HERE

Crusty Topped Bloomer
TIGER LOAF

THIS RECIPE WILL ALSO MAKE 12 TIGER TOPPED ROLLS
WHICH WILL BAKE FOR 25 MINUTES.

This is a simple white bloomer loaf that has a tasty crunchy top
which once you have tried it you will be hooked.

Ingredients

FOR THE DOUGH:
- 500g strong white flour
- 7g dried yeast
- 7g salt
- 15ml rapeseed oil
- 300-320ml water

FOR THE CRUNCHY TOP:
- 50g rice flour
- 4g yeast
- 1 tsp sugar
- 15ml sesame oil
- water – sufficient to mix
  to a thick paste

PREHEAT THE OVEN TO: 220 °C (FAN)

Nancy's Top Tip
*If you are new to bread baking then make just the bloom-
er without the topping, proving for 50 minutes in the oven
with the light on.*

Method

1. If you are mixing your dough by hand place the flour, salt, yeast and oil in a roomy mixing bowl then add 280ml of the water and mix to a rough dough. If the dough is very dry then add the rest of the water little by little until you have a rough sticky dough.

2. Knead the dough for at least ten minutes until it becomes stretchy, smooth and non sticky. If you are going to knead the dough in a table top mixer fitted with a dough hook - I usually place the yeast into the bottom of the bowl first then add the flour, salt, oil and finally the water

3. Add 280ml of the water then mix long enough for the dough to form a ball then add the rest of the water a little at a time.

4. Continue to knead the bread dough until smooth and stretchy – avoid adding extra flour. Kneading by hand will take at least ten minutes. I use spray oil to grease a glass bowl – transfer the dough and cover with a shower cap then leave in a warm place until doubled in size.

5. Whilst the dough is rising make the topping. In a small bowl place all the ingredients, adding sufficient water to mix into a thick paste about the consistency of whipped double cream. Set aside.

6. When the dough has risen turn out onto a lightly floured surface and shape into a bloomer and transfer to a greased baking sheet. Using the hand spread a thick coat of topping paste over the shaped dough then supply a generous sifting of flour.

7. Leave to prove for about an hour and a quarter uncovered whilst at room temperature (not in the oven with the light on as in other recipes). You will see that the paste top will start to crack as the dough expands

8. Bake at 220 degrees for 30 to 40 minutes until the top is crisp and brown.

Let Me Show You...
Watch My 'Recipe' Video
SCAN HERE

Crusty Dinner Rolls
DARK RYE AND FENNEL

MAKES 12

These incredibly tasty rolls will be well received at a meal with friends: for sandwiches, with soup or cheese. I make them often as they are so delicious.

Ingredients

FOR THE DOUGH:

- 300g strong white bread flour
- 200g dark rye flour
- 10g salt
- 7g dried yeast
- 1 tbsp black treacle
- 1 tbsp oil
- 1 dessert spoonful fennel seed (I like to blitz the seeds to a powder in a grinder but they can be left whole)
- 300-320ml water

FOR THE CRUST:

- 60g rice flour
- 1 tsp sugar
- 1 tsp yeast
- 1 tbsp sesame oil
- sufficient water to form a thick paste
- extra flour for dusting

PREHEAT THE OVEN TO: 220 °C (FAN)

Method

1. Start by making the dough. Either by hand or using the dough hook of a machine mix together the dough ingredients and adding between 300-320ml water, sufficient to form a dough. Continue kneading until the dough is smooth and elastic - this will take around 10 minutes in a machine and 15-20 minutes by hand.

2. Grease a roomy mixing bowl and pop the dough into it then cover with a shower

cap and allow to double in size. This will take around an hour in a warm place.

3. Whilst the dough is rising mix the crust ingredients. Simply place all the ingredients into a small bowl then add sufficient water to form a thick paste. Set aside.

4. When the bread has risen take from the bowl and divide into 12 equal pieces - each one should be around 70g each.

5. Shape the rolls and place on one or two baking sheets. Take the paste and using the hands gently cover each roll with a layer. Once each bun is covered well then sift over a layer of white bread flour

6. Leave to prove uncovered in a warm place for one and a half hours. During the prove, the tops will start to crack as they rise and look quite interesting.

7. Preheat the oven to 220 degrees and after the long prove pop into the oven and bake for 20 minutes until browned and crispy on the top.

Wholesome Loaf

This incredibly tasty loaf has a real "feel good" about it and I like to give it a quick-easy butter glaze when it comes straight from the oven to enhance its rustic charm!

Ingredients

- 300g strong white bread flour
- 100g dark rye flour
- 100g wholemeal bread flour
- 2 tbsp mixed seeds: (pumpkin, sunflower, sesame, poppy)
- 10g salt

- 7g dried yeast
- 1 tbsp black treacle
- 1 tbsp sesame oil (or vegetable oil)
- 280-320ml water
- used butter paper for the glaze
- extra flour for dusting

PREHEAT THE OVEN TO: 220 °C (FAN)

Method

1. Start by making the dough. Either by hand or using the dough hook of a machine mix together the dough ingredients and adding between 280 and 320ml water, sufficient to form a dough. Continue kneading until the dough is smooth and elastic - this will take around 10 minutes in a machine and 15-20 minutes by hand.

2. Grease a roomy mixing bowl and pop the dough into it then cover with a shower cap or tea towel and allow to double in size. This will take around an hour in a warm place.

3. Take the risen dough from the bowl and reshape into a circle, twisting the dough so that it tightens more and more into itself. This way you will achieve a round loaf rather than a flat one.

4. Place the dough ball onto a baking sheet lined with reusable baking parchment and leave to prove for 50 minutes. I sometimes place my loaf in the microwave and keep the door shut – it keeps the air out and saves having to cover the bread.

5. Preheat the oven to 220 degrees and after the proving time – give a spray of water then pop into the oven and bake for 30 minutes until well browned.

6. Take the loaf from the oven and rub over the surface with a used butter paper – the glaze is amazing!

Let Me Show You...
Watch My 'Recipe' Video
SCAN HERE

Hot Cross Buns

MAKES 12

I adore a fresh hot cross bun, slightly warm with butter. Many recipes finish with a sticky glaze applied after baking whilst the buns are still hot. This for me can be messy, too sweet and then impossible to toast the next day without burning. My glaze is a slightly sweetened frothed egg white which is applied before baking and before the traditional crosses. The result is a dark, glossy glaze but non sticky to the touch.

Ingredients

FOR THE MIXTURE:

- 75g sultanas or mixed dried fruit and peel
- 1 tsp mixed spice
- zest and juice of 1 small orange
- soak overnight or about 2 hours in a warm place.

FOR THE CROSSES:

- 2 tbsp plain flour
- sufficient water to make a paste the consistency of thick cream

FOR THE DOUGH:

- 500g strong white flour
- 10g dried yeast
- 7g salt
- 50g caster sugar
- 150ml warm water
- 100ml milk
- 1 egg yolk (the white will be used for the glaze)
- 30g butter melted

FOR THE GLAZE:

- 1 egg white
- 1 tsp sugar

PREHEAT THE OVEN TO: 200 °C (FAN)

Nancy's Top Tips

Remember to soak the fruit

If you have the time (and you remember) soak the fruit, spice, zest and orange juice in a small bowl then cover and leave overnight in a warm place. The fruit will absorb the flavours and the juice and the resulting taste is truly luscious ! Rather than covering the bowl with cling film lay a plate over.

Don't discard stale buns

Left over hot cross buns make a fabulous bread and butter pudding. (see recipe under puddings)

Method

1. Start by placing the butter in a heat proof jug then pour over the measured warm water, then add the sugar.

2. Stir well until both dissolve, pour over the milk then add the egg yolk. Give a quick beating with a fork then add the dried yeast. Stir to combine.

3. In a machine fitted with a dough hook place first the salt then add the flour. Pour over the warm milk and egg mix then start your machine going on its lowest setting and mix for 3-4 minutes or until the dough has started to come together but is scraggy – then add the soaked fruit.

4. Keep the machine going until the dough comes together but is still quite sticky. Don't be tempted to add more flour. Keep the machine going for a further 5 minutes and the dough will start to leave the sides of the bowl and become smooth and elastic

5. Tip out onto a lightly floured surface and knead into a ball then place in a greased bowl covered in a shower cap, and leave to rise, in a warm place until doubled in size. This will take one to one and a half hours.

6. Once risen turn the dough out onto a lightly floured worktop and divide into 12

equal pieces. I think it is better to weigh the dough pieces and then you will produce perfectly uniform buns. About 80g per piece should be about right.

7. Shape each piece of dough into a ball then space equally onto two lightly greased baking sheets – six per sheet.

8. Leave to prove for 40-50 minutes until doubled in size. I place my buns in a closed oven with just the electric light on. This provides an airtight environment with just sufficient heat to prove the bread.

9. After the proving time, carefully remove the buns ready for the glazing. Preheat the oven to 200 degrees centigrade.

10. Beat up the egg white and sugar together just so that it is frothy then brush over the risen buns very gently and carefully.

11. Make a thick paste of plain flour and water then pipe this over the glazed buns.

12. Pop into the oven and bake for 12-15 minutes until dark golden, glossy and simply delicious.

13. Eat warm or cold. The next day can be toasted without the fear of burning under the grill or in the toaster.

Let Me Show You...
Watch My 'Recipe' Video
SCAN HERE

Chelsea Buns

MAKES 9

Packed with flavour, these buns are absolutely delicious. Using an enriched dough give these a try – you will not be disappointed.

Ingredients

FOR THE DOUGH:

- 500g strong plain flour
- 125ml warm milk
- 50g caster sugar
- 1 egg
- 50g soft butter
- 10g yeast
- 10g salt
- 80-100ml warm water

FOR THE FILLING:

- 150g dried fruits – try cranberries, apricots, mixed peel, cherries
- 30g marzipan chilled then grated
- 30ml marsala for soaking the fruits (or sherry)
- 1 tsp mixed spice
- 8 cardamom pods split and seeds removed and crushed
- ¼ tsp ground mace
- 1 tsp ground cinnamon
- zest of 1 orange and 1 lemon - reserve the juice
- icing sugar and lemon juice to make a drizzle icing

USE: A SQUARE CAKE TIN MEASURING 25CM X 25CM AND 5CM DEEP
PREHEAT THE OVEN TO: 200 °C (FAN)

Method

1. Start the night before and put the fruits in a bowl and pour over the marsala. Leave to infuse at room temperature until the next day. Add all the other filling ingredients to the bowl and mix well.

2. Make the dough in a table top mixer with the dough hook attached. Pour in the warm milk, sugar, yeast, egg and butter. Give everything a good stir with a fork then add the flour and finally the salt.

3. Start the machine and as the mixture comes together gradually add the water until you have a soft dough. Keep the motor going and mix until the dough is smooth, stretchy and glossy in appearance. This dough is too wet to knead so simply transfer to a greased bowl, cover with a shower cap and leave to rise until doubled in size.

4. Lightly flour a surface and turn out the risen dough. Flatten with the hands then roll out with a rolling pin until you have a rectangle approximately 35cm x 25cm.

5. Spread the filling over the rectangle then starting at the widest edge, roll the rectangle towards you encasing the filling. You will end up with a sausage – make sure the join is underneath.

6. Divide the sausage into 9 equal pieces then place in the cake tin (I line mine with a piece of non stick paper). Allow each bun space to expand.

7. Leave to prove for about 40 minutes during which time preheat the oven to 200 degrees.

8. When the buns have risen and are touching each other in the tin, transfer to the hot

oven and bake for 25-30 minutes until golden.

9. Whilst the buns are in the oven use the juices from the two fruits with half the weight in sugar (i.e If you have 100ml juice use 50g sugar).

10. Place these in a small pan, dissolve the sugar on a low heat and when the liquid is clear bring to the boil and reduce down until you have a syrup – about five minutes.

11. When the buns are baked, take from the oven and paint over with the warm syrup glaze.

12. If you want to further the appearance of your buns then mix 3 tbsp of icing sugar with sufficient lemon juice to form a runny icing.

13. Place in a piping bag and drizzle over the buns when cooled.

Sourdough

The bread baking enthusiast at some point will want to try their hand at making their own sourdough. The process is not difficult it just takes a little time and attention to detail. I remember when I made my first sourdough starter rather than leave it in the fridge whilst I went on holiday – I took it with me so that I could continue to feed and nurture it whilst I was away.

I have included details for those who may feel inspired to have a go themselves – it is very rewarding to create live yeast from what appears to be nothing!

I used to believe that only the dedicated bread bakers would have the time, commitment and inclination to embark on what is an absolute wonder of nature - and that is the natural leaven or as we tend to call it a sourdough starter.

Before you start make sure you have about a week to ten days when you can be available each day for a few minutes to keep "feeding" your new born. After that and once it has established a life of its own you can go on holiday, leave it in the fridge for a fortnight then feed it when you get back home and it comes to life again. Mine is now part of the family - I couldn't bear to let it die.

Also, if you think to yourself – it is not worth making this because I will only occasionally make sourdough bread. I use a couple of table spoons of my homemade leaven whenever I am making any bread - even my daily white loaf. Oh my word - see what a difference there is to your rise! Therefore, it is not just for special occasions – it is for everyday use too.

TO GET STARTED

1. In a small bowl mix 125g whole meal bread flour, 125g white bread flour and 125ml bottled still water.
2. Mix together with a fork making sure there are no lumps.
3. Add then a couple of slices of apple (about a quarter of a small apple - no skin or pips) - bury that in the mixture, cover with a shower cap or plate and leave at room temperature for two days.

After two days you will see that bubbles have started to appear on the top of the mixture.

1. Take your baby leaven and spoon out 4 tbsp into a clean bowl or jar.
2. Discard the remainder along with the apple.
3. Add to the new jar or bowl 3 tbsp white bread flour and about 3 tbsp bottled water (room temperature) or sufficient to mix to a fairly thick batter like consistency.

You need to repeat the last part of the method every 24 hours until you get to a stage where your leaven smells aromatic and quite pleasant rather than pungent and stinging to the nose. I think it smells like emulsion paint! You will also discover that it gets itself moving quicker and doubles in volume within 6-8 hours. It took mine about 9 days to get to this stage. After this period of time it is ready to store in the fridge or you can start to bake with it.

Thereafter - about once a week or a couple of hours before you want to use it - it needs to be refreshed. To do this simply either remove about a third of your starter and discard it. Then add a couple of tablespoons of white bread flour and sufficient room temperature bottled water to make a thick paste. Make sure all the flour is well incorporated. Leave at room temperature until you see bubbles start to form - a really active leaven will start to bubble within an hour or two.

It is now ready to use or pop into the fridge to store for a week.

Nancy's Top Tip
How should I store my bread?

Bread left out, uncovered will soon turn stale. I used to store mine in a plastic bag until I made my own Beeswax bread bag. I have given full instructions on how to make beeswax wraps and an airtight yet breathable wax bag is just perfect for keeping your bread fresh…

My Sourdough Bread

If you want to spend time making a loaf of sourdough then you will love this recipe. Once you have thought about making it then you will need 24 hours for it to materialise! And it is worth the effort I promise.

Let us say you want your loaf for Saturday evening…

FRIDAY AFTERNOON ABOUT 2PM

Refresh your starter or natural leaven. It should get bubbling after 3-4 hours.

FRIDAY EVENING ABOUT 8PM

Or before going to bed - make the sponge.

1. In the bowl of your mixer place 150g white flour, 50g rye flour, 100g of your natural leaven and 200ml warm water.

2. Give a really good mix making sure there are no lumps then cover the bowl with a shower cap and leave in the kitchen overnight. The next morning - just look at the bubbles!

3. 10am: Fit the dough hook to your mixer then add 150g white bread flour and 7g salt to your bubbling sponge. Mix well for 3-4 minutes until everything is well combined then turn up the speed of your mixer and continue until the dough comes together, is stretchy and silky.

4. Turn out onto a floured surface and start to knead your dough. It is quite sticky to begin with so you may find it easier to oil your hands. Transfer to a greased bowl and leave to rise until doubled in size - about an hour.

5. 11.30am: Turn the dough out again onto a floured surface, knead, shape into a ball and place in a greased bowl.

6. 12.30pm: 2nd kneading – repeat the 11.30am knead

7. 2.00pm: 3rd kneading – repeat the 11.30am knead

8. 3.30pm - 4th and final kneading, now shape the dough and place in a well floured proving basket

9. 5.00pm: Baking

10. Leave to prove for 1 hour then transfer to a baking sheet and bake for 30 minutes. Start with your oven at its highest setting then turn down to 200 degrees after 20 minutes.

11. 6.00pm: Eating!

If you don't have a proving oven you can place your dough into your electric oven with just the light on. This creates sufficient heat for a good rise.

Let Me Show You...
Watch My 'Recipe' Video
SCAN HERE

Stromboli

MAKES 9

Everyone I know who has heard of this amazing bread absolutely loves a Stromboli as it ticks all the boxes. Great for snacks, lunch, BBQ's, with soup, salads – you name it. I use all kinds of fillings, bacon, egg and sausage being a real favourite but this one is quite traditional using typical Italian ingredients. The dough is sufficient for two Stromboli but you will need to double the filling ingredients. I tend to make a Stromboli and a small loaf with the other half of the dough.

Ingredients

FOR THE DOUGH:

- 500g strong white bread flour
- 7g dried yeast
- 10g table salt
- 10ml rapeseed oil or olive oil
- 300-320ml water

FOR THE FILLING:

- 100g or about 8 slices parma ham
- fresh basil leaves (good handful) remove any stalks
- 125g mozarella
- 50g grated cheese
- 6 sundried tomatoes chopped
- 1 tbsp mixed dried herbs
- olive oil or rapeseed oil 1-2 tbsp
- freshly grated black pepper
- sprinkling of sea salt flakes and oil for finishing

PREHEAT THE OVEN TO: 200 °C (FAN)

Nancy's Top Tip

Enjoy onion without the unwanted side effects

I love raw onion as a garnish on salads but the strong after taste is unpleasant and then I wish I hadn't eaten it.

Raw onion gives a great crunch to salads but too much of it can be difficult to digest and the aftertaste is with you forever. Here are a couple of tips to ensure you can enjoy your garnish with no after effects.

Place thinly sliced onion rings in a small shallow bowl then sprinkle over ½ tsp sugar and 2-3 tbsp vinegar. Leave for about half an hour. Your onion will still be crunchy but will have been sweetened and the harshness taken away by the vinegar. Any vinegar will be fine but cider vinegar or white wine vinegar give a lovely flavour. Malt vinegar will be perfect if you have no other to hand.

Save your jar of pickled beetroot vinegar then drop a few onion rings in there- not only does the vinegar sweeten the onion it also takes on a dark red colour. Great for salads...

Method

1. Put the flour, yeast, salt and oil into the bowl of a table top mixer fitted with a dough hook then add about 280ml of the water and mix until dough is formed. Add more water as necessary.

2. Knead until the dough is smooth and stretchy. Place in a greased bowl covered in a shower cap and leave to rise until doubled in size (about 1 to 1 ½ hours depending on the temperature in the room).

3. In the meantime prepare the filling and have everything in front of you ready to use.

4. When the bread dough has risen, take from the bowl, divide into two and turn one half out onto a floured tea towel then roll into a rectangle measuring about 10 inches x 14 inches. (25cm x 35cm)

5. Sprinkle the dried herbs over the dough then layer the filling ingredients over. I start with the ham then the basil leaves followed by the sun dried tomatoes, mozzarella cheese, grated cheese, a grating of pepper then a drizzle of oil.

6. Starting at the wide end and using the tea towel as an aid – start to roll up the Stromboli finishing with the seam underneath. Tuck the ends under then transfer to a baking sheet lined with re-useable baking parchment.

7. Leave to prove for 30-40 minutes.

8. Before baking, using a metal skewer, make 5 or 6 air holes.

9. Bake at 200 degrees for 30-35 minutes until golden brown.

10. A brush with a little oil and a sprinkling of sea salt over the hot Stromboli with give it a yummy finish.

11. Delicious served hot or cold – with soup, alongside salads and great outdoor food.

Let Me Show You...
Watch My 'Recipe' Video
SCAN HERE

No Knead Bread
GARLIC AND CORIANDER

FOR A LARGE TRAY SERVING
UP TO 8-10 PEOPLE

For those new to bread baking or without a machine then this is a great crowd pleaser. Easy to make, no kneading required but you do need to forward plan. This super tasty dough matures for 24 hours in the fridge before being baked.

Ingredients

- 400g white bread flour
- 5g dried yeast
- 340ml lukewarm water
- 30ml rapeseed oil or olive oil

- 7g salt
- 50g butter
- 3 cloves garlic crushed
- 3 tbsp fresh finely chopped coriander

USE: A SHALLOW TRAY MEASURING 26CM X 36CM (APPROX.) WELL GREASED OR USE LINING PASTE.

PREHEAT THE OVEN TO: 220 °C (FAN)

Method

1. Start the day before. In a roomy mixing bowl place the flour, yeast, water and oil (the salt will be added later).

2. Mix well with a spatula or wooden spoon until the dough is rough and shaggy but well combined then cover the bowl with a shower cap and leave in a warm place for 10 minutes. I place mine in the oven with just the light on as this creates just the right amount of heat for a rise. The salt is not added yet as we want to give the yeast a chance to get working and salt impedes the rising of the yeast.

3. After 10 minutes, remove the shower cap and add the salt, give a good stir, back on with the shower cap and into the cold oven for 20 minutes.

4. Take from the oven again and this time rub one hand with oil and give this very soft wet dough ten turns ! Hold the bowl in the left hand and using the right, oiled hand (so that the dough doesn't stick) imagine your hand is a large spoon and bring the dough from the outside edge to the inside of the bowl, turning the bowl 45 degrees as you go. Do this just ten times then back on with the shower cap and into the cool oven for 20 minutes

5. Repeat this again only this time instead of placing the dough back into the oven it will be transferred into a plastic box which has been well oiled. I have a square box with a lid.

6. Push the dough into the corners of the box, pop the lid on and place into the fridge and leave overnight and up to 24 hours!

7. The next day take the dough from the fridge and invert onto the baking tray which has been well oiled or brushed with lining paste. Use oiled hands to push the dough around the tin so that it covers the tray in an even layer.

8. Back into the oven with just the light on and allow to

prove for 1.5 hours. The dough will rise and at the end of the proving time you can push any large bubbles down.

9. Preheat the oven to 220 degrees (fan) and pop the dough into the oven and bake for 20 minutes.

10. Whilst it is baking melt the butter and garlic then add the coriander. I blitz my butter garlic and coriander briefly so that the everything is well mixed.

11. Take the bread from the oven and brush over the blitzed garlic butter and coriander

12. Pop it back into the oven and bake for a further 10 minutes. Take from the oven and slice into squares and serve warm or cold. This bread freezes well too.

Let Me Show You...
Watch My 'Recipe' Video
SCAN HERE

Brioche

FOR A LARGE LOAF

Truly beautiful – soft, rich, so tasty and delicious on its own, toasted, served with bacon or pate and makes a great base for many desserts and the best bread and butter pudding. Brioche is special.

Ingredients

- 7g dried yeast
- 40ml whole milk
- 30g caster sugar
- 250g strong white bread flour
- 1 tsp salt
- 3 eggs
- 175g salted butter at room temperature

PREHEAT THE OVEN TO: 200 °C (FAN)

Nancy's Top Tip
Leftover Brioche will make the most beautiful Bread and Butter Pudding which can be used in place of the bread in this recipe.

Method

1. I have a wide 2 lb loaf tin but this recipe can be baked in two x 1 lb loaf tins. The tin must be well buttered (or use lining paste). Brioche is so much easier to make if you have a table top mixer fitted with a dough hook. The brioche needs a warm place to rise and prove and I find the oven with just the light on generates just the right amount of heat.

2. In the bowl of your mixer place the yeast, milk, sugar – give a quick stir then add the flour and salt followed by the three eggs. With the machine on a low setting mix until the ingredients are well combined. This may take 5 minutes or so. Lift the dough hook from the mix and it should be stretchy though raggy in appearance.

3. With the machine still on a low speed add the soft butter little by little until well combined. The machine speed can now be increased slightly for another five minutes or so until the mix then becomes smooth, very stretchy and glossy in appearance.

4. Use a spatula to scrape the very sticky dough into a greased bowl then cover with a shower cap and place in the oven (with only the light on) to rise until doubled in size. This will probably take as long as two hours.

5. Sprinkle a little flour onto the work surface then transfer the risen dough and I find it easier to use a bench scraper rather than my hands to gently knock the dough back. Form into a rough ball and place back into the bowl. Cover again with the shower cap and place in the fridge overnight to rest.

6. The next day transfer the chilled dough onto a lightly floured surface and it will be so easy to work with. Knead gently then divide into even sized balls. I placed four into my tin – if you are using 2 x 1lb tins then use two balls in each.

7. Cover again with the shower cap and pop back into the oven (with just the light on) and allow to prove until doubled in size and almost reaching the top of the tin. This can take between one

and a half to two hours depending on the ambient temperature.   Towards the end of the proving time remove the brioche from the oven and preheat ready for baking.

8. Preheat the oven to 220 degrees c (fan). When ready to bake - remove the shower cap and carefully.

9. Place into the preheated oven then immediately turn down to 200 degrees c (fan) and bake for 25 minutes until the loaf is risen, golden and smelling amazing.

10. Remove from the tin and cool on a wire rack.

Let Me Show You...
Watch My 'Recipe' Video
SCAN HERE

Yorkshire Teacakes

MAKES 12 TEACAKES OR 6 GOOD SIZED TEACAKES
AND A 1 lb TEA LOAF TO FREEZE BEFORE PROVING.

A traditional Yorkshire teacake is totally moreish. It has a dark, well baked crust and is best eaten fresh on the day of baking but totally delicious toasted the next day and served warm with lashings of butter.

Ingredients

- 7g yeast
- 450g white bread flour
- 240 ml milk
- 1 egg
- 5g salt
- 40g caster sugar
- 40g lard or butter (melted and cooled)
- 100g fruit (I use chopped apricots and cherries but currants, sultanas etc. are fine)
- ¼ tsp cinnamon and ½ tsp fresh grated nutmeg
- grated zest of 1 lemon plus the juice

PREHEAT THE OVEN TO: 200 °C (FAN)

Nancy's Top Tip

Freezing a tea loaf

The tea loaf can be baked and then frozen once cooled if preferred. If thawing the frozen dough, remove from the freezer bag and thaw in the oven with just the light on for 5-6 hours after which time the dough will be well risen and proved. Place into a preheated oven and bake for 25 minutes.

Non sticky glaze for bread

Beat an egg white with 1 tsp caster sugar for a shiny, dark and non sticky glaze for your teacakes. Brush just a little of this glaze over the proved cakes just before they go into the oven. If you like to toast your teacakes this glaze will not burn.

Method

1. In the bowl of a table top mixer fitted with a dough hook place first the yeast then the flour and then the rest of the ingredients minus the lemon juice.

2. With the machine on its lowest setting bring the mixture together to a rough shaggy mix then turn up the speed and mix for about 10 minutes. The dough will look very sticky and wet – if it doesn't and has formed into one large ball then add the lemon juice.

3. Continue to mix in the machine until the dough firms up, comes together, is smooth and leave the sides of the mixing bowl.

4. Transfer the dough to a greased bowl, cover with a shower cap and then leave to rise in a warm place for 1.5 to 2 hours. It will double in size.

5. Remove the dough from the bowl and divide into two. Shape one half and place into a well greased 1 lb loaf tin and pop straight into the freezer.

6. Shape the remainder of the dough into equal sized balls and leave to prove for 50 minutes until doubled in size. A Yorkshire teacake is flat rather than round so after shaping roll flat with a rolling pin and place onto a baking sheet.

7. Bake the loaf for 25 minutes until golden and the teacakes for 15-18 minutes until golden. Delicious buttered on the day of baking then afterwards toasted.

Let Me Show You...
Watch My 'Recipe' Video
SCAN HERE

Cakes

Cakes

Everyone loves cake and a child's birthday cake is a delight to make and if you make your own it is of course cheaper and although the decoration can seem daunting, just do it.

When your child has grown up, I promise you the cake that will be remembered will not be the bought, specially themed 'unicorn cake' with all bells and whistles.

You will reminisce about that chocolate cake covered in runny chocolate that didn't quite set which was covered in smarties. The candles were stuck into the runny chocolate and everyone had to sing happy birthday really quickly before the wax ran onto the cake.

The thing is you made it – and the next one you make will be better. The chocolate will set and you will put the candles in little holders.

Don't worry - there is a time for spinning sugar, tempering chocolate and obtaining the perfect mirror glaze but this book is aimed at taking you to a level where all the basics have been mastered and you have a confidence and desire to move on to bigger things.

Cake Making Methods

There are several cake making methods that fit different types of cake. A Victoria sponge cake, probably the most widely used is made differently to a swiss roll for example and rich fruit cakes, although the mixing method may be similar to a Victoria sponge needs to be baked much lower and slower in order to be moist and tasty. I will cover and discuss a number of cake making methods and throw in a few relevant popular recipes as we go along.

Making a sponge using the 'Creaming Method'

If you want to make the perfect sponge cake this is probably the method you should choose. Whether you make a simple lemon drizzle cake, a three tier sponge wedding cake, Christmas cake or fondant fancies – this is how you will get started…

Most recipes give scant instructions and assume the baker knows exactly what the perfect sponge should be. For me – the perfect sponge cake is soft, springy, not dry, not cracked or overbaked and of course tasting delicious.

An overbaked sponge will have a dark crust on its sides, bottom and maybe even the top. The perfect sponge should be the same colour all over.

I always use soft margarine – I believe it makes a lighter sponge. Use butter if you prefer.

Cake ingredients should all be at the same temperature, preferably room temperature so take the margarine out of the fridge about an hour before you need it (unless the weather is really hot). Eggs should never be kept in the fridge.

The perfect temperature for your ingredients is about 20 degrees c (room temperature). If your ingredients are too cold they will find it more difficult to emulsify and mix together and may curdle.

Ingredients

- 125g soft margarine or butter
- 125g caster sugar
- 2 large eggs at room temperature
- 125g self raising flour
- 1 tsp vanilla extract

Equipment

- a hand held electric whisk
- a medium sized mixing bowl
- a spatula and a metal spoon

USE: 2 X 6INCH SANDWICH TINS – USE LINING PASTE AT THE EDGES AND A CIRCLE OF GREASEPROOF PAPER CUT EXACTLY TO FIT THE BASE

PREHEAT THE OVEN TO: 190 °C (FAN)

Method

1. Using the medium sized, roomy mixing bowl – mine is Pyrex - place the margarine and the sugar. Using the electric hand whisk then whisk the two together until light and fluffy. Do not rush this step. In fact I whisk for about two minutes then stop whilst I collect and weigh out all the other ingredients. This then allows the sugar to dissolve slightly into the margarine or butter.

2. Continue to whisk again until the mixture is pale, light and mousse like.

3. This next stage is where my unique technique is applied.

Lift the whisks out of the mix and the hole that is left – drop into this one of the eggs.

4. Place the whisk over, switch it on low speed and do not move it at all. Keep that whisk attachment in exactly the same place, increasing the speed as you go. You will see the mixture turn from a curdled state, a bit like scrambled eggs into a smooth creamy consistency.

5. At this point you can then move the whisk around the bowl and incorporating the rest of the butter and sugar. Repeat this with the second

egg, scraping the sides of the bowl with the spatula before restarting the whisk. Your finished batter will be smooth, light, thick and gorgeous – I always think it has the look and colour of melted ice cream. Following this method will ensure you get the perfect mix, no curdle, no need to add flour to bind during mixing and no need to incorporate additional raising agent to make your cake rise.

6. With the light, mousse mixture which is successfully full of air you now need to incorporate the flour and any flavourings. I always sift the flour even though we are told that modern flours do not require it. However, if there are any lumps this quick procedure ensures no problems and by sifting more air is introduced into the batter.

7. Once the flour has been added you can finally add any flavours – this cake I will add the vanilla.

8. Using a large metal spoon slowly and carefully fold in the flour. Imagine the bowl of mix is a clock face. The spoon is the big hand! Take the spoon from 12 o'clock to 6 o'clock then from 6 o'clock back up to 12 o'clock. Turn

Nancy's Top Tip

Beware flavours can make your mixture curdle

I have been asked many times why flavours (that includes fruit, nuts, citrus, coffee etc.) have to be added at the end. The reason is that some flavours can cause a curdle – certain spices and certainly citrus cause curdling but once the flour has been added to the batter any flavours can be added with confidence knowing that the mixture is stable.

the bowl a quarter turn then repeat again. I find it easier to move the bowl a quarter turn at a time but maintaining the same movement with the spoon into the mixture.

9. When everything is fully combined take a pair of digital scales and place the empty sandwich pan onto it.

10. Spoon 3 large spoonfuls into the pan then the same into the other then carefully equal out the remainder of the mix.

11. This is important as you want your cakes to be uniform but also they will bake together so you want to make sure one is not more baked than the other.

12. Pop the cakes into the oven and bake for 18-20 minutes only. After 18 minutes have a look at your cakes. The perfectly baked sponge will be a sunny golden colour and will be starting to brown. It will have risen evenly and the centre of the sponge will be firm to the touch.

I try to give EXACT baking times because I find recipes confusing if the baking time given has something like a 15 minute window, i.e. bake from 30-45 minutes. That is not helpful.

Ovens do vary though so if after a quoted baking time in one of my recipes your cake isn't quite right then adjust your oven by 15 degrees one way or another.

For example, if at the time given in the recipe your cake is risen, brown at the sides and cracked in the middle then your oven is too hot.

If your cake seems risen but the centre does not spring back when touched (i.e. your finger leaves a mark) then the cake is under done and should be left for another 5-10 minutes.

Take your perfect cakes from the oven and place onto cooling trays. As soon as you can manage to handle the cake tins without blisters to your hands then carefully slide a knife around the outside edge then turn out onto the cooling tray. I try to do this immediately as I do not want my cake to continue baking in the tin, not even for a minute.

Allow the cakes to cool completely before filling and decorating.

Avoid cooling your cakes upside down as the cooling tray will leave marks in the sponge which will affect the presentation of your cake. Decide which cake sponge will be the top then lay a clean tea towel over the top and quickly flip it over so that the presentation sponge turns out briefly onto the tea towel. Remove the tin then flip over and place the cake presentation side up on the cooling tray. No cooling ridges.

Nancy's Top Tip

Not all ovens are the same

Some ovens, particularly older electric ovens (like mine) can be quite fierce and can burn the sides of the cake which are nearest the sides of the oven. In addition, if your cake tins are of a thin gauge and maybe quite old this can cause your cakes to bake too quickly. This can cause your cake to rise up in the middle, form a dome and then a crack. Your perfect sponge should be almost flat on the top, no crack and no burnt sides. Make a simple heat diffuser by wrapping a collar of kitchen foil around the outside of your cake tins. I take a strip of foil, fold it into four lengthways then secure this around the tin once filled with batter. The cake will then bake evenly. Use your foil collars again and again.

Cakes soon dry out so once cool if you don't intend to fill and decorate straight away I like to cover in a piece of greaseproof paper, secured with elastic bands - place in a tin and keep in a cool place.

Large Cake Mixing

When mixing large celebration cakes I will use a table top mixer and here are my tips for avoiding a curdle.

Cream together the butter and sugar using the whisk attachment. Mix on a high speed until light and fluffy. Place the eggs for the recipe in a jug then blitz with a hand blender or beat well to disperse any solid bits. With the motor of the mixer on a high speed I then add the egg in the thinnest slowest yet continuous stream. Even though your arm is aching do not be tempted to rush the egg. Once incorporated then change the attachment to the paddle and on a very low speed fold in the flour and flavourings.

If the mixture does start to curdle then add a spoonful of flour and mix on a high speed until the mixture has emulsified and looks smooth again before adding further egg.

Whisked Sponges

Whisked sponges are used for swiss rolls, certain dessert recipes and particularly top end cakes and patisserie. A light and lovely swiss roll can fit the bill on so many occasions. Serve it as dessert, decorate to suit any celebration such as Easter and Christmas, a beauty for afternoon tea and with a little bit of thought when it comes to fillings can be a very low fat cake option. Whisked sponges are very quick to make and to bake – a swiss roll for example will take only around 8 minutes to bake. A whisked sponge is a great choice for those people with a gluten intolerance. Gluten free flour works a treat in a whisked sponge.

Whisked sponges because they contain little or no fat soon dry out so they need to be eaten within a day or two and the filling needs to be moist and wholesome. A swiss roll is beautiful in that with every bite there is cream and sponge. A whisked sponge is super easy to make and once mastered you will show it off again and again.

Chocolate Fudge Cake

SERVES 6-8 PEOPLE

A cake for any occasion – this moist chocolate cake with a fudge filling and frosting is easy to make and is a favourite with the whole family.

Ingredients

FOR THE CAKE:

- 125g soft margarine or butter
- 120g caster sugar
- 1 tbsp golden syrup or black treacle
- 2 eggs
- 130g self raising flour
- 1 tsp vanilla extract
- 30g cocoa powder mixed to a paste with 100ml milk
- 50g dark chocolate melted and cooled (optional)

FOR THE FUDGE FILLING AND FROSTING:

- 100g caster sugar
- 100ml evaporated milk
- 125g plain chocolate or chocolate chips
- 20g butter
- ½ tsp vanilla extract

USE: 2 X 16CM (6 INCH) LOOSE BOTTOM SANDWICH TINS GREASED AND BASE LINED.

PREHEAT THE OVEN TO: 170 °C (FAN)

Nancy's Top Tip

How do I measure 1 tbsp syrup?

Syrup, treacle, malt extract and honey are difficult to measure accurately but here is a tip...

Take a small heatproof jug and fill with boiling water then pop a metal spoon in then and leave a few minutes. Open the tin or jar of sticky syrup, honey or malt extract then take the spoon from the water, give it a shake to remove surplus water then take your spoon of syrup. The heat from the spoon will prevent the syrup sticking – the spoon will leave the tin cleanly and then will just fall off the spoon into your mix. If you need more than one spoonful pop the spoon back into the water to clean and reheat.

Method

1. In a roomy mixing bowl cream together the margarine/butter with the sugar until light, pale and fluffy.

2. Whisk in the eggs one at a time, beating really well between each addition followed by the golden syrup.

3. Fold in the flour then once it is well mixed in add the vanilla and cocoa paste. Mix really well then stir in the cooled melted chocolate if using.

4. Divide between the two tins and bake for 20-25 minutes or until the sponges are risen and springy to the touch.

5. Remove from the tins when cool enough to handle then make the fudge filling.

TO MAKE THE FILLING...

1. In a small saucepan place the evaporated milk and the sugar and pop onto a low heat and stir until the sugar dissolves.

2. Once the mixture is smooth Turn the heat up and bring to the boil then reduce the heat and allow the mixture bubble busily for 5 minutes exactly.

3. In a small bowl break up the chocolate into small pieces then pour over the hot milk/ sugar mix.

4. Stir until the chocolate dissolves then add the vanilla and butter and mix well until you have a shiny thick fudge.

5. Allow to cool then use one third to sandwich the cakes together and the rest to coat the top and sides.

Nancy's Top Tips
My fudge separated
Simply whisk 1 to 2 tbsp evaporated milk into the fudge and it will return to a smooth, silky state. I have made this fudge filling many times and this happened to me only the once.

Let Me Show You...
Watch My 'Recipe' Video
SCAN HERE

Lemon Drizzle Cake

MAKES 2 (1 for now and 1 for a friend or the freezer)

This cake is probably one of the most popular, the easiest and certainly one of the cheapest to make – each cake costing no more than 70p.

Ingredients

FOR THE CAKE:

- 165g soft margarine or butter
- 165g caster sugar
- 3 eggs
- 165g self raising flour
- zest of a large lemon finely grated plus half of the juice

FOR THE CRUSTY TOPPING:

- juice of the other half lemon
- 50g granulated sugar

USE: 2 X 1LB LOAF TINS GREASED AND BRUSHED WITH LINING PASTE.

PREHEAT THE OVEN TO: 170 °C (FAN)

Method

1. In a roomy mixing bowl cream together the margarine/butter and sugar until light and fluffy.

2. Add the eggs one at a time whisking well between each addition.

3. Fold in the sifted flour then add the grated zest and juice.

4. Divide equally between the two tins then bake at 180 degrees centigrade (fan) for 25-30 minutes until the cakes are risen, firm to the touch and golden in colour.

5. Remove the two cake tins to a cooling tray and leave for just five minutes. Mix the granulated sugar and

lemon juice together then brush over the tops of the hot cakes. Leave the cakes in the tins to cool completely.

6. The sugar will cool to a crunchy crust and then you can easily remove the cakes from the tins.

7. Time for a delicious slice – put the kettle on !

Nancy's Top Tips

Ring the changes in flavour

Orange Drizzle Cake - Use a large orange in place of the lemon and make the cake in exactly the same way.

♥

What if I don't have the right size tin

This recipe will make an 8 inch round cake or 7 inch square cake which can then be finished off with the crunchy glaze. *The Ready Reckoner* in the book will give many options for adapting recipes to fit the size of tin you possess.

Let Me Show You...
Watch My 'Recipe' Video
SCAN HERE

Barbados Banana Bread

SERVES 8 PEOPLE

Inspired on a holiday to this beautiful island, this is my take on the deliciously moist banana bread which was served to us at breakfast!
It is delicious and a great recipe for using up over ripe bananas. I have included a lime water icing and crunched banana chips but this is optional. This cake will freeze well so double the quantities and make one for now and one for later.

Ingredients

- 60ml vegetable oil
- 1 egg
- 50g brown sugar
- 1 ripe banana
- ¼ tsp freshly grated nutmeg
- ½ tsp mixed spice ground
- 1 piece stem ginger in syrup finely chopped
- 2 tbsp ginger syrup juice (from jar above)
- 90g self raising flour

FOR THE CRUNCHY TOP:

- 2 tbsp icing sugar
- Lime juice (sufficient to make a runny icing)
- 1 tbsp dried banana slices crunched to a crumb

USE: 1 LB LOAF TIN GREASED AND BRUSHED WITH LINING PASTE.
PREHEAT THE OVEN TO: 170 °C (FAN)

Method

1. In a medium bowl place the oil, egg, brown sugar, banana, dried spices and chopped ginger and the ginger syrup.

2. Mash everything together with a fork or blitz with a stick blender if you have one, to this thick mixture then fold in the flour.

3. Transfer the thick batter into the loaf tin then bake for 30-40 minutes until risen and firm to the touch.

4. Whilst still warm apply a coating of runny icing using either a spoon or piping bag and before it sets sprinkle over the banana chips.

5. Leave to cool completely.

Nancy's Top Tip

I have over ripe bananas but don't have the time to bake today...

Peel your bananas, pop them into a bag and freeze.
When you have the time to bake you can thaw them and use.

Let Me Show You...
Watch My 'Recipe' Video
SCAN HERE

Cherry Almond Traybake

MAKES 12 SLICES

Easy bake and fit enough for any occasion – children love to make these. Great for afternoon tea, these little slices are moist and simply divine.

Ingredients

FOR THE CAKE:

- 185g soft margarine or butter
- 185g caster sugar
- 3 eggs
- 100g self raising flour
- 100g almond flour or ground almonds
- 1 tsp almond extract
- 60g glace morello cherries

FOR DECORATION:

- 180g fondant icing sugar
- ½ tsp almond extract
- 2-3 tbsp boiling water
- marzipan or fondant coloured red (about 20g)
- green food colouring

USE: 8 INCH SQUARE TIN
PREHEAT THE OVEN TO: 165 °C (FAN)

Method

1. Start by prepping the cherries. Wash the cherries then cut each one into eighths. Dry them on kitchen paper then dust in flour by placing them in a small bowl and adding 1 tsp flour. Stir them around so that each cherry chip is covered. This will prevent your cherries sinking to the bottom of the cake during baking.

2. In a large roomy mixing bowl whisk together the soft butter or margarine with the sugar until light, pale and fluffy. Add the eggs one at a time whisking well between each addition.

3. Fold in then the flour, ground almonds or almond flour and almond extract and when everything is well combined stir through the cherries.

4. Transfer the mixture to the prepared tin and bake for 30 minutes until slightly risen, pale golden in colour and firm to the touch.

5. Cool on a wire rack and then I turn my cake upside down so that the base of the cake is uppermost and completely flat.

TO MAKE THE FROSTING...

6. To mix the icing sift the icing sugar into a bowl then add the almond extract and boiling water just 1 tbsp at a time, stirring really well until you achieve a thick yet runny smooth icing.

7. Take 2 tbsp of the icing and colour green and set aside but do cover the bowl or place in an icing bag so that your icing doesn't form a skin.

8. Pour the remainder of the icing over the cake and smooth to the edges. Leave to set.

9. Decorate with green coloured icing for stalks and tiny red coloured marzipan or fondant formed into tiny balls for the cherries.

Nancy's Top Tip

How do I cut neat slices when the cake is so soft and fresh.

When wanting to cut your fresh cake cleanly just pop it into the freezer for around 20 minutes.
Take out of the freezer and see how easy and firm it is.
It is now possible to cut the finest neat slices or squares - tidy!

Let Me Show You...
Watch My 'Recipe' Video
SCAN HERE

Coconut & Lime Traybake

MAKES 12 SLICES

Coconut and lime are a great combo but so often coconut cake can be dry. To ensure we have a lovely moist slice of cake I am pre-soaking the desiccated coconut before baking. This cake will keep well in a tin and is great when the weather is hot as the frosting is not heat sensitive.

Ingredients

FOR THE CAKE:

- 50g desiccated coconut
- 1 lime
- 3 tbsp lime cordial
- 120g soft butter or margarine
- 110g caster sugar
- 2 large eggs or 3 medium
- 145g self raising flour
- 1 tbsp plain thick full fat yoghurt

FOR THE FROSTING:

- 1 lime
- 120g sifted icing sugar
- ½ tsp lime cordial
- 1 tbsp cold water

FOR THE DECORATION:

- 2 tbsp desiccated coconut lightly toasted
- finely grated lime zests tossed in 1 tsp caster sugar

USE: 8 INCH (20CM) LOOSE BOTTOMED CAKE TIN GREASED AND BASE LINED WITH PAPER.
PREHEAT THE OVEN TO: 175 °C (FAN)

Method

FOR THE CAKE...

1. Start by placing the coconut in a small bowl then add the zest and juice of the lime plus 3 tbsp lime juice cordial.

2. Give a good stir and set aside.

3. In a roomy mixing bowl cream together the butter/ margarine and caster sugar

until light, pale and fluffy.

4. Add the eggs one at a time whisking well between each addition.

5. Fold in then the self raising flour and finally add the coconut and yoghurt.

6. Transfer to the prepared tin and bake at 175 degrees c (fan) for 20-25 minutes until pale golden.

7. Take from the oven and leave in the tin to cool.

8. When the cake has cooled, remove from the tin and peel back the paper from the sides.

9. Spread the icing over the top then decorate with the sugared lime zests and toasted coconut.

FOR THE DECORATION...

1. Finely grate the zest from the lime (we will be using the segments in the frosting) then place in a small bowl and scatter over 1 tsp caster sugar.

2. Stir well then leave in a warm place for about an hour. The zests will dry and become crunchy and sweet – they will absorb some of the sugar.

3. Place the coconut in a dry frying pan and roast for a few minutes over medium heat. Caution, keep the coconut moving around in the pan as it can soon catch and burn.

4. As soon as it has turned pale golden turn out onto a cold plate – don't leave it in the hot pan.

FOR THE FROSTING...

1. After zesting the lime for the decoration crumb – segment the lime by cutting off the top and base of the lime then carefully remove the layer of pith. It is then easy to remove the fruit segments leaving behind the membrane that separates the little segments.

2. Break these segments into small pieces and place into a bowl with any lime juice, the lime cordial and 1 tbsp cold water.

3. Add the sifted icing sugar a few tbsp. at a time until you achieve a thick icing about the consistency of double whipped cream.

Let Me Show You...
Watch My 'Recipe' Video
SCAN HERE

Lemon Swiss Roll

SERVES 8 PEOPLE

Ingredients

FOR THE SPONGE:

- 75g caster sugar
- 3 eggs
- 75g plain flour
- 1 tsp lemon extract

FOR THE FILLING:

- 150g lemon curd
- 150ml double cream

USE: A LARGE BAKING SHEET LINED WITH NON STICK BAKING PARCHMENT. THE TIN AND BAKING PARCHMENT NEED TO MEASURE 26CM X 37CM X 2CM DEEP (10 INCHES X 14 INCHES X ¾ INCH DEEP)

PREHEAT THE OVEN TO: 175 °C (FAN)

Method

TO MAKE THE SPONGE...

1. In a large roomy bowl whisk together the eggs and the caster sugar until the mix has become thick and mousse like, is pale and leaves a trail when you take the whisk out of the mix. I always use a hand held electric whisk for this.

2. Sieve the flour over the top and add the lemon extract then with a large metal spoon gently fold in the flour. This takes a few minutes to get right – don't rush it. You need to retain the air. Mix slowly and in large stirs. Don't be tempted to speed things up as you see unmixed flour regularly appear in the batter. Slow, regular stirs and then you will see that the batter has thickened, is smooth and no flour remains.

3. Turn the mixture out onto the baking sheet lined with the parchment and using an angled palette knife or the back of a spoon gently

push the mixture into a large rectangle leaving just a tiny margin around the side of the parchment. This batter is not runny and will stay where you put it. It is important that you smooth it out evenly across the sheet so that it is an even thickness all over.

4. Make sure the batter is as thick at the edges as it is in the middle. It will not find its own level whilst baking – it will stay put! The mixture will not run in the oven so don't be afraid to go close to the edge.

5. Pop the tray straight into the oven and bake for 8-10 minutes keeping a close eye over your precious sponge.

6. Take it from the oven when it is golden in colour and slightly risen.

7. When the tin is cool enough to handle but before the sponge has cooled, sprinkle caster sugar over the surface then lay a piece of paper non-stick baking parchment over the top, then a baking sheet and quickly flip the whole thing over.

8. Peel the baking parchment from the cooked sponge and then carefully roll the warm sponge using the new piece of parchment as an aid.

9. Leave to cool in the rolled up position.

10. When ready to fill the sponge whisk the double cream to soft peaks then stir in the lemon curd. *(See my all in one easy Lemon curd recipe in the fillings section.)* I like to mix the cream and curd quite loosely so that there are streaks of lemon running through.

11. Take the cooled sponge and gently unroll. Leave it on the paper for now but just make sure it hasn't stuck to the paper anywhere. Your good sprinkling of caster sugar should have prevented it.

12. Spread the creamy lemon mix over the sponge in an even layer then use the paper again to help re-roll and bring together your swiss roll. For perfect presentation trim the ends with a sharp serrated knife and enjoy them as a snack reward for your good work.

13. Dust over a further sprinkle of caster sugar then transfer to a presentation plate making sure the seam is perfectly hidden underneath.

Nancy's Top Tip
Rolling a Swiss Roll

It is important to remove the backing paper from the sponge and then roll up whilst still warm. This prevents the sponge from cracking. Your finished Swiss roll will amaze your friends – it will be swirly, smooth and beautiful.

Let Me Show You...
Watch My 'Recipe' Video
SCAN HERE

Pistachio & Raspberry Ripple Swiss Roll

SERVES 6-8 PEOPLE

This is a delightful bake and can be served with afternoon tea or as a dessert. I use frozen raspberries for this Swiss roll which makes it a year round favourite in our house.

Ingredients

FOR THE CAKE:

- 3 eggs
- 75 icing sugar sifted
- 75g plain flour
- 30g pistachio paste

FOR THE FILLING:

- 250g mascarpone cheese
- 150ml double cream
- 70g icing sugar
- 3 tbsp raspberry coulis

USE: YOU WILL NEED A BAKING TIN MEASURING 26CM X 37CM X 2CM DEEP (10INCHES X 14INCHES X ¾ INCH DEEP) LINED WITH NON STICK BAKING PARCHMENT.

PREHEAT THE OVEN TO: 180 °C (FAN)

Method

TO MAKE THE SPONGE...

1. Whisk together the eggs and sugar for 5-8 minutes until thick and mousse like and the whisk leaves a trail on the top of the mixture.

2. Fold in the sifted flour and finally the pistachio paste. It is a good idea to loosen the pistachio paste with a little of the cake batter – it makes it easier to fold in. Transfer to the prepared tin, smooth out and bake at 175 degrees (fan) for 8-10 minutes.

3. Transfer the sponge still in the tin to a cooling rack and leave for 5 minutes.

4. Whilst still warm turn dust the baked surface of the sponge

with caster sugar then lay a piece of paper over and use a second cooling tray or baking sheet as an aid, flip over then peel off the original baking paper.

5. Carefully loosely roll up the sponge in the second piece of baking paper then leave and allow to cool completely. This prevents the roll cracking later.

TO MAKE PISTACHIO PASTE...

It is available to buy but if you want to make your own, let me show you! Blitz together 40g pistachio nuts, 15g ground almonds, 2 tsp almond extract, 2 tsp Amaretto, 1 tsp vegetable oil and green food colour, sufficient to make a dark green paste (makes 60g).

TO MAKE THE COULIS...

1. Make the coulis by blitzing 100g frozen raspberries then passing through a sieve.

2. The coulis should be very thick so if it is a bit runny reduce it down by boiling for a few minutes in a pan then allow to cool. Alternatively, you could use raspberry jam thinned with a little water but the coulis is better as I don't add any sugar. The tartness of the fruit is just divine amongst the filling.

TO MAKE THE FILLING...

1. Whisk the cream to soft peaks in one bowl and in the other bowl whisk together the mascarpone cheese and icing sugar.

2. Fold the two together and then lastly ripple through the raspberry coulis or jam. Do not over mix – you need a strong ripple effect.

3. Unroll the cooled Swiss roll and spread the cream inside then re roll.

4. For decoration a few chopped pistachio nuts and a dusting of freeze dried raspberry powder but you can use a dusting of icing sugar along with fresh raspberries and chopped pistachios.

Nancy's Top Tip

How to roll a Swiss Roll

It is important to remove the backing paper from the sponge and then roll up whilst still warm. This prevents the sponge from cracking. Your finished Swiss roll will amaze your friends – it will be swirly, smooth and beautiful.

Let Me Show You...
Watch My 'Recipe' Video
SCAN HERE

Cherry Chocolate Roulade

SERVES 6-8 PEOPLE

A delicious moist, non cracking, truly chocolatey roulade filled with black cherry jam and fresh whipped cream then topped off with fresh chocolate dipped cherries.
Fit for any occasion.

Ingredients

FOR THE SPONGE:

- 75g Plain flour
- 30g Cocoa powder
- 1 tsp coffee powder mixed with 2 tbsp hot water
- 1 tsp vanilla extract
- 3 eggs
- 75g caster sugar

FOR DUSTING:

- 2 tbsp caster sugar and 1 tsp cocoa powder mixed together

FOR THE FILLING:

- 3 tbsp black cherry jam mixed with 1/2 tsp almond extract
- 300ml double cream whisked with 1 tbsp icing sugar and 1 tbsp amaretto (optional)
- 10-12 fresh stoned cherries
- 30g White chocolate melted in 30 second burst in the microwave. (Stir well between each session. Overheating will cause your chocolate to seize but we can rescue it.)

USE: A SHALLOW TIN - MINE MEASURES 26CM X 37CM X 2CM DEEP (10INCHES X 14INCHES X ¾ INCH DEEP) - LINED WITH NON STICK BAKING PARCHMENT.

PREHEAT THE OVEN TO: 175 °C (FAN)

Method

FOR THE CAKE...

1. Start by lifting the plain flour and cocoa powder together.

2. Whisk together the 3 eggs and caster sugar until light, mousse like and when the whisks are taken from the mixture they leave a trail for a number of seconds.

3. Add half of the flour, sifting a second time - then the coffee and vanilla. Fold together slowly and carefully to ensure as much of the air is retained as possible.

4. Fold in the second half of the flour and when all is well combined transfer to the prepared tin.

5. Use the back of a spoon or an angled palette knife to even the mixture and push to the sides and corners of the tin. This mixture will not find its own level in the oven.

6. Bake for just 8 minutes then check to make sure your sponge has risen slightly and is springy to the touch.

7. Take from the oven and place the tin on a cooling rack. Leave for a few minutes but whilst still warm it must be removed from the tin.

8. Sprinkle over the surface the caster sugar and cocoa mix then place a clean piece of paper over and a second cooling rack then flip the whole lot over so that the original cooling rack is on the top.

9. Remove the original rack, the tin and the baking paper. Using the new piece of paper as an aid roll up the warm sponge and paper and leave rolled up until completely cool.

FOR THE FILLING...

1. To prepare the filling whisk the double cream with the icing sugar and amaretto if using until soft peaks are formed. Set aside.

2. Mix the cherry jam and almond extract together.

3. Stone the fresh cherries then holding the stalks, dip into the melted white chocolate and leave to set on a piece of baking parchment.

4. When ready to assemble - unroll the roulade, spread over the jam, cover then with the whipped cream and carefully re-roll.

5. Trim the ends to neaten the roulade, transfer to a presentation plate then decorate with a dusting of sugar/cocoa mix, a drizzle of white chocolate and the dipped cherries.

Christmas Cake

RICH FRUIT CAKES

For many people a real family tradition is the home made Christmas Cake. A very fond memory for me is spending the day with my grandmother busily prepping all the ingredients for Christmas bakes. Many of us have their tried and trusted recipe, been in the family for years and it is totally delicious.

For those who have never made their own Christmas cake, I urge you to try mine. It fits in nicely with today's busy routines in that the fruit can be prepped in the morning before heading out to work, i.e. soaked in citrus and alcohol and then left for the day in a bowl covered (leave it for up to a week if you've got other things to do). The mixing is straight forward and then best of all – the cake bakes during the night whilst you sleep. It bakes in a very low oven for ten hours. You will come downstairs the next morning to that warm comforting aroma of Christmas spice.

Take your cake out of the oven, leave it in the tin on a cooling rack then when you come home from work remove it from the tin, leave the baking paper on as it helps to keep everything moist, wrap in foil and pop into a tin until nearer to Christmas. There is no need to feed this cake – it bakes at such a low temperature that there is no drying out.

Last but not least – the cost!

An 8 inch Christmas cake will cost around £7 to make. Christmas cakes, especially mini cakes make great little gifts and this recipe will adapt and make 9 x 3 inch cakes.

Nancy's Top Tip

Do I need to buy special small tins for mini cakes

Mini Christmas cakes can work out to be expensive. Instead, save small baked bean tins. Remove the top and the base with a can opener and you will be left with a metal sleeve. Remove the label of course, give it a good wash then line with a ribbon of baking parchment and place on a baking sheet lined with paper. Don't worry that there is no base to the tin – the mixture is very thick and will not leak out at the bottom.

SERVES 8-10 PEOPLE

I usually make my Christmas cake in October and store until two weeks before Christmas. My cake needs no feed because the low slow bake ensures there is no drying out and the cake is moist. If you have a table top mixer this cake is so easy to make you will never buy one again.

Ingredients

- 1 kg mixed dried fruit and peel
- 100g French morello flavour glace cherries (washed, dried and cut into thirds)
- 4 tbsp cointreau, brandy, sherry or juice from the orange (after zesting)
- finely grated zest of 1 orange and 1 lemon
- 250g salted butter
- 250g dark brown soft sugar

- 1 tbsp golden syrup or black treacle
- 5 eggs (beaten together in a mixing jug)
- 250g plain flour
- 1 tsp ground mace (or 1.5 tsp ground nutmeg)
- 1 tsp mixed spice
- 1 tsp ground ginger
- half tsp ground cinnamon

YOU WILL NEED A 9 INCH (23CM) TIN, GREASED AND LINED BOTH BOTTOM AND SIDES.

PREHEAT THE OVEN TO: 100 °C (FAN)

Nancy's Top Tip

This recipe will also make 9 x 3 inch mini Christmas cakes which will need to bake for 5 hours.
This same recipe also makes a 20cm large hemisphere cake pan which will bake for 10 hours.

Method

1. First thing in the morning put the mixed fruit and cherries in a large bowl and add the cointreau or other liquid, fruit zests and juices, stir and cover with a plate or lid then leave until the evening. The fruit can be left in a cool place for a number of days and even up to a week.

2. In the evening when you are ready to mix – cream together the butter and brown sugar until pale, light and fluffy. Gradually incorporate the beaten egg a little at a time followed by the syrup or treacle and continue to mix.

3. I often use a table top mixer when making a Christmas cake. Start with the whisk attachment and cream the butter and sugar. Beat the eggs together in a jug and blitz with a hand blender to make sure the egg is well blended and has no stretchy bits. A good beating with a hand whisk will work just as well. With the machine on a medium speed pour the egg in a very thin and steady stream, increasing the speed of the whisk as the mixture becomes thinner. This method should avoid any curdling. If you see that the mixture is starting to split (curdle) then add a tablespoon of the measured flour, bring the mixture back to a smooth consistency then continue adding the rest of the egg.

4. When all the egg has been incorporated gently fold in the rest of the flour which has been mixed with the spices.

5. Finally, fold in the fruits.

6. Transfer the mix to the prepared tin and bake for 10 hours.

7. I usually put the cake into the oven at 10pm and take it out at 8am the next day. Allow the cake to cool completely in the tin then remove, leave on the papers, wrap in foil and store in a tin until ready to decorate at Christmas .

Let Me Show You...
Watch My 'Recipe' Video
SCAN HERE

Simnel Cake

SERVES 6-8 PEOPLE

Prior to becoming an Easter bake the Simnel Cake used to be made by girls in service at the early part of the last century and taken home as a gift on Mothering Sunday.

Ingredients

- 125g butter or margarine at room temperature
- 60g caster sugar
- 60g light soft brown sugar
- 2 eggs
- 150g plain flour
- ½ tsp baking powder
- pinch salt
- 1 tsp mixed spice
- 75g ready to eat apricots chopped into small dice (about the size of a sultana)

- 200g mixed dried fruit with peel
- 75g glace cherries cut into halves
- finely grated zest and juice of 1 large lemon
- 300g golden marzipan and icing sugar for rolling out.
- 1-2 tsp apricot jam for brushing over the cake to secure the marzipan.

Nancy's Top Tip
If you don't have the two sugars in stock use all caster sugar.

USE: 6 OR 7 INCH (16-18CM) CAKE TIN, LINED WITH PAPER
PREHEAT THE OVEN TO: 125 °C (FAN)

Method

1. Start the night before (if you remember) but no worries if not. Place the dried fruit into a small bowl then grate over the lemon zest then the juice. Give the whole lot a stir then cover and set aside until the morning. The fruit will plump up and absorb the liquid.

2. When ready to bake start by washing the cherries in a sieve then dry on kitchen paper and set aside. Preheat the oven to 125 degrees (fan)

3. In a roomy mixing bowl cream together the butter/margarine and sugars until light and fluffy. If using brown sugar make sure there are no lumps. Add the eggs one at a time – whisking well between each addition. Take a spoonful of the measured flour and add to the cherries in a small bowl. Stir them around so that the cherries are well separated and each one coated in flour.

4. Sift together the remaining flour, baking powder, salt and spice – stir together to combine then fold this into the cake batter. Next add the fruit and lastly the cherries.

5. Spoon 450g (or half of the mixture) into the base of the prepared cake tin then smooth out with the back of a spoon.

6. Roll out 125g of the marzipan to a circle. Sprinkle icing sugar on the work surface to prevent it sticking then use the base of the tin as a template and I use a pizza cutter to cut out a circle. Ideally your circle should be just slightly smaller than the cake tin so you will need to trim your circle once the tin has been removed.

7. Place this circle of marzipan over the raw cake mix then top off with the rest of the batter and smooth out.

8. This cake needs to bake evenly with no rise and no burnt or overbaked sides. A foil collar will do the trick here. Take a length of foil, fold in half lengthways then wrap around the outside of the cake tin. The foil will be higher than the cake tin. Secure with string.

9. Pop the cake into the oven and bake for 1 hour then turn the temperature down to 100 degrees c (fan) and continue to bake for another three hours.

10. The cake will be a dark

golden colour, firm to the touch with a flat top.

11. Take the cake from the oven and allow to cool in the tin.

12. Remove from the tin when cold, remove the lining papers then transfer to a cake board or cake stand.

13. Roll out the remainder of the marzipan using icing sugar to prevent sticking and use the tin again to cut out a second circle. Brush the top of the cake with the jam then secure the marzipan. Flute the edges and decorate with the marzipan trimmings.

14. The marzipan balls on the top I think are better if they are not large and clumsy. I used just 3g of marzipan per disciple. Toasting the balls with a blow torch, as well as being traditional also gives the marzipan a lovely flavour.

Happy Easter & Happy Mother's Day

Let Me Show You...
Watch My 'Recipe' Video
SCAN HERE

Date & Orange Cake

OTHER CAKE BAKING METHODS

There are a couple of other cake making methods which I want to mention that are not often used. I call them forgotten cakes. Many of us now have labour saving gadgets, mixers and blenders that benefit us enormously but then these traditional methods, even though they are easy and make brilliant cakes are not often used.

Boil and Bake Method

The great thing about cakes made using this method is that there is hardly any washing up! The recipe's fats and liquids are boiled together in a pan, cooled and then the eggs and flour are added. A quick stir and into the tin – job done.

Rubbing in Method

If you like to make pastry you will adore my second "forgotten" method. My grandmother made fantastic pastry but rarely did she make cakes. When she did make a cake it was using this method probably because the two methods are so similar. The mixing of the cake starts with the fat being rubbed into the flour then the sugar, eggs and flavours are stirred through. If you are new to cake making and maybe have very little equipment then this method is for you. No creaming, no curdling and no mixer required.

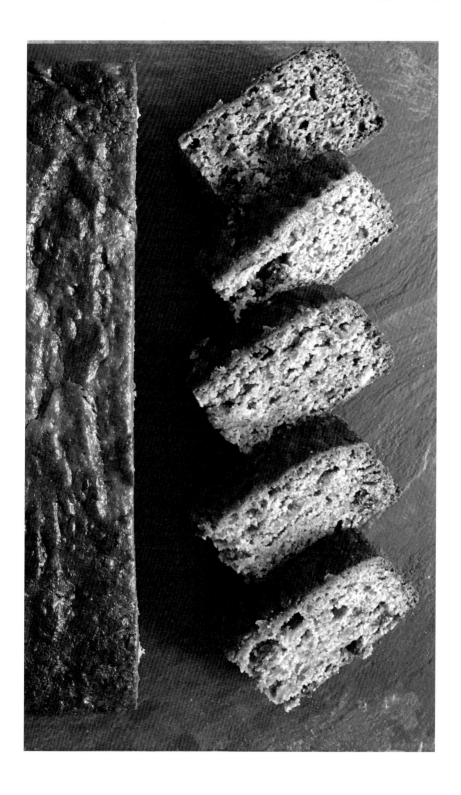

SERVES 6-8 PEOPLE

This is a traditional cake made using the 'boil and bake' method. It has no additional sugar only that naturally in the dried fruits and the sugar contained in the condensed milk. It is easy, cannot fail and actually improves with keeping. This cake will keep for several weeks in a tin. I like it sliced thinly into fingers and served alongside other cakes, scones and patisserie for Afternoon Tea.

Ingredients

- 120g chopped dates
- 180g mixed dried fruit
- 140g butter
- finely grated zest of 2 oranges
- 150ml juice from the 2 fruits (I got 120ml so make up with water or breakfast juice)

- 400g tin condensed milk
- 150g self raising flour
- ½ tsp salt
- 1.5 tsp ground ginger or 1 tbsp fresh grated ginger
- 2 eggs

USE: 20CM (8 INCH) SQUARE CAKE TIN FULLY LINED
PREHEAT THE OVEN TO: 150 °C (FAN)

Nancy's Top Tip
Buy fresh ginger once a year!

How many times have you bought fresh ginger for a recipe and cut off what you need, popped it into the fridge and when you need it again a week or two later you go to the fridge only to find it has wrinkled and dried up and has to be thrown away – then you go out to buy some more...

TIP: When you buy your fresh ginger root pop it straight into a freezer bag and pop into the freezer. When you need ginger for your recipe take from the freezer, grate what you need (skin and all) then pop it back into the freezer for next time. You will never be out of fresh ginger again!

Lemongrass and horseradish work the same too.

Method

1. In a medium sized pan place the fruit, butter, orange zest, juice and condensed milk. Stir regularly over a low heat until the butter has melted then turn up the heat and bring the mixture to the boil.

2. Once bubbling – cook for four minutes then take off the heat and give it a really good stir. I like to then blitz my mixture with a hand blender to break down the fruit a little but this is entirely up to you. Place the lid on the saucepan and leave to cool completely.

3. Once the mixture is cold stir in the two eggs making sure they are well incorporated and thus loosen the mixture.

4. Finally fold in the sifted flour, salt and ginger.

5. Transfer the thick mixture into the tin and smooth out.

6. Bake at 150 degrees c fan for 1 hour until the cake is slightly risen and firm to the touch.

7. Allow to cool completely in the tin then turn out and store in an airtight tin. The flavour of this cake improves if it is stored for a day or two.

Let Me Show You...
Watch My 'Recipe' Video
SCAN HERE

Orange & Ginger Cake

SERVES 4-6 PEOPLE

This cake is utterly delicious, keeps well in a tin for at least a week and in fact improves after sitting in a tin for a couple of days after baking. This cake is made using the 'rubbing in' method which is not seen often these days – a handy cake to make if you have little equipment.

Ingredients

- 200g self raising flour
- pinch of salt
- 40g butter at room temperature cubed
- 40g lard at room temperature (or use all butter if you prefer) cubed
- 100g caster sugar
- 1 heaped tablespoon marmalade
- finely grated zest of 1 large orange plus the juice
- 1 tsp ground ginger
- 100ml milk
- 1 egg
- 80g stem ginger (from a jar of stem ginger in syrup)
- 1 tbsp demerara sugar or sugar nibs to sprinkle over

USE: 18CM CAKE TIN (7 INCH) – BRUSHED WITH LINING PASTE AND BASE LINED

PREHEAT THE OVEN TO: 180 °C (FAN)

Nancy's Top Tip
Smooth top - no cracks!

When baking deep cakes, that is those that will not be sandwiched together with a filling if the cake does not bake evenly then the cake will dome and crack on the top. The sides may be dry and hard. When baking cakes of this type wrap a piece of kitchen foil, folded lengthways around the outside of the cake tin. This foil diffuses the heat and allows the cake to bake evenly with delicies moist sides and a flat top.

Method

1. Preheat the oven to 180 degrees centigrade (fan).

2. Start by prepping the stem ginger – wash under the cold tap, dry on kitchen roll then cut into small dice.

3. Take then 1 tbsp of the weighed self raising flour and dust the ginger to coat thoroughly. Set aside.

4. In a medium sized bowl place the self raising flour, salt, butter and lard then rub in together just as you would for pastry. The mixture needs to be looking like fine breadcrumbs.

5. Add then the ginger, sugar, zest, marmalade, juice and give a stir.

6. Add then the egg followed by the milk.

7. Add the milk a little at a time until you achieve a soft dropping consistency. You will probably need all the milk but add it gradually just in case.

8. Finally fold in the chopped ginger.

9. Transfer to the prepared tin then sprinkle over either the demerara sugar or the sugar nibs.

10. Bake for 35-40 minutes until the cake is golden, risen and springy to the touch.

11. Leave to cool in the tin for about 20 minutes before turning out onto a wire tray to cool completely.

12. Wrap in foil and store in a tin for a couple of days but if you just cannot wait to eat it – enjoy !

Nancy's Top Tip

Oh no!
My cake is overbrowning!

Your cake may looked baked as it is brown on the top but there is still 10 minutes baking time left according to your recipe. Do not be tempted to take the cake out of the oven. Instead, change your oven from 'fan' to 'conventional' cooking then take a piece of foil larger than the cake, fold it into four and tear out a hole that will be in the centre of the foil. Carefully open your oven door and lay the foil over the cake. The cake can then continue to bake and cook through without further browning.

Let Me Show You...
Watch My 'Recipe' Video
SCAN HERE

Raspberry Ripple Cupcakes

MAKES 12

Easy bake and fit enough for any occasion – children love to make these. I use frozen raspberries for the cakes and then top off with a fresh one.

Ingredients

FOR THE CAKES:

- 130g Soft margarine or butter
- 130g Caster sugar
- 1 tsp vanilla extract
- 2 large eggs
- 130g Self Raising flour
- 70g Frozen raspberries broken into crumbs

FOR THE CREAM:

- 150g Butter at room temperature
- 270g Sifted Icing sugar
- 1 tsp vanilla extract
- 2 large tbsp. thick full fat plain yoghurt
- Pink food colouring
- 12 fresh raspberries

USE: 12 HOLE MUFFIN TIN LINED WITH PAPER CASES.
PREHEAT THE OVEN TO: 175 °C (FAN)

Method

1. In a roomy mixing bowl cream together the margarine/butter, vanilla and sugar until light and fluffy then add the eggs one at a time beating well between each one. Fold in the flour then finally stir through the frozen raspberry crumbs.

2. Divide the mixture between the 12 paper cases – a large dessert spoonful each is just about right.

3. Transfer to the oven and bake for 17-20 minutes until risen, pale golden in colour and springy to the touch.

4. Cool on a wire tray and remove from the muffin tin when cool enough to handle.

5. For the cream, whisk the butter and vanilla until it is pale and soft then add the sifted icing sugar in three parts whisking well between each addition.

6. Finally whisk in the yoghurt. You should have a light, smooth fluffy buttercream.

Nancy's Top Tip
When piping your cupcakes...

Use a reusable icing bag fitted with a star nozzle and using a long handled paintbrush paint a line of pink food colour down the inside of the bag.

Fill the bag with the butter cream and when the cakes have cooled completely pipe the buttercream over the cakes and top off with a fresh raspberry.

You will be delighted with the ripple effect when piping!

Let Me Show You...
Watch My 'Recipe' Video
SCAN HERE

Carrot & Orange Cake

SERVES 8-12

A deliciously moist carrot and orange cake filled and frosted with a smooth cream cheese filling and then decorated with glazed carrot chips and rosemary leaves.

Ingredients

FOR THE CAKE:

- 110g soft light brown sugar
- 120ml vegetable oil
- 2 eggs
- 1 orange – finely grated zest and juice
- 150g self raising flour
- 1 tsp baking powder
- 1 tsp ground cinnamon
- 1 tsp mixed spice
- 125g finely grated carrot

FOR THE VANILLA CREAM FILLING:

- 2-3 tbsp orange marmalade
- 100g butter at room temperature
- 100g sifted icing sugar
- 125g full fat soft cheese
- 1/2 tsp vanilla extract

USE: 2 18CM SANDWICH TINS GREASED AND BASE LINED
PREHEAT THE OVEN TO: 180 °C (FAN)

Method

1. Place the sugar in a roomy mixing bowl and make sure there are no lumps. Add the oil and eggs and whisk until the mixture is thickened slightly and increased in volume.

2. Sift together the flour, baking powder and spice then fold this into the mix then stir in the orange zest, juice and carrot.

3. Divide between the two tins and bake at 180 degrees c for 20-25 minutes until the cakes are golden in colour and firm to the touch. Turn out onto cooling racks and leave to go completely cold.

TO MAKE THE FROSTING...

1. Simply whisk the butter until it is creamy then add the icing sugar one spoonful at a time. Add then the vanilla and finally the cream cheese.

2. Add a quarter of the cream cheese at a time and beat well between each addition.

JAZZ UP YOUR CAKE WITH CARROT CHIPS!

Ingredients

- 50g sugar
- 30ml water
- carrot
- rosemary

Method

1. Dissolve the sugar in a small saucepan with the water.

2. Add the carrot chips then boil for 3-4 minutes until soft.

3. Take from the syrup and leave to cool on a piece of kitchen foil or parchment.

4. When ready to assemble the cake – use the marmalade and spread over the bottom cake then sandwich the two sponges together with a layer of one third of the cream then cover the top and sides.

5. Top off with the carrot chips and a blade leaf of fresh rosemary.

Coconut Passion Angel Cakes

MAKES 12

These cakes are beautifully light using only egg white in the sponge. Traditionally a cake made with egg whites is called an angel cake – so there you go.

Ingredients

FOR THE CAKES:

- 3 egg whites
- 150ml milk
- ½ tsp vanilla extract
- 150g plain flour
- ½ tsp baking powder
- 50g desiccated coconut
- 180g caster sugar
- 125g soft margarine

FOR THE CURD CREAM:

- 2 eggs
- 75g sugar
- 50g butter
- 4 passion fruit (juice required but keep the seeds)
- few drops of passion fruit flavouring (optional)
- 200ml double cream
- 10g icing sugar

USE: 12 HOLE MUFFIN TIN LINED WITH PAPER CASES.
PREHEAT THE OVEN TO: 180 °C (FAN)

Method

1. Start by making the passion fruit curd. Extract the juice from the passion fruit by cutting the fruits in half then using a teaspoon, scrape out the seeds into a metal sieve set over a small bowl. Rub the fruit juice and pulp from the seeds and set aside. Keep the seeds for decoration later.

2. Place the eggs in a medium saucepan, beat well then add all the other ingredients. Stir constantly over a low heat until the butter has dissolved then increase the heat and stir all the time until the curd thickens. Transfer to a jug or bowl and allow to cool completely.

3. To make the sponge - start by whisking the egg whites to soft peaks then in a separate bowl whisk together the margarine and

sugar until the mixture is light and fluffy. I then add about one quarter of the milk plus the vanilla and about one quarter of the flour sifted with the baking powder and keep mixing until everything is incorporated. Repeat until the flour and milk have been incorporated and the mixture is smooth.

4. Finally fold in the coconut and the whisked egg whites.

5. Divide the mixture between the cases then bake for 18-20 minutes at 180 degrees until the cakes are risen, golden and firm to the touch. The sponges are quite pale because of the absence of the egg yolk.

6. Allow to cool completely on a cooling rack.

TO MAKE THE FROSTING...

7. To make the cream simply whisk together the double cream and icing sugar until thickened - but not too much!

8. Fold in the passion fruit curd. Pipe the cream over the cakes and top off with a few passion fruit seeds.

Lemon & Elderflower Cake

SERVES 6-8 PEOPLE

This is a wonderful cake for the summertime and a few edible flowers look simple yet stunning. If you like cake but the thought of sweet sickly buttercream puts your teeth on edge then this frosting is for you. Light, smooth and not overly sweet this little cake is a delight.

Ingredients

FOR THE CAKE:

- 125g soft margarine or butter
- 125g caster sugar
- 2 eggs
- 125g self raising flour
- finely grated zest of 1/2 lemon and all of the juice
- ½ tsp Sicilian lemon extract

FOR THE 'NOT TOO SWEET BUTTERCREAM':

Sufficient to fill and coat the cake. If you just want to fill the cake make half the quantity.

- 250ml whole milk
- 3 tbsp cornflour
- 180g soft butter
- 170g icing sugar
- 4 tbsp elderflower cordial
- grated zest of half a lemon

USE: 2 X 6 INCH SANDWICH TINS GREASED AND BASE LINED
PREHEAT THE OVEN TO: 180 °C (FAN)

Method

1. To make the cake. Cream together the margarine (butter) and sugar until light and fluffy then add the eggs one at a time whisking well between each addition.

2. Fold in the flour which has been sifted then add the lemon zest, extract and juice.

3. Divide between the two tins and bake for 18-20 minutes until the cakes are pale golden, risen and firm to the touch.

4. Remove from the tins when

cool enough to handle and leave to go completely cold.

5. To make the cream – Place the milk and cornflour in a small saucepan and heat gently stirring all the time until the mixture thickens. Transfer to a heatproof bowl, cover in cling film and leave to go completely cold.

6. In a separate bowl whisk the butter until creamy then add the icing sugar in three parts, whisking really well between each addition. This is important if you are to have a smooth cream.

7. Take then the cold paste and whisk this into the buttercream just one spoonful at a time again whisking really well between each addition. Finally whisk in the elderflower cordial and lemon zest.

8. Sandwich the cakes together then apply a thin crumb-coat to the sides and top of the cake.

9. Chill for an hour then spread over the rest of the frosting and decorate as you wish.

Let Me Show You...
Watch My 'Recipe' Video
SCAN HERE

Chocolate & Amaretto Festive Cupcakes

MAKES 12

I really recommend these little treats. The chocolate sponge is light with the lovely amaretto flavour coming through. If like me you are put off my frostings that are too sweet then this one is for you. Decorate them as you like but I piped a little rope work on the top and then finished off with marzipan leaves and berries.

Ingredients

FOR THE CAKES:

- 100g dark chocolate (75% cocoa solids will give the best flavour)
- 150ml whole milk
- ½ tsp almond extract
- 25ml amaretto
- 125g caster sugar
- 60g soft butter
- 2 eggs
- 150g self raising flour sifted

FOR THE FROSTING:

- 100ml whole milk
- 2 tbsp cornflour
- ½ tsp vanilla extract
- 100g icing sugar
- 100g soft butter

USE: A LARGE DEEP 12 HOLE MUFFIN TIN LINED WITH PAPER CASES. PREHEAT THE OVEN TO: 175 °C (FAN)

Method

TO MAKE THE CAKES...

1. In a pan pour the milk and 40g of the sugar. Bring to simmering point and pour into a bowl which contains the chocolate which has been broken into small pieces. Give a good stir and when the chocolate has fully melted, set to one side.

2. Cream together the remaining sugar and butter until light and fluffy then add the amaretto and almond extract then add the eggs one at a time.

3. Fold in the flour and chocolate mix. You will have a very runny batter so I pour mine into a jug before transferring into the cupcake cases. The mixture needs to fill the case about 2/3rds.

4. Transfer to the oven and bake for 18-20 minutes until risen and springy to the touch.

5. Remove from the muffin tin and leave on a rack to cool.

TO MAKE THE FROSTING...

6. Place the milk and cornflour in a small saucepan over a medium heat and whisking all the time allow the mixture to thicken.

7. Transfer to a bowl and leave to go completely cold.

8. In a medium bowl whisk together the butter and icing sugar – incorporating the icing sugar a little at a time and whisking well between each addition.

9. Add the vanilla extract. Whisk for about 4 minutes until it is pale and fluffy then add the milk paste a spoonful at a time – whisking between each addition.

10. Transfer to a piping bag and use as required.

Let Me Show You...
Watch My 'Recipe' Video
SCAN HERE

Chocolate, Vanilla & Strawberry Drip Cake

SERVES 6-8 PEOPLE
A celebration cake loved by children!

Ingredients

FOR THE SPONGES:

- 500g soft butter or margarine
- 500g caster sugar
- 50ml vegetable oil
- 1.5 tbsp vanilla extract
- 9 eggs
- 650g self raising flour
- 40ml milk

FOR THE BUTTERCREAM:

- 250g sott butter
- 450g icing sugar
- 4 tbsp freeze dried strawberry powder
- 50g cream cheese
- 3 tbsp whole milk

FOR STRAWBERRY ITALIAN MERINGUE BUTTERCREAM:

- 375g caster sugar
- 120ml water
- 3 egg whites
- 330g salted butter
- 4-6 tbsp freeze dried strawberry fruit powder

FOR THE CHOCOLATE DRIP:

- 200g Dark Chocolate
- 200g Double cream
- Coloured sprinkles to decorate

USE: 2 X 9 INCH (23CM) DEEP SPRINGFORM CAKE TINS GREASED AND LINED.

PREHEAT THE OVEN TO: 130 °C (FAN)

Method

1. Cream together the butter/ margarine and the sugar until light and fluffy.
2. Beat the eggs together and add the vanilla and oil. Add the egg mix a little at a time to the creamed butter beating well between each addition. If the mixture starts to curdle add 1 tbsp flour from the 650g.
3. When all the eggs have been incorporated, add the flour and fold in until you have a smooth mixture then finally add the milk.
4. Divide between the two tins then bake for 1 ¼ hours. Leave to cool in the tins for 15 minutes then remove and leave to cool completely on wire racks. You may want to level the tops of your cakes with a knife or cake wire if they have risen up in the middle slightly during baking.

TO MAKE THE BUTTERCREAM...

5. Cream the butter well then add the icing sugar in three parts, beating really well between each addition.
6. Add the strawberry powder, cream cheese and the milk. Whisk well until the cream is light, smooth and fluffy.

7. Use the buttercream to sandwich together the two cakes then apply a coating to the top and sides. Pop into the fridge for at least two hours to firm up.

TO MAKE THE CHOCOLATE DRIP...

8. Chop the chocolate into small pieces and place into a heat proof jug. Heat the double cream in a small saucepan and when it starts to form bubbles take it off the heat and pour over the chocolate in the jug.
9. Stir well until the chocolate has dissolved and the resulting ganache is smooth and shiny.
10. Allow the chocolate to cool and thicken to the consistency of single cream then pour over your chilled cake and with the aid of the back of a spoon or a small angled palette knife work at steering the drips so that they are fairly uniform around your cake.
11. Pop back into the fridge to firm up for about 15 minutes then finish the decoration with sweets, sprinkles, macaron – the possibilities are endless.

Nancy's Top Tip
Piping fears...

You are delighted and so proud. You have made a perfect cake – soft light sponges, smooth gorgeous buttercream... Your cake is filled and sitting resplendent on its cake board. The last touch has to be done. The final personalised piping!
Happy birthday piped in chocolate is fearful and once on the cake it cannot be removed. The whole thing could be ruined!

-

Try piping onto a piece of baking parchment or greaseproof paper. Have as many tries as you need then pipe your perfect lettering on paper.
(You know it will fit because you measured it beforehand.)
Pop the whole thing into the fridge and once set carefully remove with an angled palette knife and transfer where you want it onto the cake.

Let Me Show You...
Watch My 'Recipe' Video
SCAN HERE

Pecan & Apple Cake

SERVES 8 PEOPLE

This cake is a real delight. It is light yet moist and has a delicious cinnamon frosting but best of all I think is the little apple surprise inside every slice.

Ingredients

FOR THE CAKE:

- 175g soft margarine or butter
- 175g caster sugar
- 3 eggs + 1 egg yolk
- 175g self raising flour
- 25g pecan nuts chopped finely and toasted (or simply mixed chopped nuts)
- 1 tsp ground cinnamon
- pinch of salt
- 2 small dessert apples peeled, cored and cut into quarters (I prepare these right at the end so that they don't lose their colour). make small cuts into the apple starting at the outside and towards the core but not all the way through – this aids the cooking process.

FOR THE SWISS MERINGUE BUTTERCREAM FROSTING:

- 1 egg white
- 30g Light brown soft sugar and 40g Caster sugar
- 125g Unsalted butter cut into dice at room temperature
- ½ tsp ground cinnamon
- 1 tsp vanilla extract
- 8 toasted pecan nuts to decorate

USE: YOU WILL NEED A DEEP 9 INCH (22CM) SPRING FORM CAKE TIN GREASED AND BASE LINED

PREHEAT THE OVEN TO: 175 °C (FAN)

Method

TO MAKE THE CAKE...

1. Whisk the margarine/butter and sugar until light and fluffy then add the eggs one by one, plus the egg yolk - saving the white for the frosting.

2. Sift the flour, salt, spice and baking powder and fold in gently.

3. Finally add the toasted nuts.

4. Transfer the mix to the prepared cake tin and level out.

5. Quickly prepare the apples and starting at the join of the tin (or some recognisable place) - place the apples, core side down into the mix – at 12 o'clock, 6 o'clock, 2 o'clock, 4 o'clock, 8 o'clock and 10 o'clock (or spaced evenly 8 times).

6. Push them into the mix cut side uppermost so that you can still see about half of the apple.

7. Bake for 35-40 minutes until the centre of the cake is springy to the touch and golden brown.

8. The apples should almost disappear and be covered by the cooked cake.

9. Take the cake from the tin but before you do, place a wooden toothpick as a marker at the place where you placed the first piece of apple and where the tin seam was.

10. Allow to cool thoroughly before frosting.

TO MAKE THE SWISS MERINGUE FROSTING...

1. Put the egg whites and sugar in a bowl over a pan of barely simmering water and keep stirring until the sugar is dissolved.

2. With an electric hand whisk – whisk the mixture for about 6 minutes until you have a thick pale caramel coloured mix.

3. Take from the pan and continue to whisk until cool.

4. Place the room temperature butter in a separate bowl and whisk until well creamed then add the whisked up whites a large spoonful at a time, whisking between each addition. You will achieve a deliciously smooth frosting which will be applied to the cake when cool. Finally whisk in the vanilla and cinnamon.

5. When ready to decorate cover the top of the cake in the frosting then the sides, making special note of where you inserted the wooden skewer. I think the frosting looks better not too perfect.

6. Place one pecan nut above where you have inserted your skewer then it is easy to determine where the other seven need to go. In this way each serving will contain a piece of apple.

Let Me Show You...
Watch My 'Recipe' Video
SCAN HERE

Cake Fillings & Frostings

I considered this chapter heading and immediately felt overwhelmed before I even start to write. There are so many to choose from and so many flavours. I have decided that maybe the most straight forward is to start with the easiest and progress through to the more complex.

The thing is, once you have mastered the art of making the smoothest fillings you will be totally put off by very sweet, gritty frostings that put your teeth on edge. By the end of this chapter you will be well equipped to take on the lot!

I try through all of my recipes to consciously work on reducing sugar and fat where appropriate. I like to decorate cakes simply without resorting to piles of sugary sweets and chocolates – for me such cakes are 'heartstoppers' not 'showstoppers'.

A slice of cake is not prohibitive – I can think of nothing more delicious just now than a piece of my carrot and orange cake with a cream cheese frosting decorated simply with a slither of fresh glazed carrot.

Buttercream

I like this filling – it is smooth and rich but uses less butter than other basic buttercreams. This filling will sandwich and decorate an 8 inch (20cm) chocolate cake or decorate 12 mini cakes or cupcakes. It pipes well and will keep up to one week in the fridge. Allow to return to room temperature before using as it sets quite firm.

Ingredients

FOR A CHOCOLATE
BUTTERCREAM FILLING:

- 450g icing sugar
- 150g unsalted butter
- 30g cocoa
- 30ml milk
- 30ml brandy

Method

1. It is important that the butter is creamed really well until it is really soft and fluffy.

2. I like to sift the cocoa and icing sugar together then there are no streaks in your finished cream.

3. Add the icing sugar mix little by little until eventually you have a consistency which is crumbly in appearance.

4. Pour in milk and brandy slowly and whisk until light and fluffy.

Nancy's Top Tip
Alter the flavours to suit your cake.

FOR A COFFEE BUTTERCREAM FILLING:

- 450g icing sugar
- 150g unsalted butter
- 2 tbsp instant coffee dissolved in 2 tbsp hot water
- 1 tsp vanilla extract

FOR A LEMON BUTTERCREAM FILLING:

- 450g icing sugar
- 150g unsalted butter
- finely grated zest of 1 large lemon
- 50ml lemon juice
- 1 tsp lemon extract

Italian Meringue Buttercream

For me – this is the queen of cake fillings.

Light, not too sweet, smooth, pipes well and utterly gorgeous. When I make wedding cakes I always use this beautiful frosting. However, she does have issues – the cream can be lumpy, it can curdle and can literally turn to soup!

I remember learning to make this buttercream using the conventional method only to find I added the butter at a time when the meringue was too warm, or the butter may have been too warm but either way the whole lot collapsed and turned to liquid.

I have encountered every disaster when making this cream but I promise you if you follow my straight forward simple instructions you will produce a perfect 'IMBC' every time.

Why? Because I have decided to do things a little differently...

So here's how !

Ingredients

- 1 egg white
- 125g caster sugar
- 3 tbsp water
- 110g butter (at room temperature)

YOU WILL NEED: A TEMPERATURE PROBE AND A HAND HELD ELECTRIC WHISK.

This is a small but sufficient amount to fill and decorate a 6-8 inch cake.

Method

1. In a small saucepan place the caster sugar and water.

2. You will need two large mixing bowls, one for the egg white and one for the butter.

3. Dissolve the sugar into the water on a low temperature. Do not stir but simply swirl around upon itself in the pan. When fully dissolved bring to a boil then pop the temperature probe into the pan.

4. When the temperature reaches 105 degrees centigrade, start to whisk the egg white. Whisk until the white reaches the soft peak stage by which time the sugar solution should have reached a temperature of 119 degrees c.

5. Take off the heat and with the whisk running pour the sugar in a slow steady stream into the egg white. Keep whisking continually, scraping the sides of the bowl as you go until the meringue finally cools to body temperature. You will be able to pop your finger into the mix and it feels neither warm nor cold. This will take about 8 minutes. When cool set aside.

6. Using the same whisk and in the other bowl cream the butter to smooth then add the meringue, a little at a time until fully incorporated.

7. Finally whisk in your flavouring. The result will be unbelievably delicious cream which will keep in the fridge for up to 7 days. It will firm up in the fridge so before using allow it to return to room temperature then give a whisk to return it to its former glory.

When making large amounts of this cream you will find it easier to use a table top mixer.

Make sure the bowl and whisk are absolutely clean with no grease otherwise your egg whites will not whisk up to their full potential. I find it easier to warm a Pyrex jug then transfer my sugar syrup into it so that I have better control when pouring the hot liquid onto the meringue.

The machine can be left running for around ten minutes until the meringue has cooled. I bring the IMBC together by hand – whisking the butter up in a separate bowl with a hand held electric whisk then adding the meringue one spoonful at a time.

Nancy's Top Tip

Avoid curdling when making Italian Meringue Buttercream

The secret to success is to ensure that the butter and meringue are both at the same temperature before mixing them together. I have found that creaming the butter rather than adding it in chunks avoids any problems. If however your cream curdles during the mixing do not stress. Take a large spoonful of your curdled mix – pop it into a non metallic bowl then microwave for a few seconds only until you see the mixture turn to liquid. Take a hand held electric whisk and blitz the liquid into the curdled cream. Miraculously you will see the cream return to its former glory.

DIFFERENT FLAVOURS FOR THE CREAM QUANTITY GIVEN...

LEMON - whisk in the zest and juice of 2 lemons
COFFEE - dissolve 2 tbsp coffee powder with 1 tbsp hot water
CHOCOLATE - 2 tbsp cocoa mixed with 4 tbsp milk

DRIED FRUIT POWDERS are really good as they are intense in flavour. 1 tbsp added as it is or mixed with water to bring to a paste will flavour this cream too.

Nancy's Top Tip

Getting butter to room temperature from cold

Room temperature butter is essential for creaming with sugar or for making IMBC but when you realise you forget to take it from the fridge – or maybe your kitchen is as cold as a fridge. Here is a quick way to soften butter ready for creaming or spreading.

Take your piece of cold butter, place it on a flat plate or piece of paper and find a glass bowl or glass tumbler that when turned upside down covers it comfortably. Rinse the bowl or glass under the cold tap so that it is dampened. Pop into the microwave for 1 minute. Take the hot glass (use a towel to hold it) and pop it over the piece of butter then leave it there for 4-5 minutes. Your butter will be soft enough to use with no melting or oiliness.

Let Me Show You...
Watch My 'Recipe' Video
SCAN HERE

Chocolate Swiss Meringue Buttercream

Standard buttercreams can be gritty, lacking flavour and certainly too sweet. A Swiss meringue buttercream is easy to make, smooth, silky, full of flavour and the best news – no thermometer or special kit is required.

This amount makes sufficient to top off 18 cupcakes or fill and coat an 8 inch sandwich cake.

Ingredients

- 140g soft light brown sugar
- 2 egg whites
- 250g butter at room temperature
- 120g dark chocolate
- 1 tsp vanilla extract
- 2 tbsp cocoa mixed to a paste with 2-3 tbsp milk

YOU WILL NEED: A HAND HELD ELECTRIC WHISK.

Method

1. Start by melting the chocolate as this needs to be cool before using.

2. Break up the chocolate (or use chocolate chips) and place in a small non metal bowl.

3. Pop into the microwave and I found 3 x 20 second bursts, stirring in between was sufficient to cause the chocolate to melt.

4. Stir then Set aside.

5. Place the sugar in a roomy mixing bowl and press out any lumps with the back of a spoon. Add then the two egg whites and give everything a good stir.

6. Transfer the bowl over a pan of recently boiled water. Continue to stir for about five minutes. The mixture will be dark and gritty to

begin with but then as the sugar dissolves, the mix will appear paler, about the colour of caramel.

7. Once there is no gritty feel to the mixture (rub a little of the mixture between a thumb and forefinger and it should feel smooth) then take the electric whisk and mix, still over the heat until the mixture thickens, turns pale in colour and doubles in size.

8. Take the bowl off the pan of water and transfer to a cloth on your work surface to prevent it slipping or sliding. Continue to mix until the meringue, whilst still being thick, pale and gorgeous will be cool. This can take about 5 minutes. It is important that the meringue is not still warm.

9. Once you have a cool meringue set it aside.

10. In another bowl whisk the soft butter until creamy then add the cooled meringue one large spoonful at a time, whisking well between each addition. Finally add the flavours, the cooled melted chocolate, the vanilla and the cocoa paste.

11. This cream is silky, not too sweet and delicious and will keep up to one week in the fridge. It pipes well, smooths and will not disappoint.

Quick Curd

A massive favourite of mine and the extra few minutes it takes to make will make such a difference to your finished cake and its filling. When adding a lemon, lime or passion fruit cake filling I often make a lovely zingy fresh quick curd.

The curd can be used on its own but I prefer it whisked into fresh cream for a swiss roll or to top off a trifle, whisked into mascarpone cheese for a gorgeous less sweet filling or added to an Italian meringue or swiss meringue buttercream.

The method is simple, everything goes into the pan together. The curd must be allowed to cool before using.

Lemon Curd

- 2 eggs
- 75g caster sugar
- 50g soft room temperature butter (cut into dice)
- finely grated zest and juice of 1 large lemon

Lime Curd

- 2 eggs
- 75g caster sugar
- 50g soft room temperature butter (cut into dice)
- finely grated zest and juice of 2 limes

Passion fruit Curd

- 2 eggs
- 75g caster sugar
- 50g soft room temperature butter (cut into dice)
- 4 passion fruit (extract the juice – reserve seeds for decoration)
- few drops of passion fruit flavouring (optional)

Nancy's Top Tips

Choose wrinkled passion fruits

Wrinkled passion fruits are ripe and have more juice than smooth ones. To extract as much juice as possible: Cut the passion fruits in half over a metal sieve standing over a bowl. Scoop out the seeds with a teaspoon then push with a metal spoon until the juice and pulp leave the seeds.

A quicker way to get the pulp out of a passion fruit

Cut the fruits in half over the goblet of a food processor, scoop out the seeds and flesh. Blitz for a minute or two then pour the whole lot through a sieve. This method is quicker especially if using a number of passion fruits. The blitzing releases the fruit pulp from the seeds resulting in a quick sieve!

Let Me Show You...
Watch My 'Recipe' Video
SCAN HERE

Creme Patissiere

This delicious thick and creamy custard filling has so many uses and made using my simple "one stage" method will have you filling and topping off your éclairs, fruit tarts, cakes, trifles and meringues effortlessly.

Use as it is in open fruit tarts and éclairs or fold into 300ml whipped double cream for a gorgeous filling or topping for your trifle, pavlova or cake.

To make 400ml – enough for 1 large or 12 small open fruit tarts

Ingredients

- 3 egg yolks
- 1 tsp vanilla extract
- 50g caster sugar
- 25g cornflour
- 15g soft butter
- 250ml whole milk

Method

1. Place the egg yolks into a small saucepan (off the heat) and beat together using a small whisk.

2. Add then the vanilla, sugar and cornflour and mix to a smooth paste.

3. Gradually add in the milk, a little at a time and when all is well combined add the butter.

4. Place over a low heat and stir all the time until the butter melts. Increase the heat slightly and still stirring allow the custard to thicken.

5. When it thickens, take off the heat, beating all the time then transfer to a cold bowl and cover with a sheet of crumpled greaseproof paper and allow to cool.

6. Alternatively, if you are using the crème patissiere in open fruit tarts the warm custard can be poured directly into the baked pastry shell and left to cool.

Let Me Show You...
Watch My 'Recipe' Video
SCAN HERE

Free
From

Digestive Biscuits

GLUTEN FREE

SERVES 8-12

Ingredients

- 50g rice flour
- 25g ground almonds
- 25g dried polenta
- pinch salt
- ½ tsp baking powder
- 20g soft brown sugar
- 25g butter at room temperature (salted)

- ¼ tsp / large pinch chinese five spice or ground star anise
- 1 tbsp maple syrup (or golden syrup)
- milk to bind (about 1 tbsp)

YOU WILL NEED: YOU WILL NEED A BAKING SHEET LINED WITH REUSABLE BAKING PARCHMENT

PREHEAT THE OVEN TO: 175 °C (FAN)

Method

1. Mix all the dry ingredients together in a mixing bowl then rub in the butter as you would for pastry.

2. Then add the maple syrup and sufficient milk to form a stiff dough. Between two sheets of plastic (e.g. Cut across the bottom and one side of two freezer bags so that you have two large plastic sheets), roll out the dough to 3mm (1/8 inch) thickness

3. Place the dough once rolled out into the fridge to chill for about 10 minutes still enclosed between the plastic sheets. Take from the fridge, peel off the top layer of plastic then using a 6cm cutter cut out your biscuits, re-rolling the trimmings as necessary.

4. If the dough gets sticky simply pop it back into the fridge for 5 minutes to firm up.

5. Transfer your biscuits onto a baking sheet lined with reusable baking parchment.

6. Prick the biscuits with a fork then place in the fridge until the oven heats up. They need to chill for about 15 minutes.

7. Heat the oven to 175 degrees then bake the biscuits for 8-10 minutes until just starting to colour. Use an angled palette knife to life and transfer the biscuits on to a wire rack to cool.

Let Me Show You...
Watch My 'Recipe' Video
SCAN HERE

Summer Cake
LOW FAT & SUGAR FREE

SERVES 8-10 PEOPLE

A generous slice of beautiful creamy cake doesn't have to be bad for you. This whole cake including the cream contains just 200g refined sugar and 164g fat. TREAT YOURSELVES!

Ingredients

FOR THE CAKE:

- 4 large eggs
- 150g caster sugar
- 1 tsp vanilla extract
- 75g cornflour
- 75g plain flour
- 1 tsp baking powder
- 50g butter (melted and cooled – still runny)

FOR THE LOWER FAT VANILLA CREAM:

- 3 egg yolks
- 1 tsp vanilla extract
- 50g caster sugar
- 25g cornflour
- 250ml whole milk
- 300ml whipping cream (lower in fat than double cream)

FOR THE DECORATION:

500g fresh late summer fruits (blackberries, raspberries, blueberries, strawberries, plums, kiwi)

USE: DEEP 9 INCH (23CM) LOOSE BOTTOMED CAKE TIN GREASED AND BASE LINED.
PREHEAT OVEN TO: 175°C (CONVENTIONAL)

Method

1. In a large roomy mixing bowl whisk together the eggs, vanilla and sugar until light, mousse like and doubled in size. You can place your mixing bowl over a pan of simmering water and this will speed up the mixing. When you lift the whisk out of the mix it will leave a trail. If that is not happening, continue whisking some more.

2. Sift over the flour, cornflour and baking powder and fold in gently taking care not to knock out that valuable air. Pour in the cooled melted butter and stir this briefly through the thick mix- just a few stirs is all it needs. Transfer to the prepared tin and bake for 30-35 minutes until the cake is well risen and golden brown. Your cake may start to darken after about 15-20 minutes and if so lay over a piece of foil with a hole in the centre. This will protect the cake from over browning

3. When baked take the cake from the oven and leave on a cooling rack still in the tin for about 15 minutes. The cake will leave the sides of the tin. Run a knife around the edges and remove then leave to cool completely.

Nancy's Top Tip:

Get ahead and make the pastry cream in advance. The pastry cream can be made up to three days in advance and kept in the fridge.

TO MAKE THE CREAM...

1. Start by making the thick pastry cream. Place the egg yolks, vanilla, sugar and cornflour in a medium sized saucepan and mix to a thick paste.

2. Gradually pour over the milk and stir well. Place over a medium heat and keep stirring all the time until the mixture heats and thickens.

3. Take from the heat, give a good beating then transfer to a heat proof bowl, cover and leave to go completely cold.

4. When cold whisk the whipping cream in a large bowl until thick and standing in peaks then whisk it into the cold pastry cream, little by little until you have a very thick smooth vanilla flavoured frosting.

5. Transfer your cooled cake to a cake board and slice in half horizontally so that you have two sponges.

6. Spread a layer of cream to sandwich the two cakes together then use the remainder of the cream to cover the top and sides

7. Chill in the fridge for a couple of hours to firm up.

8. Decorate with as much fresh fruit as you can

Let Me Show You...
Watch My 'Recipe' Video
SCAN HERE

Malt Loaf

(NEARLY) FAT FREE

MAKES 2

Malt loaf is a classic and very easy to make. Don't feel guilty about wanting to spread butter on it - there is hardly any fat in this recipe. Malt loaf is best kept in a tin for 2-3 days before eating to allow the flavours and the squidgy moistness to develop.

Ingredients:

- 150g chopped dates
- 150g sultanas
- 150ml hot tea
- 190g malt extract
- 1/2 tsp salt

- 70g dark muscovado sugar
- 2 eggs
- 1 tsp mixed spice
- 50g butter or margarine at room temperature
- 250g self raising flour

USE: 2 X 1LB LOAF TINS GREASED AND LINED OR BRUSHED WITH LINING PASTE
PREHEAT THE OVEN TO: 120 °C (FAN)

Nancy's Top Tip:

Try the finely grated zest of an orange or lemon to enhance the flavour. Use the juice too but then reduce the amount of tea used for soaking the fruits.

Method

1. So easy - place the dates and sultanas in a small bowl and pour over the hot tea.

2. Leave to steep until cool then add the malt extract, salt, sugar, mixed spice, butter and eggs - in fact everything except the flour.

3. I then use a stick blender to blitz everything together to a runny batter.

4. Fold in the sieved flour and mix well then divide the mixture between the two tins

5. Bake for 1 hour 15 minutes until the cakes are firm and springy to the touch.

6. Take from the oven - place on cooling trays and leave to go cold in the tins.

7. Transfer to a tin for 3-4 days to ripen.

8. Served sliced with butter.

FOR NANCY'S LINING PASTE...

1. Simply take equal quantities of Vegetable shortening or soft butter, Plain flour (or gluten free flour) and Vegetable or sunflower Oil. I use 100g of each then store in a jar in the fridge.

2. Whisk together the soft fat and flour until you have a smooth paste then add the oil. Brush this thick paste inside your cake tin to save paper lining.

Coffee & Walnut Cake

GLUTEN FREE

SERVES 8

I have tried gluten free cake in the past and have to say I have found it either dry, almost sawdust like in texture or alternatively heavy and lacking depth of flavour.

Ingredients

FOR THE CAKE:
- 125g soft margarine or butter
- 125g caster sugar
- 2 eggs
- 35g walnuts blitzed to a paste in a food processor or coffee grinder
- 1 tbsp mayonnaise
- 50g rice flour
- 50g gluten free plain flour
- 1/2 tsp salt
- 2 tsp baking powder
- 1/2 tsp xanthan gum
- 1.5 tbsp instant espresso powder or instant coffee mixed with 1.5 tbsp hot water

ITALIAN MERINGUE BUTTERCREAM:
- 1 egg white
- 1 tbsp instant expresso powder or instant coffee mixed with 1 tbsp hot water
- 125g caster sugar
- 3 tbsp water
- 110g butter (at room temperature)

SIMPLE BUTTERCREAM:
- 100g soft butter
- 180g sifted icing sugar
- 2 tbsp full fat cream cheese
- 2 tbsp instant espresso or instant coffee powder or granules mixed with 2 tbsp hot water

USE: YOU WILL NEED 2 X 16CM (6 INCH) LOOSE BOTTOMED SANDWICH CAKE TINS GREASED AND BASE LINED.
PRE-HEAT THE OVEN TO: 175°C (FAN)

Nancy's Top Tip:

I think I will go so far as to say you will not be able to tell the difference here between gluten free and a cake baked with wheat flour. My family could not tell the difference - in fact nor could I...
This cake is totally successful and that is a promise!

Method

1. In a roomy mixing bowl whisk together the margarine/ butter and sugar until light and fluffy. Add the egg yolk then the eggs one at a time, whisking well between each addition.

2. Mix together the mayonnaise and the walnut paste then whisk this into the egg/ sugar mix.

3. In a separate bowl sieve together the rice flour, gluten free flour, baking powder, salt and xanthan gum.

4. Sieve a second time into the cake mix then add the coffee and water and fold everything together.

5. Divide between the two tins and bake for 18-20 minutes. The cakes will be well risen, soft and springy to the touch.

6. Remove from the tins and cool on cooling racks

7. Whilst the cakes are cooling make the cream.

TO MAKE THE ITALIAN MERINGUE BUTTERCREAM...

1. Dissolve the caster sugar in a small saucepan with the 3 tbsp water. Start on a very low heat then once the syrup is clear you can increase the heat and bring to a temperature of 119°C.

2. Whilst the sugar syrup is reaching temperature whisk the egg white in a medium sized clean mixing bowl until soft peaks are formed.

3. When the sugar is to temperature pour it in a steady stream over the egg white.

4. Keep your whisks going all

the time and continue to whisk until the meringue cools down and you are able to pop your finger into it and it feels neither warm nor cold.

5. In a separate bowl whisk the butter until it is soft and smooth then add a large spoonful of the meringue and whisk until well combined. Continue to incorporate the meringue into the whisked butter and finally whisk in the coffee.

Alternatively, if you prefer a quicker, simpler filling for your cake:

TO MAKE THE SIMPLE BUTTERCREAM...

1. In a roomy mixing bowl whisk the soft butter until really creamy then add the icing sugar in three separate parts whisking really well between each addition.

2. Finally whisk in the cream cheese and coffee mix. Enough to fill and decorate the top of the cake.

6. When the cakes have cooled you will have enough filling to sandwich the cakes together and decorate the top. Arrange the sugared walnuts over the top into the whisked butter and finally whisk in the coffee.

7. When the cakes have cooled you will have enough filling to sandwich the cakes together and decorate the top. Arrange the sugared walnuts over the top.

FOR DECORATION...

1. 8 walnut halves dusted in icing sugar then toasted lightly in a dry frying pan.

Let Me Show You...
Watch My 'Recipe' Video
SCAN HERE

Choco-Fudge Slices
LOW SUGAR

MAKES 12-16 SLICES

I decided to include these deliciously moist slices into this chapter because they are quite different in that they contain lots of stewed apple, are low in fat and can easily be made gluten free.

I store apples over the winter but by February they are starting to look a bit tired yet they are perfect for baking and cooking. If you have no stored apple then dessert apples will be fine and even better than those eating apples from the fruit bowl that you would otherwise probably throw away.

Ingredients

FOR THE CAKE:

- 250g apple puree (about 4 medium sized apples) needs to be cold
- 100g soft margarine or butter
- 180g caster sugar
- 2 eggs
- 35g cocoa powder mixed to a paste with 175ml milk
- 1 tsp ground cinnamon or ½ tsp Chinese five spice
- 250g self raising flour

FOR THE FUDGE TOPPING:

- 100g double cream
- 100g dark chocolate (I use bourneville)

USE: 1 SQUARE 8 INCH (20CM) CAKE TIN GREASED AND LINED. PREHEAT THE OVEN TO: 180 °C (FAN)

Nancy's Hot Tip:
Whenever I make these slices I ask family and friends to guess the "secret ingredient" – no-one ever detects the apple!

Method

1. Start by preparing the apples. Peel then slice off the flesh into a non-metallic bowl until you have about 250g. I use the microwave to cook mine in 3 minute bursts – stirring between each session. The riper the apples the quicker they will cook. Keep mashing with a fork until you have a smooth pulp then leave to go completely cold.

2. Place the cocoa powder in a small bowl then gradually add a little milk and mix to a smooth paste then add the remainder of the milk. Set aside

3. In a roomy mixing bowl and I use an electric hand whisk cream together the margarine/butter and sugar then add the eggs one at a time. Fold in the sifted flour and spice.

4. Add the chocolate paste and apple puree and stir everything together until well combined.

5. Transfer to the prepared tin and bake at 180 degrees for 30-35 minutes until the cake is springy to the touch and slightly risen in the middle. The cake may crack but don't worry

6. Remove from the oven and allow to cool on a wire rack. Take from the tin as soon as it is cool enough to handle.

TO MAKE THE FUDGE TOPPING...

1. Place the double cream into a small saucepan and bring to the boil then pour over the chocolate which has been broken up and placed in a heatproof bowl.

2. Stir continuously until the chocolate has dissolved and the mixture is smooth and shiny.

3. When the cake has cooled completely I like to take a second cooling rack and invert my cake so that the very smooth underside becomes my top.

4. Pour over the cooling fudge top and smooth with a knife over the top and sides.

5. When completely cold cut into 16 even slices.

Lemon Cake
VEGAN

I wrote this recipe following a message received from a desperate mum with a little girl who was 8 years old and had never had a birthday cake ! The reason for this was that the child had an egg allergy and was therefore unable to eat standard cakes. Many egg free cake recipes are pale and heavy in texture but after a number of attempts I came up with this delightful sponge that was enjoyed by the whole family. This cake is also a good standby if you find yourself out of eggs!

Ingredients

- 300g self raising flour
- 30g custard powder (adds colour and depth of flavour to the sponge)
- ¼ tsp salt
- 1 tsp bicarbonate of soda
- 110g caster sugar
- 200ml almond milk
- 140ml vegetable oil
- 30g golden syrup
- finely grated zest and juice of 1 lemon
- 1 tsp lemon extract

USE: YOU WILL NEED 2 X 8 INCH (20CM) SANDWICH TINS GREASED AND BASE LINED.
PREHEAT THE OVEN TO: 165 °C (FAN)

Nancy's Top Tip

Don't throw away those zested and juiced lemon halves just yet... Lemon juice is a fantastic natural limescale remover. If you have noticed that the spouts of your taps are cloudy due to limescale build up simply use your lemon halves to cup around the base of the tap and leave overnight. The limescale will simply dissolve away.

Method

1. In a roomy mixing bowl sift together the self raising flour, custard powder, bicarbonate of soda and salt.

2. Stir in the sugar then add the finely grated lemon zest. Make a well in the centre.

3. In a mixing jug combine the milk, oil, golden syrup, lemon juice and lemon extract – the mixture will separate but don't worry.

4. Mix by hand with a large spoon and start to add the liquid in thirds, stirring well between each addition. You will mix to a fairly thick yet smooth batter.

5. Divide between the two tins (I prefer to weigh the mixture) then transfer to the oven and bake for 20-25 minutes until the cakes are risen and golden.

6. Transfer to cooling racks and allow to cool in the tins for about 20 minutes before turning out and cooling completely.

7. Fill with jam and a vegan cream or really jazz up if this is a celebration cake.

Let Me Show You...
Watch My 'Recipe' Video
SCAN HERE

Sausage Rolls
MEAT FREE

MAKES 24 COCKTAIL SAUSAGE ROLLS
12 REGULAR SIZED

I love sausage rolls but had never contemplated or tried a vegetarian option until I was asked during my Challenge. I experimented with various flavours because the last thing a sausage roll should be is bland. These are absolutely perfect – packed with flavour and of course meat-free!

Ingredients

- 300g Puff Pastry
- 2 tbsp oil
- 1 small onion finely chopped
- 2 cloves garlic chopped
- 100g chestnut mushrooms roughly chopped
- 80g fresh white breadcrumbs
- 20g butter
- 50g grated cheese
- 1 can red kidney beans, rinsed and drained
- Salt and pepper
- 1 tsp ground mace
- 2 tsp dried sage
- 12 juniper berries crushed
- 4 tbsp brown sauce or tomato sauce
- 2 tbsp finely chopped fresh herbs (chives, parsley, sage, thyme, mint – a mixture of any of these)
- 1 egg
- Egg yolk mixed with 1 tbsp water for glazing

PREHEAT THE OVEN TO: 200 °C (FAN)

Nancy's Top Tip

HOW TO CUT AN ONION?

Ever wondered how chefs obtain those tiny dice of onion?
You need a sharp knife.

Start at the root end of the onion and cut off any tiny dried up roots but leave the core on.
Turn to the other end of the onion and slice off the top and peel off the skin. Cut the onion in half north to south.

Take one half and lay it cut side down on a chopping board with the core to your left. (If you are right handed) Take the point of the knife and follow nature's little cutting lines and cut from the core end to the right of the onion. The thinner the lines the smaller the dice will be so be patient. The onion will hold together because everything is anchored by the core.

The next part – hold the onion half in the left hand, still cut side down on the board and make horizontal slices in the onion. If the onion is small you may only be able to make one, if it is larger then two or three.

The final stage is the exciting bit. With your half onion still firmly in tact and holding it with the left hand then make vertical slices. Your onion will come away in the tiniest of dice perfect for cooking.

Repeat with the other onion half. Once you have mastered this skill you will never go back to thick lumpy chunks of onion in your cooking.

Method

1. In a medium sized frying pan heat the oil then add the finely chopped onion and fry gently for 10 minutes until the onion is softened

2. Add the garlic and mix well. Add the mushrooms to the pan and continue to fry until they start to colour.

3. Transfer to the bowl of a food processor. In the same pan melt the butter until foaming then add the breadcrumbs and stir regularly until the breadcrumbs are nicely browned. Transfer these to the food processor too.

4. Add all the remaining ingredients to the food processor then blitz until you have a thick paste. I then fill a piping bag with the filling to make constructing the sausage rolls much easier. Refrigerate until ready to use.

5. On a lightly floured surface roll out the pastry into a rectangle measuring approximately 50cm x 20cm. (20inches x 8 inches) I then use a pizza cutter to straighten all of the sides and cut into half lengthwise. You will now have two long strips of pastry. Brush egg down one long side of each strip then pipe the filling down the centre of each piece of pastry.

6. Fold the unglazed side of the pastry over the filling then roll the filled half of the pastry strip over so that it encloses the egg washed side underneath, forming a seal. Repeat with the second strip.

7. Cut each roll in half then transfer to a baking sheet and pop into the freezer for 20 minutes to half an hour.

8. Take from the freezer then egg wash all four lengths of filled pastry then with a sharp knife cut sausage rolls to the desired lengths. You will realise that the part freezing of the sausage rolls makes them much easier to cut

9. Either freeze for baking later or pop into a preheated oven at 200 degrees for 20-30 minutes until golden brown.

Let Me Show You...
Watch My 'Recipe' Video
SCAN HERE

Spinach and Ricotta Lasagne

MEAT FREE

SERVES 8 (OR MAKES 2 SMALL PORTIONS)

The whole family will love this and having one in the freezer is a perfect "go to" meal which can be popped into the oven and cooked from frozen.

Ingredients

- 1 banana shallot or small onion chopped small
- 3 cloves garlic chopped
- 30g butter
- 1 tsp dried mixed herbs
- 500g baby leaf spinach (if using spinach with large leaves then remove the stems)
- 250g ricotta cheese
- salt and pepper
- 300g tomato passata with 1 tsp sugar, ½ tsp salt and ½ tsp dried mixed herbs added.
- 6-8 fresh lasagne sheets (about 300kg)

FOR THE SAUCE:

- 50g butter
- 50g plain flour
- 750ml whole milk
- 1 tsp freshly grated nutmeg
- salt and white pepper (tsp of each)
- 120g grated mozarella or cheddar cheese
- 2-3 tbsp grated parmesan

USE: LARGE OVEN PROOF DISH.
MINE MEASURES 30CM X 25CM X 5CM DEEP
(OR TWO SMALLER DISHES: 25CM X 16CM X 5CM APPROX.)
PREHEAT THE OVEN TO: 200°C (FAN)

Method

1. Choose your largest casserole pan and melt the butter over a low heat then add the chopped onion, garlic and dried herbs.

2. Fry for about 5 minutes then add the spinach. (If you have washed your spinach before using make sure it has drained and dried)

3. Pop a lid on the casserole pan and leave to sweat down for 5 minutes.

4. Remove the lid, give a good stir then cook without a lid for a few minutes so that any liquid in the pan evaporates.

5. Take off the heat then stir in the ricotta cheese and seasoning. Set aside.

6. In a medium saucepan place the sauce ingredients. You will need the butter, cut into cubes, the flour, milk, nutmeg and salt and pepper.

7. Stir over a low heat until the butter melts then increase the heat and stir continually until the sauce thickens to the consistency of single cream or custard. Take off the heat and set aside.

8. Now is the time to assemble the lasagne.

9. Start by spreading about two thirds of the seasoned passata over the base of the dish.

10. Cover with a single lasagne sheet (or sheets if making a large one) then add half of the spinach and ricotta mix and two to three large spoonfuls of sauce.

11. Cover with another lasagne sheet(s) then the rest of the spinach mix, the rest of the tomato and a further few spoonfuls of white sauce

12. Add another lasagne layer then finish with a final white sauce layer followed by the grated mozzarella and a grating of parmesan. Chill or freeze until required.

13. Bake for 40 minutes, in pre-heated oven at 200 degrees, from chilled until dark golden brown and bubbling.

14. Bake for 50 minutes to 1 hour from frozen. Take from the oven and allow to stand for 10 minutes before serving.

Let Me Show You...
Watch My 'Recipe' Video
SCAN HERE

Muesli

SUGAR FREE

SERVES 12-15 SERVINGS

If you have ever examined the ingredients on the back of your pack of muesli you may be astounded at the amount of sugar included and, believe it or not, dried milk powder!

My sugar free version is now a breakfast staple in our house and once you've tried it – there is no going back.

Ingredients

- 300g porridge oats
- 45g oat bran
- ½ tsp each salt, ground cinnamon and nutmeg
- 45g toasted flaked almonds
- 70g pecan nuts or walnuts (chopped)

- 150g mixed seeds (pumpkin, sunflower, poppy, chia, sesame and goji berries for colour)
- 40g desiccated coconut or coconut flakes
- 100g chopped ready to eat apricots

Nancy's Top Tip

A 60g serving is just about right and pre-soaking in a little milk then topped off with yoghurt is delicious. Try soaking overnight in apple juice then topping off with a blob of yoghurt – Yummy!

Method

I mix everything in a large bowl together then transfer to a large Tupperware container with a pourer.

Let Me Show You...
Watch My 'Recipe' Video
SCAN HERE

Summer Pudding Terrine
GLUTEN FREE

SERVES 4-6

If you like summer pudding I promise this is the best you have ever tasted! Sometimes there is a sort of bitter after taste but with this recipe there is a depth of flavour and lusciousness and not too heavy on the sugar either ! I used a mixture of berries ready in the garden but also used frozen blackberries. Frozen fruit works well.

Ingredients

- 4-5 large slices sliced white bread crusts removed (use gluten free bread for a gf dessert)
- 600g fresh summer berries (redcurrants, blackcurrants, strawberries, raspberries, blueberries, blackberries) – reserve some for decoration – use a few frozen berries too...
- 20g caster sugar
- 30ml blackcurrant cordial
- 30ml water
- zest and juice of 1 orange
- 1 tbsp fruit jam
- 20g French morello flavour glace cherries chopped (with scissors)

USE: YOU WILL NEED 2 X 1 LB LOAF TINS AND TWO SHEETS OF PLASTIC TO BE USED FOR LINING THE TINS. THESE CAN BE WASHED AND REUSED WHEN ROLLING OUT BISCUITS OR PASTRY.
PREHEAT THE OVEN TO: 200 °C (FAN)

Method

1. In a medium saucepan place the sugar, cordial, orange juice, zest and water. Dissolve over a low heat until the sugar has dissolved then add the cherries, the jam and all the berries apart from the very soft raspberries and the soft strawberries.

2. Bring to the boil, simmer for a couple of minutes until just soft - take off the heat then add the strawberries and raspberries, stir and leave to one side.

3. Line the loaf tin with one large piece of plastic having oiled the tin first. The plastic will then stick to the tin and be easier to line - allow it to overlap the edges.

4. Use a rolling pin to flatten the bread a little then line the tin making sure there are no gaps. Pile the fruit mixture into the tin – pack it in really tightly. Reserve a little juice for serving and patching up any white bread showing later.

5. Cover with bread, fold over the plastic then place the second tin over the top and weigh down with weights from kitchen scales.

6. Place in the fridge and leave for 12 hours or overnight.

7. When ready to serve - remove the weights etc. and upturn on an oblong plate, remove the sheet of plastic.

8. Brush or pour juice over any white bits and serve garnished with fresh berries, crème fraiche, ice cream or double cream. Wash the sheet of plastic to use again later.

Pastry

Pastry

When we examine cooking and baking skills, pastry making seems to be the one that causes the most problems. Thinking about the reasons I believe, it is because pastry is precise; there are rules and these things alone can make people nervous.

I often describe a 'top end' pastry as a beautiful young woman even though a little aloof. She is dressed in all her finery – she is perfect to look at, slim and absolutely stunning. She appears superior and not approachable, totally out of your league. After a friend introduces her to you and after a little time you get to know her and find out that she is easy to work with, not in the least bit complicated, needs to be approached positively and once your nervousness has passed – you have a friend for life.

The making of pastry was taught to me by my grandmother and the first thing I learnt to make was a deep custard tart and I was probably about 8-10 years old.

My childhood wasn't great. My mother left when I was 13 and I found myself looking after a house from that early age. Looking back my grandmother tried to hold things together for us and I spent hours with her, days in fact. Her house was always warm, smelling of food and there was always lots to do. On the other hand the house where I lived with my father and brother seemed barren and only as homely as I could make it.

Pastry then of course was always made by hand. These days I use my food processor which mixes it in seconds but the recipe is just the same whichever method is used. A basic shortcrust pastry is simply flour, fat and liquid – that's it! But the quantities have to be exact. The right amount of liquid is key to successful pastry.

I have looked at many pastry making recipes and methods but I have yet to find a recipe that will give EXACT quantities when it comes to the amount of liquid to be added. A standard quote will be "add sufficient liquid to bring everything together to make a dough". A better recipe may say "add between 2 tbsp and 4 tbsp" – this is not EXACT – we need to be exact! Too much liquid and the dough will be sticky meaning more flour will have to be added, more handling is required and before we have even started, already our exact ingredient quantities have changed. This dough will have been overworked resulting in a tough crust. On the other hand too little liquid and the dough will be crumbly, difficult to form into a dough, will break when rolling out and will have such a crumbly (short) texture that it will easily break and not hold a filling.

The perfect pastry – shortcrust - is the most versatile of all pastry and can be used in your pies, tarts and quiches. Once you have mastered short crust pastry – the others will be easy to learn. Thin and crispy, baked all the way through and utterly delicious. We have all seen some poor pies and quiches with thick overworked pastry, grey and raw underneath with a pale anaemic crust. Here's how to achieve perfection.

FLOUR

I use plain flour for shortcrust pastry. Some use self raising flour but the raising agent will encourage the dough to puff up during baking and become thicker even though it may have a softer texture. My pastry (and yours) will be paper thin.

SALT

I add just a tiny pinch of salt to the flour because I use salted butter.

FATS

When mixing pastry in a food processor the fats need to be well chilled. If mixing by hand the fats need to be at room temperature to make 'rubbing in' more convenient. The type of fat is really down to taste. For a sweet shortcrust pastry I use all butter whereas for a savoury pie I will use half butter and half lard.

METHODS OF MAKING PASTRY

My method is simple and there is no guess work involved. Firstly, switch the button on your digital scales from kg to lbs or get the old pounds and ounces weights from the back of your cupboard for your balance scales. The rule now is simple: Use half fat to flour and for every ounce of fat to be used, you will be using 1 tbsp liquid. And that's it.

Nancy's Top Tip
How big is an egg yolk?

When using an egg yolk for a richer pastry each egg yolk counts as 1 tbsp. Beat your egg yolk with the rest of the measured water.

The method in a nutshell...

1. Place the flour and salt (lets say 8 oz) in the bowl of your food processor with the blade attachment. Then Add 4oz fat well chilled and cut into small cubes. Blitz for only 4-5 seconds just long enough for the mixture to look crumbly. Remember pastry likes to be cool and hates to be handled.

2. Turn off the machine then measure out 4 tbsp icy cold water

3. Turn the machine on again and pour that cold water in a thin steady stream and keep the machine going until the dough comes together in a ball – about 10 seconds.

4. Take the dough from the machine and pop into the fridge, wrapped in greaseproof paper or a beeswax wrap (see Home Time: Sustainable Hints & Tips) I am not using cling film. This dough will need to cool off, firm up and relax for about half an hour. Leaving the pastry to rest allows the gluten to develop making it easier to roll out.

5. Once the dough is rested now is the time for rolling out. How many times have you seen a work surface covered in flour ready to roll out the rested dough? I no longer do this because I want to keep the flour and fat quantities exact. I have two sheets

of plastic and I use them again and again. The plastic needs to be not too thick and not too thin that it creases. I have found a freezer bag to be the perfect thickness. Cut down one side and across the bottom and you have your first sheet. Repeat with a second bag.

6. Lay one piece of plastic on the work surface, place your ball of dough in the centre then your second piece over the top and start rolling. The beauty of this method is that you can lift the pastry up, turn it around, try it for size over your tin and all the time the plastic holds it in place. You can lift it up to the light and see 'thick' bits that need to be smoothed out. When the weather or your kitchen are very warm you can slide the whole lot into the fridge for 10 minutes to firm up.. Even better – there is no worktop to wipe down.

7. When ready to line your tin, take your chilled pastry, peel off one side of the plastic and using the other piece of plastic as an aid, lay the pastry down into the tin. You can then shape the dough into the tin with the fingers moulding the plastic right into the corners. No holes in the pastry as the plastic is protecting it.

8. Chill for about 10 minutes before peeling off that second piece. Wipe or wash the plastic sheets and store ready for your next pie or tart.

Let Me Show You...
Watch My 'Pastry' Video
SCAN HERE

School Dinners Meat Pie

SERVES BETWEEN 12 AND 16 PEOPLE

I love this pie – it can be made in advance and baked when the family arrive. It is also very economical yet everyone loves it, particularly children. It actually reminds me of school dinners which I adored! (School dinners of 50 years ago by the way).

This pie can be frozen unbaked if required and then defrosted in the fridge or even baked from frozen. I serve this pie with mashed potatoes and peas – also you will need some lovely gravy. Again I freeze left over gravy which is ideal with this pie. I make two pies in 20cm square loose bottomed cake tins. The secret is to cut the vegetables very small.

I often make a pie for now and one for the freezer.

Ingredients

TO MAKE THE FILLING:

- 1kg minced steak
- 125g lardons or bacon cut into small pieces
- 2 tbsp vegetable oil
- 2 onions chopped small
- 2 carrots chopped small
- 2 celery sticks chopped small
- 2 cloves garlic chopped
- 400ml chicken or beef stock

- 100ml red wine
- 2 tbsp dark brown sugar
- 2 large potatoes diced small (1cm)
- 2 tbsp plain flour
- 3 tbsp hp sauce
- salt and pepper
- 3 tbsp chopped fresh parsley and 1 tsp dried thyme
- 100g grated cheese

PREHEAT THE OVEN TO: 100 °C (FAN)

Nancy's Top Tip

How do I keep my bunch of parsley fresh?

*Fresh herbs sold in plastic packets are great for the recipe you are making today but then you leave any leftovers in the packet and pop them into the fridge. The next time you see them they are black, slimy and unfit for use. When you have used the herbs you need, take the remainder from the packet and wrap in a piece of kitchen paper which has been sprayed with water.
Wrap then in a beeswax wrap (see Home time: Sustainable Hints & Tips) then pop back into the fridge.
Your herbs will now keep over a week.
PS: Basil hates the fridge
– keep it in a cool place wrapped as stated.*

Method

TO MAKE THE FILLING:

1. In a large casserole pan add the oil then fry the onions on a low heat for 10-15 minutes until soft and translucent.

2. Add the carrot, celery, garlic and potato and stir well. Cook for a further 5-10 minutes then take off the heat. In the meantime heat a frying pan and fry the lardons until well brown and crisp – transfer to the casserole pan.

3. Dry fry the mince in batches and add this to the casserole. By dry frying I mean, have the pan really hot, add no fat and add about two handfuls of mince at a time – no more or else it will boil and not fry. The mince needs to have a brown crust before transferring to the casserole.

4. Add the sugar to the casserole pan then the flour and stir well, adding seasoning.

5. De-glaze the frying pan with the red wine and add this to the casserole. Turn off the heat. De-glazing means pouring the wine into the hot pan and it will bubble and fizz but at the same time will take all the lovely meat particles from the bottom of the pan.

6. Finally add the stock and

dried thyme to the casserole and give everything a good stir. Bring to a gentle simmer then transfer to a low oven (100 degrees) or a slow cooker for 5 hours with a lid. You can cook the meat quicker on a higher heat if you wish. Pop your casserole into the oven at 180 degrees for 1 hour and 30 minutes.

7. After the cooking time remove the lid. The meat filling needs to be thick and wholesome.

8. Stir well then add the fresh parsley and grated cheese. Allow the filling to cool completely – taste and check the seasoning.

Nancy's Top Tip

Season to Taste

I have read this so many times in recipes but how do I know my food tastes the best it can be without over or under doing the salt and pepper? This applies to casseroles, pie fillings, soups well in fact anything that needs to be seasoned well. Take a ladle of the sauce and place in a separate bowl. Add more salt and pepper and taste. If this sample dish tastes better than your original then you know to add more seasoning. If on the other hand it is too salty or there is too much pepper then you know your original panful is seasoned well enough.

Too late – I have oversalted!

Do not worry – there is a rescue. A tablespoon of jam will counteract saltiness in food, so if you have oversalted your gravy, casserole or stew. Stir through raspberry jam or redcurrant jelly and no one will ever know.

Ingredients

TO MAKE THE PASTRY:

- 1lb 12 oz plain flour
- 7oz butter diced
- 7oz lard diced
- 1 egg and sufficient cold water to make 14tbsp total liquid

- ½ tsp salt
- egg yolk mixed with 1 tsp water to use as an egg wash

PREHEAT THE OVEN TO: 200 °C (FAN)

Method

TO MAKE THE PASTRY:

1. I use a food processor to make pastry. Place the flour and salt into the bowl with the blade attached. Add the chilled fats which have been cubed. Blitz for just about 10 seconds until the mixture resembles breadcrumbs then with the motor running pour the liquid in a steady stream and allow the dough to form a ball.

2. Remove from the machine, divide into four (or six if making a lattice top) equal pieces, pop into a plastic bag or wrap in cling film and chill for half an hour.

3. On a lightly floured surface, roll out 1 piece of the pastry into a rough square shape large enough to fit the tin then bottom line one of the two tins – fill to the top with the cold meat filling then roll out a second piece and top off the pie with a pastry lid, sealing the top and bottom together by wetting the edge with a damp finger.

4. Crimp the edges and make a few air holes in the pastry lid.

5. Egg wash then chill until required. Repeat with the second pie

6. Preheat the oven to 200 degrees.

7. Egg wash the pies once more then bake for 35-45 minutes until golden brown.

8. Leave to stand for 10 minutes before taking from the tin and cutting into portions and serving.

Nancy's Top Tip

Egg washing the pastry twice gives a deeper, richer glaze to the pastry.

How to make a lattice top to your pie

Roll out two 20cm pastry squares and cut into strips as shown on the video. There is sufficient pastry in the recipe to make two latticed pies. You will have left over pastry (freeze it) if you pop on a plain lid.

The pie filling needs to be really thick and wholesome.

If after the cooking time you appear to have a thin filling give it a good stir then pop into a high oven (200 degrees) for 1 hour without a lid to thicken up. Leave to go completely cold before assembling the pies

Never fill a pie with a hot filling...

When working with pastry every part of the process has to be cold. A hot or warm filling will warm the pastry and your finished pie will probably be undercooked at the bottom.

Let Me Show You...
Watch My 'Recipe' Video
SCAN HERE

Chicken and Tarragon Pie

SERVES 6 PEOPLE

Chicken pies can be dry and lacking in flavour. I poach my chicken breasts briefly before cooking this pie – the chicken is moist and flavoursome. This is an absolutely delicious pie, ideal for mid-week family eating and equally good enough to serve in the evening to friends.

Ingredients

FOR THE FILLING:

- 1 small onion finely chopped
- 20g butter and 1 tbsp oil
- 4 skinless chicken breasts
- 150g button chestnut mushrooms sliced
- small handful dried wild mushrooms (10g) steeped with 200ml boiling water for 30 minutes then drained and chopped (keep the mushroom liquor)
- small bunch fresh tarragon – use about 2 tbsp leaves torn from the stalks or 1 tbsp dried
- 4 spring onions finely chopped
- 60g frozen peas
- 20g flour, 20g soft butter, 2 tsp dry mustard powder, salt and pepper
- pinch ground mace (or 1 tsp grated nutmeg)
- 80ml double cream
- 400ml chicken stock
- 200ml white wine
- 1 egg (to glaze the pie)

Ingredients

FOR THE BASIC SHORTCRUST
PASTRY:

- 16oz plain flour
- 4oz salted butter cut into cubes and well chilled
- 4oz lard cut into cubes and well chilled
- 8 tbsp chilled water
- salt

USE: A SQUARE 8 INCH (20CM) LOOSE BOTTOMED CAKE TIN
OR 9 INCH (23 CM) PIE DISH OR 2 X SHALLOW 8 INCH (20CM)
PIES MADE ON PLATES. GREASE WELL OR BRUSH WITH LINING
PASTE – IT IS PERFECT FOR PASTRY AS WELL AS CAKES.
PREHEAT THE OVEN TO: 200 °C (FAN)

Nancy's Top Tip

TIP: How do I get rid of onion and garlic smells
from my chopping board?

Take half a freshly cut lemon and rub the cut
side across the chopping board 'to and fro'.
The lemon will neutralise any odour from your smelly veg!

Method

TO MAKE THE PASTRY:

1. In a food processor blitz the flour, salt and fats to the breadcrumb stage then gradually add the chilled water and continue with the motor running until a ball of dough is formed.

2. Divide in two then wrap in greaseproof paper or beeswax wrap and chill for at least half an hour.

3. In a saucepan bring the white wine and stock to a gentle simmer then add the chicken breasts, cover with a lid and poach for 15 minutes on the lowest heat.

4. Remove from the liquid, allow to cool slightly then chop into 2cm chunks then set aside.

5. In a large frying pan heat the oil and butter then fry the onion gently for 10 minutes until golden and soft. Add the finely sliced mushrooms and chopped wild mushrooms. Fry for a few minutes only before adding the butter, flour, mustard powder, mace and salt and pepper.

6. Stir for a minute or two to cook the flour then add sufficient liquid from the stock pan little by little until you have a thick sauce (you will need about 150-200ml stock).

7. Transfer this mixture to a large bowl then add the spring onions, peas, fresh tarragon leaves, 50ml of the cream and the poached chopped chicken. Stir thoroughly and leave to go completely cold. The filling should be quite thick.

8. Use the frying pan to slightly reduce the remaining stock and wine then add 30ml cream, stir, season and taste then serve with the pie. If the sauce needs thickening simply mix 1 tbsp cornflour with cold water to a thin paste then stir into the hot sauce.

Method

TO MAKE THE PIE:

1. Roll out the pastry then line the greased tin. Put the cold filling inside with a pie blackbird if your pie tin is deep then roll out the pastry lid, dampen the edges then place the lid over and seal the edges and decorate.

2. Egg wash the pie then chill for half an hour.

3. Egg wash again then bake for 40-45 minutes at 200 degrees until the pie is golden.

4. Serve hot on warmed plates.

Nancy's Top Tip
TIP: Quick Plate Warmer

Your meal is ready to plate up but you have forgotten to warm the plates. Provided you have a microwave oven and your plates do not have any silver or gold trim you can warm them instantly. Spray each plate with a little water then stack them on top of each other in the microwave for 30 seconds – that is sufficient for two plates. More plates need more time – 4 plates probably a minute.

Let Me Show You...
Watch My 'Recipe' Video
SCAN HERE

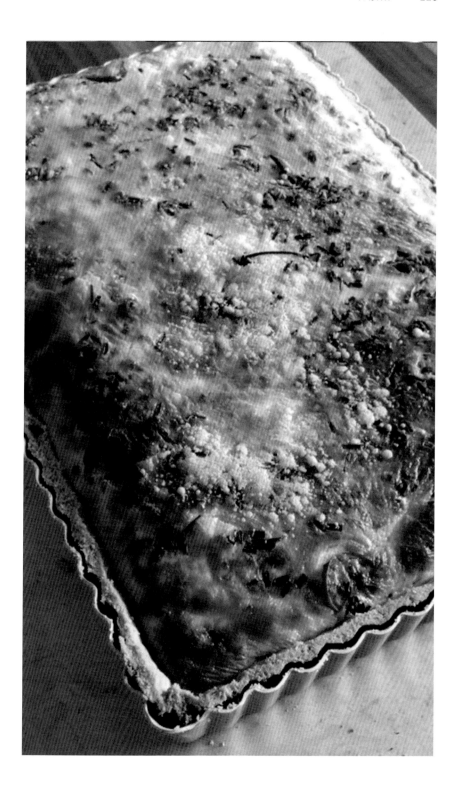

Cheese and Onion Flan

Thin, light crispy pastry is an essential and I have a few tips ensuring success. Cheese and onions are perfect partners and are delicious in this family bake.

Ingredients

FOR THE FILLING:

- 2 large onions
- 1 tbsp butter and 1 tbsp vegetable oil
- 3 tbsp water
- 1 tsp finely grated nutmeg
- 150g cream cheese
- 4 eggs
- 200g grated strong cheddar cheese
- 150ml whole milk
- salt and pepper
- 3 tbsp finely chopped chives

FOR THE PASTRY:

- 6oz plain flour
- pinch of salt
- 3oz chilled lard (or butter) or half of each
- 3 tbsp chilled water

USE: A 9 INCH (23CM) LOOSE BOTTOMED FLAN TIN LIGHTLY GREASED OR FOR A REALLY DEEP FLAN AN 8 INCH 20CM TIN 5CM DEEP
PREHEAT THE OVEN TO: 180 °C (FAN)

Nancy's Top Tip

When baking a quiche, flan, custard tart or lemon tart – in fact anything with a very runny filling I tend to fill the pastry shell half full then transfer it to the oven on a low shelf. Once in place I then fill it to the very top knowing there will be no spills.

Method

1. Start by cooking the onions for the filling. In a roomy frying pan gently heat the butter and oil together then add the finely sliced onions. Give a good stir and fry gently uncovered for 3-4 minutes.

2. Add then the 3 tbsp water and the nutmeg, cover with a lid and cook on the gentlest heat for 10 minutes. After the cooking time, remove the lid, stir again – check that the onions are soft and tender then transfer the cooked onions to a large cold bowl and set aside.

TO MAKE THE PASTRY:

1. Place the flour and salt in the bowl of a food processor then add the chilled cubed fat and blitz for a few seconds until the mixture resembles fine breadcrumbs. With the motor running, pour in the water and allow the dough to come together in a ball then remove from the machine, wrap in greaseproof paper and chill for at least half an hour. Preheat the oven to 180 degrees(fan).

2. Once the pastry has rested roll out thinly (I find it easier to roll between two sheets of thin reusable plastic) and line the prepared flan tin allowing the surplus pastry to overhang the edges of the tin.

3. Chill for 15 minutes then prick the base of the pastry shell with a fork, line with baking paper and baking beans then bake blind for 15 minutes.

4. After the baking time remove the tart from the oven and carefully lift off the baking paper and beans. Have a look at your pastry base.. It should be dry and pale golden. If it looks grey and waxy then pop it back into the oven for 2-3 minutes to completely dry out.

5. Once you are happy with your pastry shell you can trim the over hanging edges of the pastry with a serrated knife then. To make sure the pastry shell is completely waterproof paint over the base with the beaten egg taken from the eggs to be used for the filling. Pop back into the oven and bake for a further 2 minutes.

TO MAKE THE FILLING

1. Place the eggs, cheese, cream cheese, whole milk and seasoning into the bowl with the onions and mix well. I prefer a smooth filling so I blitzed my filling with a stick blender. Add then the chopped chives.

2. Take the trimmed pastry shell and pour in the filling. Slide the tart back into the oven and bake for 35 minutes until dark golden and set. If you bake a deep flan then allow about 50 minutes turning the temperature of the oven down to 150 degrees for the final 20 minutes to avoid over browning.

3. This tart is easier to cut once cooled.

Let Me Show You...
Watch My 'Recipe' Video
SCAN HERE

Courgette Quiche

SERVES 8-10 PEOPLE

Growing courgettes is easy and once they get going you will have so many! They are best harvested while small and before the seeds form inside. This recipe is a looker but courgettes on their own are pretty tasteless so I have bumped up the flavour with green pesto and finely grated parmesan cheese. It tastes so good!

Ingredients

FOR THE FILLING:

- 2 tbsp green pesto
- 50g finely grated strong cheddar cheese
- 4-5 small courgettes
- 3 eggs
- 300ml single cream
- salt and white pepper
- freshly grated nutmeg (about 1 tsp)
- 1-2 tsp finely chopped fresh mild red chilli

FOR THE PASTRY:

- 6oz plain flour
- 3oz chilled butter cut into dice
- pinch salt
- 1 egg yolk mixed with 2 tbsp cold water

USE: A LOOSE BOTTOMED FLAN TIN 9 INCHES (23CM) IN DIAMETER AND 1 INCH (2.5CM) DEEP LIGHTLY GREASED.
PREHEAT THE OVEN TO: 190 °C (FAN)

Nancy's Top Tip

TIP: If you are afraid your liquid filling may overfill your quiche - fill it as full as you dare then bake for ten minutes by which time the filling will have settled, you can then open the oven door and pour in any you have left over from the jug.

Method

1. Start by making the pastry. In a food processor place the flour and salt, add the chilled butter then blitz for a few seconds just until the mixture resembles fine breadcrumbs. With the motor running add the egg mix in a steady stream and allow the machine to run until the dough forms a ball. Wrap in greaseproof paper or beeswax wrap then chill for 30 minutes.

2. Place the pastry between two sheets of plastic, roll out large enough to comfortably fit the tin, then peel off one sheet of plastic, fit the pastry into the tin and chill again

3. Peel off the second sheet, prick the base all over with a fork, fill with paper and baking beans then chill again until the oven reaches a temperature of 190 degrees (fan).

4. When the oven has reached temperature bake the tart blind for 15 minutes then remove from the oven, trim the pastry overhang using a serrated knife whilst warm and then brush the inside with beaten egg (taken from the mixture for the filling) and pop back into the oven for 3 minutes to set.

5. Take from the oven and set aside. When the pastry case has cooled a little spread the pesto over the base of the tin then sprinkle the cheese over and a grating of white pepper and salt.

6. To prepare the courgettes, using a vegetable peeler, take ribbons from the courgettes and roll these - not particularly uniform. Have some rolled tightly and others rolled loosely - just adds interest to your finished tart.

7. Starting around the outside and finishing in the centre arrange the little courgette rolls then sprinkle over a grating of white pepper.

8. Whisk together the eggs and cream in a jug, season with salt and pepper, add the nutmeg then carefully pour this over the filling. So that the courgettes are defined during baking it is important not to bury them with the egg and milk. I fill each hole carefully - time consuming I know but it is worth it.

9. Sprinkle over the chilli pieces then pop into the oven, turn down to 180 degrees (fan) and bake for 25-30 minutes until just starting to brown.

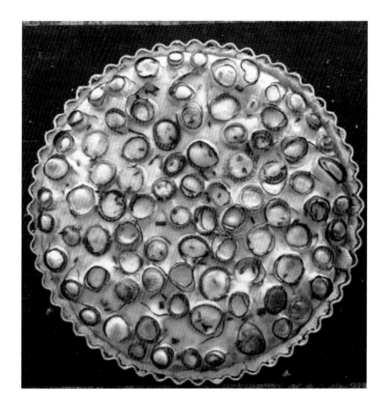

Single Serve Whole Apple & Blackberry Pies

SERVES 6

I love to create little bakes that need no special tins, can be single serve and that look amazing. If you want a job for a rainy day – this one is perfect! These pies will freeze unbaked but apply the egg wash before freezing.

These individual pies can look top end and then served up with pride to your friends and family. They can be enjoyed with cream, custard or ice cream and they are a winner. You will be serving a whole, cored skinless apple filled with blackberries and covered in a sweet shortcrust pastry.

Ingredients

FOR THE PASTRY:

- 12oz plain flour
- 6oz butter cold
- 6 tbsp egg yolk and water (2 egg yolks and 4 tbsp cold water)
- 1 tbsp icing sugar

FOR THE FILLING:

- 6 medium sized dessert apple
- 1 tbsp lemon juice
- 1 cinnamon stick
- 18-20 frozen blackberries and 2 tbsp white chocolate chips
- beaten egg yolk to wash over the finished pies and egg white for glue

USE: 6 EVEN SIZED DESSERT APPLES
PREHEAT THE OVEN TO: 190 °C (FAN)

Method

FOR THE APPLES:

1. You will need a pan large enough to hold the apples.

2. Fill it to just over half way with water, add the lemon juice and the cinnamon stick. Bring the pan of water to the boil. Whilst the water is heating, core the apples then gently score the skin of the apple all around the circumference, half way up with a sharp knife. Just score the skin, don't cut through to the apple flesh. As each apple is cored, pop it into the pan of water. The lemon juice in the water will prevent discolouration of the apple.

3. Bring the apples to the boil and cook for 5 minutes. This is the tricky bit because it really depends how hard the apples are to start with as to how long they need to cook. I have found that five minutes is just right. Using a slotted spoon take each apple from the water and leave to cool on kitchen paper.

4. When cool enough to handle and using a vegetable knife carefully lift and peel off the skin. Leave your apples then to go completely cold. Keep the cinnamon stick for later.

TO MAKE THE PASTRY:

1. Rub together the flour and butter until the mixture resembles fine breadcrumbs.

2. Alternatively, if you have a food processor place the flour, icing sugar and butter in the bowl with the blade attachment fitted. Blitz until the mixture resembles breadcrumbs then with the motor running add the liquid. Allow the dough to form into a ball then wrap and leave to rest in the fridge for half an hour

3. Take the dough from the fridge then divide the dough into six equal pieces

WHEN READY TO ASSEMBLE THE APPLE PIES:

1. Work on one apple at a time. Have a baking sheet lined with reusable baking parchment or paper. Roll out a piece of the pastry and cut out a circle large enough to sit the apple on comfortably with an overhang that can be pushed up and around the bottom of the apple. Using a small oval or round cutter then cut out a number of shapes (you will need a lot!)

2. Place the cold peeled apple onto the pastry circle then force 2-3 frozen blackberries down the centre core cavity, popping 5-6 white chocolate chips in there too. The white chocolate sweetens the fruit whilst preventing the blackberries bleeding too much during baking

3. Use a small paintbrush and egg white and working from the bottom in a clockwise direction, patiently stick the pastry pieces onto each other and around the apple – overlapping as you go and not leaving any raw apple showing.

4. When you get to the top of the apple try using a shard from the cinnamon stick that was boiled earlier and cut out two pastry leaves to decorate the pie.

5. Once complete pop the apples into the fridge to chill and firm up.

6. Preheat the oven to 190 degrees

7. Brush the apples with egg yolk and bake for 25-30 minutes until the pastry is golden.

8. Serve warm.

Let Me Show You...
Watch My 'Recipe' Video
SCAN HERE

Blackberry Pie

SERVES 8

Blackberry pie baked well is one of Britain's classics. The most common problem is that the juice from the fruits runs from the pie, bubbles over the top or leaks so badly after the first slice is cut that the pastry is soggy and not pleasant.

A slice of fruit pie should be full of fruit, not overly sweet, cuts well, no wet or soggy bottom and no leaking juices. Not as easy as it sounds and blackberries are probably the most difficult fruit to accomplish the perfect pie.

Here is my recipe - perfect in every way.

Ingredients

FOR THE PASTRY:

- 7oz plain flour
- 1oz icing sugar
- pinch salt
- 4oz chilled butter cut into dice
- 4 tbsp egg (1 egg and 1 egg yolk beaten together)

FOR THE FILLING:

- 400g fresh blackberries
- 2 tbsp semolina
- 20g grated white chocolate
- 2 tsp sugar
- For washing the pastry- left over egg white and vanilla sugar (or granulated)

USE: A 9 INCH (23CM) PIE TIN LIGHTLY GREASED AND TWO FREEZER BAGS SLIT BOTTOM AND ONE SIDE.
PREHEAT THE OVEN TO: 200 °C (FAN)

Method

1. In a food processor place the flour, salt, sugar and chilled butter and blitz until mixture resembles bread crumbs. With the motor running add the egg in a steady stream and allow the dough to form into a ball. Wrap in greaseproof paper or beeswax wrap and chill for minimum of half an hour.

2. Lay one sheet of plastic on the worktop, place half of the pastry in the centre, place the other sheet over the top then roll out the pastry. No extra flour required and no sticking to the surface.

3. When the pastry is large enough to fit in the tin, chill for a couple of minutes then remove one sheet of plastic, line the pastry tin and with the other plastic sheet uppermost, mould the pastry into the tin.

4. Chill again for a few minutes before peeling off the second sheet. Trim the edges then repeat with the second piece of pastry - keep it in the plastic and pop into the fridge whilst you prepare the filling.

5. Take the pastry lined tin then sprinkle the semolina over the base.

6. Add the blackberries followed by the grated white chocolate and sugar

7. Dampen the edges of the pastry with water then take the pastry top, peel off one side, then lay the pastry over the pie. Secure the edges, trim the pastry, crimp and then chill until the oven reaches temperature.

8. Heat the oven to 200 degrees (fan) with a baking sheet on the middle shelf. When the oven is at temperature, take your pie from the fridge and brush with the left over egg white then sprinkle with vanilla sugar (if you have it) or granulated sugar.

9. Bake for 25 minutes until the pie is golden. The juices are prevented from leaking as they are soaked up by the semolina.

10. Leave the pie to cool before cutting and when it is just warm slice and serve with vanilla ice-cream or fresh cream or custard.

Let Me Show You...
Watch My 'Recipe' Video
SCAN HERE

Rich Chocolate Tart

SERVES 8-10

Totally delicious, rich and decadent. This tart can be decorated simply or lavishly depending on your mood, the occasion or the season.

Ingredients

FOR THE CHOCOLATE PASTRY:

- 4oz plain flour (00 flour is best)
- 1oz cocoa powder
- 1oz icing sugar
- pinch salt
- 3oz chilled butter cut into dice
- 1 egg yolk and 2 tbsp egg white (beat the white up to frothy to make it easier to measure)
- 1/8 tsp ground star anise or chinese five spice (optional)

FOR THE CHOCOLATE FILLING:

- 300g dark chocolate chopped
- 150ml milk
- 150ml double cream
- 2 tsp vanilla extract
- 2 eggs

USE: A LOOSE BOTTOMED FLAN TIN 9 INCHES (23CM) WIDE X 1 INCH (2.5CM) DEEP LIGHTLY GREASED.
PREHEAT THE OVEN TO: 190 °C (FAN)

Nancy's Top Tip

TIP: If you find chocolate pastry too difficult

Chocolate pastry is a little more difficult to handle and needs to be rolled out really thinly because it tends to puff up in the oven. If you don't feel confident make this tart using a straight forward sweet shortcrust pastry as follows.

- 5oz Plain flour
- 1oz Icing sugar
- pinch salt
- 3oz chilled butter cut into dice
- 1 egg yolk mixed with 2 tbsp cold water

Method

TO MAKE THE PASTRY:

1. In a food processor simply place all the dry ingredients then blitz briefly until well combined.

2. Add the chilled butter and blitz for a few seconds only until the mixture resembles breadcrumbs. With the motor running, add the egg yolk and the 2 tbsp egg white (no more) and allow the dough to form into a ball. Take the fairly sticky dough from the machine and wrap in greaseproof paper then chill for at least half an hour.

3. Do not roll out using flour as this will streak and colour

your dark chocolate pastry.

4. Take two sheets of thin plastic. I use two cut open freezer bags (cut along the bottom and one side), I use them over and over again

5. Place the pastry in between the plastic sheets and start to roll out the pastry until it is large enough to cover your flan tin. If the pastry is sticky between the plastic pop it back into the fridge for 10 minutes to firm up.

6. Peel off one piece of plastic and with the pastry adhered to the other piece, lay the pastry face down into the tin. Use your fingers along the

plastic to mould the pastry into the corners of the tin.

7. Chill for another 10-15 minutes before peeling off the second sheet of plastic.

8. After peeling off the second plastic, prick the base with a fork then line the chilled case with paper and baking beans. The pastry can overlap the edges of the tin and be trimmed after blind baking.

9. Blind bake for 15 minutes then remove from the oven and carefully lift the paper and beans.

10. The pastry can now be trimmed with a serrated knife whilst warm and set aside whilst the filling is prepared.

11. Lower the oven temperature to 100 degrees

TO MAKE THE FILLING:

1. Break the chocolate into small pieces and place in a roomy bowl along with the vanilla.

2. In a small saucepan add the milk and cream, place over a gentle heat and allow to come up to simmering point.

3. Pour the warmed milk over the chocolate pieces and stir well until the chocolate is melted and the mixture is smooth and shiny.

4. Allow to cool down slightly then stir in the eggs. Give everything a good mix then pour into the cooked, trimmed pastry case

5. Make sure your oven has cooled right down then pop the tart into the very low oven and bake for 50 minutes.

6. Leave to go completely cold then decorate to your choosing. Raspberries are fabulous.

Let Me Show You...
Watch My 'Recipe' Video
SCAN HERE

Custard Tart

MAKES 9

A classic bake but can be difficult to get right. My recipe and tips will ensure crisp and light sweet shortcrust pastry baked all the way through and filled with a smooth nutmeg and vanilla flavoured creamy custard.

Ingredients

FOR THE PASTRY:

- 9oz plain flour
- 1oz icing sugar
- pinch salt
- 5oz chilled butter cut into 1 cm dice
- 2 egg yolks and 3 tbsp icy cold water

FOR THE CUSTARD FILLING:

- 25g caster sugar
- ½ tsp vanilla extract
- ½ grated nutmeg
- knob of butter (15g)
- 100ml double cream
- 150ml whole milk

2 eggs

USE: A 12 HOLE DEEP MUFFIN TIN LIGHTLY GREASED AND A BAKING SHEET
PREHEAT THE OVEN TO: 190 °C (FAN)

Method

TO MAKE THE PASTRY:

1. Place the flour, salt and sugar in the bowl of a food processor with the blade attached. Add the chilled butter and blitz for only a few seconds until the mixture resembles fine breadcrumbs.

2. Mix the egg yolks with the water in a small jug and

with the motor running, pour the liquid in a steady stream and allow the dough to come together. Take from the mixer, pop into a plastic bag and chill for at least half an hour.

3. Once the dough has firmed up and rested take from the fridge and I prefer to roll out between two sheets of plastic as then no additional flour is required. Roll out the pastry to about the thickness of a £1 coin then use a 4 inch (10cm) cutter to cut out 9 circles. Re-use trimmings as necessary.

4. You may find it easier to mould the cut out pastry circles around the end of your rolling pin and then lower this into the muffin tin. The pastry will then fit perfectly and there is no danger of it cracking, or splitting   by putting your fingers through.

5. Pop the tray of pastry into the fridge to firm up whilst your oven comes to temperature. Heat the oven to 190 degrees centigrade (fan)

6. Once the oven has come to temperature - line each of the cups with a paper bun case (slightly smaller than a cupcake case) then fill with either rice, lentils or baking beans. Pop straight into the oven and bake "blind" for 14 minutes.

7. Take from the oven and have ready a baking sheet. Hold onto those little paper cases and lift the pastry shells from the muffin tin. The pastry will adhere to the paper but you need to do this whilst the pastry is hot otherwise the paper cases will release themselves from the pastry and the shells will stay in the tin.

8. Place the pastry shells onto the baking sheet and then once cooled slightly, you can remove the paper cases and lentils.

9. Pop the pastry shells back into the oven to completely bake through and dry out for just 2-3 minutes more

10. Take the pastry shells out of the oven and immediately drop the oven temperature to 140 degrees c (fan). I even leave the oven door open for about 30 seconds to allow some of the heat to escape.

TO MAKE THE FILLING:

1. Place the cream, milk, sugar, butter and vanilla in a small saucepan and heat gently, stirring all the time. It needs to be heated only to the point where the sugar and butter dissolve so when there is no gritty feel to the bottom of the pan take it off the heat. Don't let it boil.

2. In a 1 pint jug beat the two eggs then pour over the warm milk mixture in a thin steady stream. Grate over about half of the nutmeg and mix this in too.

3. Pour the mixture into the little pastry cases, filling them as full as you can. You may find it easier to fill the cases once the tray is in the oven then there is no chance of them spilling but be careful – don't burn yourself. Sprinkle over more grated nutmeg then bake for just 13-15 minutes.

4. Take from the oven when the centre of each tart still has a slight wobble when you move the baking sheet – the custard will firm up as it cools. An overbaked custard is rubbery and tough and may even crack.

5. Allow to cool to room temperature – delicious.

Let Me Show You...
Watch My 'Recipe' Video
SCAN HERE

Luxury Mince Pies

MAKES 12 DEEP FILLED PIES

These mince pies, even though they are mine, I have to say are the best I have tasted. The mincemeat is easy to make and the pastry quick but just needs a little careful handling. The addition of the chocolate chips and the fact that there is no suet in my mincemeat means they are less likely to bubble up during baking.

Ingredients

FOR THE MINCEMEAT

- makes 2 x 1lb jars (sufficient mincemeat for 24 pies)
- 300g mixed dried fruit and peel
- 100g ready to eat apricots cut into small pieces
- 100g dried cranberries
- 200g soft brown sugar
- ½ tsp ground mace
- 1 tsp ground cinnamon

- 2 tsp ground mixed spice
- finely grated zest of 1 orange and 1 lemon
- 4 tbsp cointreau or brandy
- 8 tbsp orange/lemon juice from the fruits
- 6 cardamom pods, split and the seeds crushed
- 50g butter
- 20g dark chocolate chips

FOR THE PASTRY:

- 9oz plain flour
- pinch salt
- 1oz icing sugar
- 5oz butter (chilled and cut into cubes)
- 1 egg yolk beaten with 4 tbsp cold water

USE: USE A 12 HOLE DEEP MUFFIN TIN

Nancy's Top Tip

TIP: How to get pastry into the bottom of a muffin tin

Mould the pastry circle around the base of your rolling pin to aid placing in the base of your deep muffin tin. You'll not then push your fingers through!

Method

TO MAKE THE MINCEMEAT:

1. Grate the zests from the fruit and put to one side.

2. In a large pan, melt the butter and the sugar and fruit juices over a low heat. When the sugar is no longer grainy, add all the other ingredients and mix well, making sure everything is well combined.

3. Stir over a low heat for about 10 minutes then take from the heat and place into warm sterilised jars or cool if using straight away.

TO MAKE THE PASTRY:

1. Put the flour and salt in food processor then add the butter and blitz for a few seconds until the butter is completely dispersed.

2. Add the icing sugar, repeat then with the motor running add 5 tbsp egg mix (no more and no less). Stop the mixer when the pastry has formed a ball.

3. Gently take from the mixer, divide into two and form into two balls then chill for half an hour wrapped in greaseproof paper or a beeswax wrap.

4. When ready to roll out – it is much easier to roll between two sheets of plastic and I use two freezer bags each with one side and the bottom cut providing two large sheets. Using this method no extra flour is needed and your pastry will be light and delicious.

5. Cut out circles with the pastry cutter large enough to line the muffin tin. I use a 3 ½ inch (9cm) cutter for the bases and a 2 ½ inch (7cm), star or snowflake cutter for the tops.

6. Fill the pastry shells with the mincemeat – about 2/3 full, dampen the edges of the pastry and gently lay the top over – do not squash it down – there is no need.

Do not egg wash the mince pies as there is enough sugar in the pastry to colour them.

7. Chill for half an hour before baking.

8. Bake at 200 degrees for 18-20 minutes until the mince pies are light golden. Allow to cool and firm up before attempting to remove them from the muffin tin.

9. Dust with icing sugar.

Nancy's Top Tips

The mincemeat can be made well in advance and will keep in jars...

You can make your mincepies and freeze in their tins. Remove from the tins and store in bags. When ready to bake, take from the freezer, pop back into the tin and bake from frozen.

If you are worried about releasing your deep filled pies from the muffin tin, a strip of baking paper placed in the tin before the pastry shell will ensure they come out easily. Even better I have found brushing the muffin tins with lining paste, allowing the mince pies to go completely cold in the tin ensures they will easily pop out. If your pastry becomes difficult to handle pop it into the fridge for 10 minutes to firm up.

If you find your filling boils over your pastry – your cases are too full.

Left over mincemeat...

When Christmas has passed and you have decided to clear out your pantry or cupboards and come across a half jar of mincemeat – you must try this fabulous little recipe. Apples from the fruit bowl passed their best are put to good use too!

Let Me Show You...
Watch My 'Recipe' Video
SCAN HERE

Viennese Tart

MINCEMEAT AND APPLE

MAKES 7 INCH (18CM) TART OR 9 IN-
DIVIDUAL DEEP FILLED PIES

Dust with icing sugar and you will LOVE these!

Ingredients

YOU WILL NEED:

- 200g sweet shortcrust pastry
- 200g mincemeat
- 3 dessert apples, peeled, cored and sliced

FOR THE VIENNESE TOPPING:

- 150g soft butter
- 40g icing sugar
- 1 tsp vanilla extract
- 150g 00 plain flour (or pasta flour)

USE: USE EITHER A 12 HOLE MUFFIN TIN OR THE PASTRY RING
PLACED ON A BAKING SHEET
PREHEAT THE OVEN TO: 190 °C (FAN)

Nancy's Top Tip

TIP: Use left over trimmings

My grandmother taught me never to throw away pastry trimmings.
About 120g left over pastry will make the most gorgeous tartlets.
Line a 12 hole tart tin with the rolled out trimmings, rolling as
thinly as you can. Chill whilst you make the filling.

Method

1. Start by cooking the apples as they need to be completely cold before using.

2. Slice the apples into a non-metallic bowl, cover with a plate and microwave for 2-3 minutes until they have reduced to a pulp. Mash with a fork and leave to go cold. No need to add sugar.

3. Use either a 12 hole muffin tin or the pastry ring placed on a baking sheet and line with the pastry. Chill.

4. Divide the mincemeat between the tartlets or place onto the base of the chilled pastry ring. Top off with the cold apple puree and pop the whole lot back into the fridge.

TO MAKE THE VIENNESE TOPPING:

1. To make the Viennese topping – Using an electric hand whisk cream the butter and vanilla well until really smooth then add the sugar.

2. Little by little incorporate the flour and you will achieve a very thick yet smooth mix.

3. Load a piping bag fitted with a star nozzle and pipe the mix over the tart or tartlets. I like to pop the whole lot back into the fridge until the oven reaches temperature.

4. Preheat the oven to 190 degrees and bake for 16-18 minutes until the Viennese tops are light golden brown.

Let Me Show You...
Watch My 'Recipe' Video
SCAN HERE

Coconut Tarts

Ingredients

- 50g soft margarine or butter
- 50g caster sugar
- 1 egg
- 50g desiccated coconut
- 1 tbsp self raising flour

Method

- Mix all together in your mixing bowl.
- Pop about ½ tsp raspberry jam in the base of each pastry shell, top off with a heaped teaspoon of mixture and bake for 18-20 minutes until golden brown.

Let Me Show You...
Watch My 'Recipe' Video
SCAN HERE

Cheat's Almond Tarts

Ingredients

- 50g soft margarine or butter
- 50g caster sugar
- 50g ground rice
- 1 tbsp self raising flour
- 1 tsp almond extract
- 1 egg

Method

- Mix all together in your mixing bowl.
- Pop about ½ tsp apricot jam in the base of each pastry shell, top off with a heaped teaspoon of mixture, scatter over a few flaked almonds and bake for 18-20 minutes until golden brown.
- Dust with icing sugar.

Let Me Show You...
Watch My 'Recipe' Video
SCAN HERE

Chocolate Crusted Passion Fruit Tart

SERVES 8-10 PEOPLE

This tart takes a little time but is a great one if you want to impress – you may remember seeing something similar in the Tent! I use a chocolate pastry which can be tricky to handle and can rise a little in the oven so it is important that you roll it out really thinly. The passion fruit custard filling is delicious and is a non -bake custard which is set with gelatine.   This is great because you can fill your tart right to the very brim. The filigree decoration is optional but I think it gives a contemporary finish to this beautiful tart.

Ingredients

FOR THE PASTRY:

- 125g 00 plain flour
- 20g cocoa
- 90g salted butter chilled and cut into dice
- 30g icing sugar
- ½ tsp chinese five spice (optional)
- 2 tbsp beaten egg yolk

FOR THE FILLING:

- 6 eggs
- 200g caster sugar
- 100g softened butter cut into dice
- 200ml passion fruit juice (about 8 fruits or 60g dried fruit powder reconstituted with water)
- 5 gelatine leaves

FOR THE FILIGREE:
- 1 egg white
- 100g icing sugar sifted

USE: A 9 INCH (23CM) LOOSE BOTTOMED TART TIN AND A THERMOMETER

PREHEAT THE OVEN TO: 200°C (FAN)

Method

TO MAKE THE PASTRY:

1. Start by making the pastry. Place the flour, cocoa, icing sugar and spice in the bowl of a food processor then add the butter and blitz for a few seconds until everything is combined. With the motor running then add the yolk and allow everything to come together. Wrap in greaseproof paper or beeswax wrap and chill for at least half an hour.

2. Roll the pastry very thinly – I roll out between two pieces of reusable plastic. If the pastry becomes difficult to handle, pop it into the fridge for 5 minutes to firm up.

3. Line the tin, prick the base all over with a fork then bake blind at 200 degrees (fan) for 10 minutes.

4. Remove the paper and baking beans and pop it back into the oven to firm up for another 3 minutes.

5. Trim the edges with a serrated knife then leave to go completely cold.

TO MAKE THE FILLING:

1. Place the gelatine leaves in cold water and allow to soak for at least 10 minutes

2. In a small saucepan dissolve the sugar and passion fruit juice together.

3. In a separate pan whisk together the eggs and whilst whisking carefully and slowly add the warm juice.

4. Place the pan on a gentle heat and continually stirring bringing the mixture to a temperature of 85 degrees centigrade. This ensures the eggs are cooked.

5. Take from the heat and add the gelatine leaves one by one, stirring between each addition.

6. Transfer the mixture into a jug first passing it through a sieve – this makes sure your custard is ultra smooth and there are no pieces of cooked egg or undissolved gelatine going into your tart

7. Add the room temperature butter and stir well until the butter is completely incorporated. Allow the custard to cool slightly then pour into the pastry case

allowing it to come right to the top of the tart. You may want to do this when the case is first put into the fridge then you don't have to move it at all.

8. When the tart is set and about 2 hours before you are ready to serve – decorate with the filigree or with fresh fruits it you wish.

9. Mix the icing by placing 1 tbsp egg white into the bottom of a small basin then add the icing sugar, sifted until you have a thick smooth paste.

10. Spoon into an icing bag and decorate.

11. Serve at room temperature. If you serve chilled you don't get the flavours.

Let Me Show You...
Watch My 'Recipe' Video
SCAN HERE

Hot Water Crust Pastry

HAND RAISED PORK PIES

MAKES 1 LARGE HAND RAISED PIES, 4 SMALL HAND RAISED PIES OR 12 PICNIC PIES

Once you have mastered the art of shortcrust pastry this method is so easy you'll wonder why you have never made pork pies before. In a nutshell it is what it says – the pastry is simply brought together by pouring hot water with fat melted in over flour then stirred with a wooden spoon until a dough is formed. Many recipes suggest working with the pastry whilst it is warm but I prefer to wait for it to cool. It firms up, is easier to roll out and an even thickness can be achieved.

My pork pie recipe is a real winner and can be formed into picnic pies, small pies or one large celebration pie.

Making your own pork pie is easier than you might think and I prefer to use a small quantity of very lean pork, leaving it cubed rather than minced. I think it results in a proper meaty, home made rather than factory produced pork pie. These pies are tasty and you will feel quite accomplished because you are not using the support of a tin. A true hand raised pie - well done!

Ingredients

FOR THE FILLING:

- 350g minced pork
- 130g lean pork (loin is a good choice)
- 40g bacon chopped small
- 4g salt
- ½ tsp white pepper

- 1/4 tsp ground mace
- 1.5 tsp dried sage
- ½ small tin anchovies
- 10 juniper berries crushed
- 1/2 tsp ground paprika
- ½ tsp black pepper

FOR THE PASTRY:

- 500g strong plain flour
- 1 egg yolk
- 150g lard
- 300ml water
- 1 tsp salt
- 1 egg yolk mixed with a little water for egg wash
- non stick baking parchment and string

PREHEAT THE OVEN TO: 180°C (FAN)

Nancy's Top Tips

TIP: How to get pies out of a tin easily

If you decide to make the picnic pies and you don't have a loose bottomed muffin tin then brushing with lining paste and leaving the pies in the tin until completely cold and firmed up will ensure they come out easily.

TIP: Adding apricots to a pie filling

Ready to eat apricots make a great addition to the meat filling. Try half filling the pie with the meat mix, then place a layer of apricot then top off with the rest of the filling.

TIP: How to add jelly to a pork pie

If you want to complete your pork pie with a jelly then simply use 200ml pork or chicken stock and 3 gelatine leaves. Soak the gelatine in cold water then add to the stock which has been heated to almost boiling. Allow to cool to body temperature then pour through the hole in the top through a little funnel (a metal icing nozzle works) into your cool pork pie. Leave to set in the fridge completely before cutting.

Method

TO MAKE THE PASTRY:

1. Put the flour into a warm mixing bowl then with a wooden spoon make a well all the way to the bottom of the bowl and drop in the egg yolk. Cover with flour.

2. In a medium saucepan, place the water, salt and lard and place over a medium heat until the lard has melted.

3. Bring to the boil then immediately pour into the bowl containing the flour.

4. Mix with a wooden spoon until the mixture starts to come together and then when cool enough to handle, tip out onto a work top and knead into a smooth dough.

5. When warm this pastry is very soft and greasy. I prefer to leave it cool completely then use it cold. It is easier to handle, makes rolling thinly more successful.

TO MAKE 12 PICNIC PIES:

1. If you are making the picnic pies then simply roll out half of the dough and use a large pastry cutter (4 inch or 10cm) to line a deep muffin tin.

2. Make sure you have enough pastry to provide an overhang that can be moulded over the pastry lid. Pack tightly with the chilled meat filling, dampen the edges of the pastry overhang then cut out and fit pastry lids using a 2 ½ inch (7cm) round cutter.

3. Fold the dampened overhand over the lid and crimp together. Pop into the fridge to then chill until ready to bake.

4. Preheat the oven to 200 degrees c then brush the tops with the egg wash and bake for 45 minutes.

TO MAKE 4 SMALL HAND RAISED PIES:

1. I find small individual 175ml metal pudding basins make excellent moulds. I use four to use as moulds for the filling. I grease them first and then line the inside with thin plastic (which I will wash and use again for rolling out of biscuits and pastry).

2. I then pack the filling inside, forcing as much into the basin as I possibly can. Transfer to the fridge and leave to firm up. An hour or so is perfect for this.

3. Take four more pudding basins and turn them upside down on the work surface. Dust each one with a little flour.

4. Divide the pastry into four pieces then take a quarter from each piece (this will be for your pie lid).

5. Roll out your piece of pastry large enough to cover the upside down pudding basin which has been dusted with flour.

6. Lay the pastry over and mould it around the outside of the tin. Give yourself a little extra pastry at the bottom as this will be needed to secure the lid.

7. Try to avoid any creases. Transfer to a tray and pop into the fridge and chill for about half an hour.

TO ASSEMBLE THE PIES:

1. Take first the pastry moulds and carefully remove the tin by twisting it slightly. The pastry shell will be able to stand unaided.

2. Take then the chilled filling, remove the plastic and place it upside down in the pastry shell (i.e. the wide part of the filling will go into the narrow part of the pastry shell). By doing this you will achieve a uniform pie rather than a pudding shaped one.

3. Roll out the piece of pastry reserved and use an 8cm (3 ½ inch) pastry cutter to form a lid.

4. Make an air hole in the centre (the wide end of a metal piping nozzle is handy for this) then place over the filling, dampen the edges and fold the edges of the

shell over the lid. Trim off any thick or uneven scraps of pastry then crimp in true pork pie style.

5. In order to maintain straight sides and a neat shape your hand raised pies will need a paper sleeve to support them during the first 20 minutes of baking. Simply take a 9 inch (23cm) length of baking parchment from the roll and fold it into three lengthways then wrap this around the pie and tie off with string.

6. Place on a baking sheet lined with either non stick baking parchment or paper. Give the top an egg wash and then chill for at least an hour. Repeat for the other three pies.

7. Preheat the oven to 200 degrees (fan)

8. When ready to bake pop the pies into the oven for 20 minutes then take from the oven and carefully remove the string and paper. Egg wash the sides and give the top a second coat of egg wash. Pop them back into the oven immediately and bake for another 40 minutes – 1 hour total baking time.

9. When baked I leave the pies to cool completely on the baking sheet before removing when completely cooled.

10. This same mix makes 1 large pork pie. Apply the method as for the small pies but mould the pastry and meat mixture using a 6 inch (15cm) solid bottomed deep cake tin.

11. Cooking time 2 hours.

Choux Pastry

MAKES 12-16 ÉCLAIRS OR 20-25 PROFITEROLES.

This delicious, light and crispy pastry is a delight and not as hard to make as some people believe.

Ingredients

FOR MAKING THE CHOUX:

- 150ml water
- 100g salted butter
- 10g caster sugar
- 1 tsp salt
- 150g plain flour sifted
- 3 eggs beaten

TO MAKE A CHOCOLATE PASTE FOR PIPING ONTO THE ÉCLAIRS:

- 100g dark chocolate
- 20g butter
- 1 tbsp water

TO MAKE THE LEMON CREAM FILLING:

- 2 egg yolks
- 75g caster sugar
- 50g cornflour
- 225ml milk
- 50g butter at room temperature
- 100ml double cream
- 50ml plain yoghurt (full fat)
- finely grated zest of 1 large lemon

TO MAKE DIPPING CHOCO-LATE FOR PROFITEROLES:

- 100g dark chocolate

PREHEAT THE OVEN TO: 200 °C (FAN)

Nancy's Top Tip

When mixing choux :-

1. Add the flour all in one go and mix quickly. I use a wooden fork which is perfect for this.

2. Add the egg gradually as sometimes, depending on the size of the eggs not the total amount is required. Check on the consistency - the paste should hang (in a "v" shape) from the end of the whisk.

3. Choux dough has a high water content which turns to steam in the oven causing the dough to puff out. A steamy environment encourages a good rise too so spray your baking sheet with a fine film of water before piping over your éclairs or spooning your profiteroles.

4. I use a star shaped nozzle for piping my choux paste. The shape of your finished baked éclairs and profiteroles will be more even as they are less able to spread.. If you worry you don't have good piping skills just spoon your blobs of choux paste onto the baking sheet for rustic, beautiful puffs of crispy deliciousness that you can then fill with cream.

Method

TO MAKE THE CHOUX:

1. Heat the water, butter, sugar and salt in a medium sized pan over a low heat until the butter dissolves then turn onto full heat and bring to a fast boil.

2. Take off the heat and immediately tip in the sifted flour and stir briskly until the mixture comes together and forms a very thick paste which leaves the side of the pan.

3. Turn into a large mixing bowl and using a hand held electric whisk mix on a low heat just to help cool it down a little. Don't be tempted to add the eggs straight away as they will cook.

4. Once the paste has cooled a little then start to add the beaten egg, little by little. Keep an eye on the consistency which is crucial to the success of your choux.

You may not need all of the beaten egg - the consistency should be such that when you lift your whisk the paste sticks to the whisk yet hangs off, i.e. it doesn't stick rigidly neither does it drop off.

5. Load your paste into a piping bag fitted with a large star shaped nozzle then you will need a baking sheet lightly greased or lined with baking parchment. I spray the surface with water then use a plastic scraper dipped in flour to mark out a regular 5 inch (13cm) length for my éclairs.

6. Pipe the choux either in an éclair shape or a large star for your profiteroles and flatten the point of your star peaks with a wet finger.

7. Bake for 18-20 minutes until your choux is risen and golden brown in colour with a crispy finish. Remove to cooling trays and allow to go completely cold before filling.

TO MAKE A LEMON CREAM FILLING:

1. Place all the ingredients apart from the yoghurt, cream and lemon zest in a medium pan and whilst constantly stirring, allow to heat gradually until the cream thickens and leaves the side of the pan.

2. Transfer to a cold bowl and cover to prevent a skin forming then leave to cool completely.

3. When the lemon cream has cooled, whisk the double cream to soft peaks then whisk everything together including the yoghurt and lemon zest. The cream is thick and delicious. Fill a piping bag fitted with a metal or plastic piping tube.

PROFITEROLES:

With a metal skewer make a hole in the side of the bun then inject sufficient lemon cream to fill the bun. I use my kitchen scales and 15-20g is just about right.

ÉCLAIRES:

With a metal skewer make three evenly spaced holes to the base of the éclair and again inject lemon cream through each of the three holes to fill the éclair. 25g is sufficient for an éclair.

TO MAKE A CHOCOLATE PIPING PASTE:

1. Dissolve all three ingredients in a heatproof bowl over a pan of hot water (not boiling) or in the microwave.
2. 30 second bursts stirring between each session should see the chocolate melted in about 90 seconds. When all amalgamated and the mixture is shiny and thick allow to cool slightly so that it holds its shape then fill a piping bag.
3. Pipe the chocolate paste over the presentation side of the éclairs and then decorate with sprinkles, melted white chocolate or fruit crumb.

TO MAKE A DIPPING CHOCOLATE FOR PROFITEROLES:

1. Melt the chocolate in a heatproof bowl over a pan of hot water then the decorating is up to you. The consistency of the chocolate needs to be that of single cream or 40 degrees c if you have a thermometer.
2. You can dip your profiteroles face down in the chocolate then carefully lift out and spin the final trail of chocolate back on itself. You will then have no drips running down.
3. Alternatively, stack your profiteroles on a presentation plate and pour the melted chocolate over.

Nancy's Top Tip

Can I make my choux buns in advance?

Choux pastry doesn't keep well so I have found that if you want to get ahead freezing the dough uncooked is probably the best way then bake them as you want them.

Uncooked choux can be frozen once piped or spooned onto your trays and then bake from frozen or once frozen the frozen dough can be placed in bags and kept in the freezer for up to three months.

Once filled choux buns or éclairs will go soggy after a two to three hours so they are best eaten fresh.

Let Me Show You...
Watch My 'Recipe' Video
SCAN HERE

Puff Pastry

MAKES A 625G BLOCK

A pastry chapter is not complete without the addition of puff pastry. Traditional puff pastry can seem complicated involving folding, resting, more folding – lots of time involved. This will lead many of us to the chilled cabinet in the supermarket to buy 500g of ready made. Before you do I urge you to try a batch of home made.. Have you seen the number of ingredients contained in a pack of ready made? My last count there were 11. Another disappointment is that many brands of puff pastry do not contain butter but are instead made using margarine and palm oil. All butter puff pastry is available but it is expensive.

Here is a quick, "all in one" home made puff pastry, only four ingredients, made with butter and cheaper and more tasty than anything you can buy.

Ingredients

- 250g plain flour
- pinch salt
- 250g salted butter cut into very small (1cm) ½ inch dice well chilled
- 125ml icy cold water to bind

Let Me Show You...
Watch My 'Pastry' Video
SCAN HERE

Nancy's Top Tip

TIP: Cleaning oven shelves.

Baking and cooking will take their toll on your oven and its shelves. My top tip will take all of the effort out of cleaning those badly burnt on drips and spills without having to go out to buy special products. Your oven shelves will clean themselves whilst you sleep.

You need a need sink large enough to hold your oven shelves or a large plastic box. Take 1 dishwasher tablet and 400g washing soda. Dissolve them both in sufficient boiling water that will cover your shelves. Submerge the warm shelves (do it when you have just finished cooking) in the solution and just leave them overnight.

The next day lift the shelves out of the water and see the baked on deposits just wipe off.
No scrubbing – in fact the job is almost exciting.

Method

1. In a roomy mixing bowl (pop your bowl in the fridge for 10 minutes before starting) place the flour and salt in and then I like to rinse my hands in cold water, dry them and then take the butter from the fridge and stir into the flour using a knife.

2. Once the butter is well distributed and coated in flour then pour in the icy cold water.

3. Use the knife again to stir everything around until the dough starts to clump together. Once you have a lump of scraggy dough then use your cold hands to briefly mould it into a ball

4. Turn out onto a floured work surface and using both a rolling pin and bench scraper form the dough into a rectangle shape.

5. Roll this rectangle to a rough measurement of 16 inches long x 6 inches wide (40cm x 15cm) then carry out what is called a "double fold". Fold the two ends into the centre

then fold the two ends into the centre once more.

6. Turn the pastry 45 degrees – roll out again to the same size and repeat. Turn the pastry once more, roll out again but this time carry out a single fold. Imagine the rectangle in thirds – fold an end third over the centre third and then the other end third over that. The Video on this page will help you enormously.

7. Like shortcrust pastry, puff pastry needs to be kept cold otherwise the fat will start to turn oily and will be difficult and sticky to handle and roll out. If you start to get into a sticky mess simply pop the whole lot into the fridge for 15 minutes and have a breather.

8. Once all the folds have been completed wrap the pastry in a cloth or greaseproof paper and chill for an hour before using. Alternatively freeze the pastry until required.

9. When baking some of the fat will run from your pastry so I find it better to bake using a lipped baking sheet otherwise your oven will suffer burnt on fat.

Let Me Show You...
Watch My 'Clean Oven' Video
SCAN HERE

Pork & Juniper Sausage Rolls

MAKES ABOUT 30 SAUSAGE ROLLS OR A LARGE PLAIT

Ingredients

- 500g puff pastry

FOR THE FILLING:

- 500g good quality pork sausage meat
- 1 heaped teaspoon fennel seeds crushed
- ½ tsp cayenne pepper
- 2 cloves garlic crushed
- 3 large fresh sage leaves finely chopped or ½ tsp dried
- 10 juniper berries crushed then chopped
- 4 spring onions chopped finely
- zest of 1 lemon
- salt and pepper
- 1 egg yolk mixed with a little water to egg wash the sausage rolls/plait

PREHEAT THE OVEN TO: 200 °C (FAN)

Nancy's Top Tip

TIP: How do I get a really deep shiny glaze on my pastry?

For a fabulous glaze apply two coats! Apply one coat of egg wash (just egg yolk with a tbsp. water) then pop the pastry into the fridge.. Apply then a second coat just before it goes into the oven to bake. Your glaze will be deep golden, shiny and crisp.

Method

Using the hands mix together all the stuffing ingredients then I find it easier to fill a large piping bag and pipe the filling for both the sausage rolls and the plait.

FOR THE SAUSAGE ROLLS:

1. Roll out the pastry into a rectangle 12 inches x 8 inches (30cm long x 20cm), neaten the edges with a pizza cutter then cut in half lengthways. Pipe a length of sausage meat down the centre of each piece of pastry.

2. Dampen the edges of the pastry with water then roll up and keep the seam underneath.

3. Apply an egg wash to the two long sausages then transfer to the freezer for just 15 minutes to firm up..

4. Take from the freezer and cut each sausage into 10-15 depending on your preferred size of a sausage roll.

5. Bake at 200 degrees for 25-35 minutes until golden brown.

6. These sausage rolls freeze very well uncooked. Open freeze the cut sausage rolls then place into bags. The sausage rolls can then be baked from frozen until golden brown. They already have their egg wash so will brown nicely.

FOR THE PLAIT:

1. Roll out the pastry to a large rectangle measuring 16inches x 12inches (40cm x 30cm) then neaten off the edges with a pizza cutter

2. Transfer the rectangle of pastry onto a sheet of baking paper or reusable baking parchment before

shaping starts.

3. With the pastry positioned "portrait style" place a score line at 4 inch (10cm) intervals so that the pastry is divided into three lengthways (don't cut through the pastry).

4. Pipe the sausage meat filling onto the centre section of

the pastry leaving a margin of 1 inch (2.5cm) top and bottom.

5. Using a pizza cutter then cut even sized strips at the two sides.

6. Dampen the pastry strips as you work and starting at the top, fold over the top margin and the bottom margin then alternating left and right wrap the sausage meat in the pastry, forming a plait

7. Chill the plait for at least half an hour then wash with egg yolk and chill for a further 15 minutes or so until the oven comes to temperature. Heat to 200 degrees (fan).

Place a baking sheet in the oven to preheat at the same time.

8. Just before placing in the oven give a second egg wash – this ensures a lovely rich deep shiny brown finish to your bake. Using the paper or baking parchment as an aid - slide your chilled plait onto the preheated baking sheet – this ensures the underneath will bake thoroughly.

9. Bake for 30 minutes.

10. This plait will freeze extremely well. Egg wash before freezing then bake from frozen for 40 minutes.

Meat Pie For One

MAKES 4 SINGLE SERVE PIES

So many recipes are for families and large numbers but I have created this single serve meat pie needing no tin. It freezes well unbaked and then can be cooked from frozen. This is a hearty plateful – real comfort food !

Ingredients

- 2-3 tbsp beef dripping or vegetable oil
- 1 onion peeled and chopped into small dice
- 1 red pepper diced
- 3 cloves garlic chopped
- 1 carrot – cut into dice
- 1 stick celery – sliced
- 100g chestnut mushrooms halved
- 500g beef skirt or braising steak cut into 2cm cubes
- 1 x 2 inch (5cm) piece oxtail (optional)

- 1 lambs kidney – chopped small (membrane removed) (optional) – flavour is greatly enhanced by the oxtail and kidney
- 25g plain flour seasoned with salt and white pepper
- ½ tsp mixed spice
- 1 tbsp tomato puree
- 2 tbsp fresh thyme or 1 tbsp dried
- 200ml beef stock
- 50ml red wine
- 1 oxo cube
- 500g Puff Pastry plus egg yolk to wash before baking

PREHEAT THE OVEN TO: 190 °C (FAN)

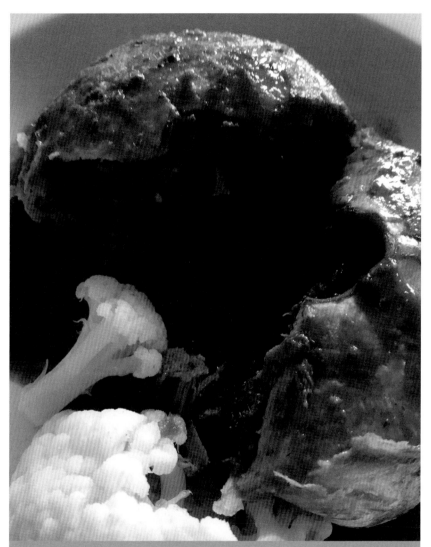

Nancy's Top Tip
TIP: Covering Hot Food

Lay a piece of kitchen paper over your bowl of hot pie filling then top off with a piece of foil – securing it around the rim of the bowl. When the filling has cooled the paper will have absorbed all of the moisture which will have prevented the foil from tarnishing and getting wet. The foil can then be used again and again. The kitchen paper will be wet and can be discarded.
No cling film in sight.

Method

1. Preheat the oven to 190 degrees (fan).

2. In a large roomy oven-proof casserole melt the fat/heat the oil then add the chopped onion and fry on a medium heat for about 10 minutes until the onions have softened but not browned.

3. Add the pepper, garlic, carrot, mushrooms and celery and stir well, keeping the heat low.

4. Place the beef, oxtail piece and chopped kidney along with the seasoned flour and spice into a large bowl and give a everything a good stir around so that all of the meat has a flour coating. Drop the meat and residual flour into the pan and stir on a high heat for a few minutes.

5. Reduce the heat and add in the beef stock, red wine, tomato puree and thyme.

6. Give everything a good stir with a wooden spoon. If there are any stuck on deposits at the base of the pan these will release as the liquid gets to work on them.

7. Give everything a good stir, put on the lid and transfer either to a slow cooker for 12 hours or into a low oven at 100 degrees c for 12 hours or conventional oven at 180 degrees for 1.5 to 2 hours or until the meat is very tender.

8. When the meat is cooked I use a slotted spoon to extract the meat and vegetables, leaving a delicious gravy behind. Check the gravy for seasoning then transfer to a small saucepan to reheat later.

9. Note: if you have used a piece of oxtail you need to find it and remove and discard the bone. The meat will just fall from it.

10. Once the filling is completely cold I crumble over a beef Oxo cube and stir this through the cold meat and vegetables. It darkens everything and adds a little more flavour.

11. Divide the pastry into four equal pieces then roll each one out to the size of a tea plate.   7-8 inches in diameter (18-20 cm) I use a pizza cutter to neatly cut around the plate then use this circle of pastry to line a large cup or soup bowl. With the pastry trimmings roll out a small circle which

will be used as a base for the pie.

12. Fill the cup/bowl with the cold meat filling then top off with the small circle of pastry. Dampen the top circle then gently fold over the edges of the larger circle, sticking them down onto the pastry. Transfer the cup/bowl to the fridge to firm up for about an hour.

13. Tap the cup/bowl and the pie will pop out, transfer it to a baking sheet lined with paper or baking parchment then make an air hole in the centre using the wide end of a metal piping nozzle. Give an egg wash and pop back into the fridge until the oven comes up to temperature.

14. Before popping the pies into the oven give them a second egg wash then Bake for 30 minutes and serve hot on warmed plates with the reserved gravy and a green vegetable. If baking from frozen bake for 40 minutes or until dark golden brown.

Nancy's Top Tip
TIP: Quick Plate Warmer

Maybe you have forgotten to warm the plates for your meal, or your oven is full and no room for plates, or you have come in with fish and chips or a takeaway and warm plates are essential. Take your plates, spray each one with water, stack them in the microwave then turn it on for just 30 seconds. Instant warm plates.

Let Me Show You...
Watch My 'Recipe' Video
SCAN HERE

Tarte Tatin

SERVES 8

A classic bake using home made or bought puff pastry. I have seen so many tarte tatins with soggy pastry, apple sliding off an unset caramel which for me, is not ideal. This recipe is a beauty and needs only a blob of vanilla ice cream to serve.

Ingredients

- 350g puff pastry
- 13 or 14 small to medium dessert apples
- 125g butter
- 200g caster sugar
- finely grated zest and juice of 1 lemon

PREHEAT THE OVEN TO: 190 °C (FAN)

Method

1. Roll out the puff pastry on a lightly floured surface until it is slightly larger than an 8 inch (20cm) heavy based Tarte Tatin tin or ovenproof frying pan and about the thickness of a £1 coin.

2. Turn the baking tin or pan upside down and make an impression on the pastry with the rim. Using this as a guide, cut a circle out of the pastry, half an inch (1 cm) larger than the pan all the way round.   Transfer the circle of pastry onto a baking sheet and set aside in the fridge until required.

3. Grate the zest from the lemon and put to one side.

4. Peel, core and halve the apples. Whilst preparing the apples have a large bowl of water to hand and squeeze in the lemon juice. Drop the apples into the water and then they will not turn brown.

5. Over a low heat melt the butter in the pan and add the sugar, stirring until it has dissolved. Do not allow the mixture to colour at all at this stage. Take from the heat and stir in the lemon zest.

6. Next, arrange the halved apples around the pan, standing them on their ends, forming an interlocking circle of fruit. Depending on the size of your applies you may have room for a second circle of apples in the centre. Make sure your apples are very tightly packed as they will shrink during cooking.

7. Place the pan on a moderate heat and once all of the butter and sugar mixture is bubbling gently, then turn down to a simmer. The juice will come out of the fruit and gradually evaporate. After a while, the apples will start to colour as the butter and sugar begins to caramelise. This will take around   45 minutes – don't be tempted to speed up the process otherwise your pan will burn and your tarte tatin will be spoiled.

8. After this long cooking time the apples will be tender and will still hold their shape. The caramel will be a golden colour. Take off the heat and leave to cool completely. I leave mine to cool to around room temperature.

9. Remove the pastry from the fridge and place over the apples, tucking it down inside the rim of the pan.

10. Place in a preheated oven at 190 degrees c for approximately 45 minutes, until the pastry is crisp, well risen and dark golden in colour.

11. Remove from the oven and leave in the pan until cooled enough to be able to handle the tin easily. This usually takes about 15 minutes.

12. To turn out, briefly loosen the apples and caramel by running a knife around the edge of the pan.

13. Place a serving plate upside down over the pan, then quickly turn the pan and plate over together. You will now have the pastry on the bottom and the apples on the top. Once turned out, the tart can be kept warm in a low oven. Best served warm with cream crème fraiche or vanilla ice cream

14. NB Is good cold for a few days afterwards.

PUFF PASTRY TRIMMINGS:

1. Never discard puff pastry trimmings. Just 200g left over pastry can be easily transformed into 8 delicious Vanilla Slices.

2. You will need an 8 inch (18cm) square loose bottomed cake tin and two baking sheets.

3. Preheat the oven to 200 degrees. Divide the pastry into two then roll each one out larger than the size of the tin.

4. Do not cut the pastry to size at this stage – that can be done once the pastry is baked.   Lay one piece of pastry on a baking sheet lined with baking parchment then cover with another piece of baking parchment and another baking sheet. Bake for 15 minutes.

5. Take from the oven and trim to the size of the tin. Repeat with the second piece of pastry. Line the square cake tin with foil and then lay one sheet of baked pastry in the base. Spread over then the crème patissiere then top off with the second square of pastry.

6. Crème Patissiere is not difficult. How many recipes have you read that involve whisking eggs and sugar together, pour over hot milk, wash the pan then return the whole mixture to the pan and continue to mix until thickens then transfer to a cold bowl and cover? My method is much simpler and everything is mixed together in one go.

7. You will need for the vanilla slices :- 3 egg yolks, 1 tsp vanilla extract, 50g caster sugar, 25g cornflour, 15g soft butter and 250ml whole milk.

8. Put the egg yolks in the pan first, whisk them together then add the rest of the ingredients.

9. Heat slowly and continually and the mixture will thicken. Take off the heat and beat well then pour over the pastry in the cake tin. Top off with the second square of pastry.

10. Cool then cut into 8 equal sized pieces. Dust over with icing sugar or water icing.

Let Me Show You...
Watch My 'Recipe' Video
SCAN HERE

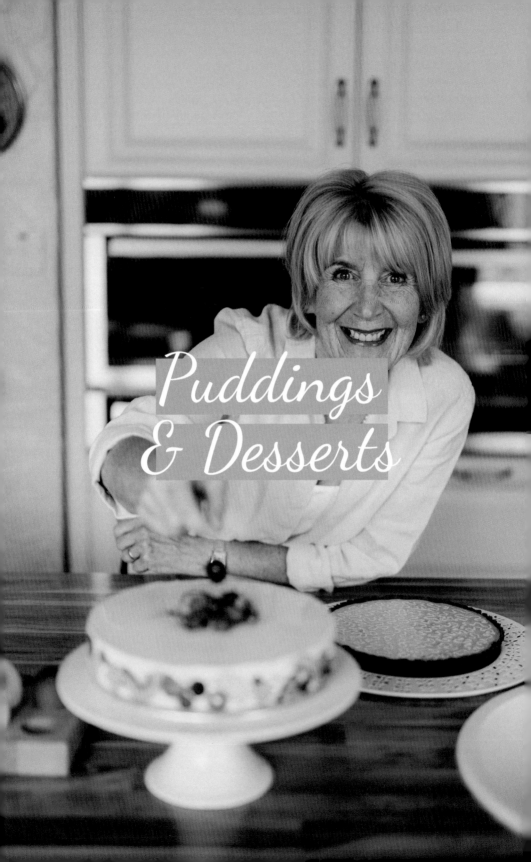

Puddings
& Desserts

Puddings & Desserts

We are continually warned about the need to reduce our sugar consumption but for me that doesn't mean we cannot enjoy pudding or dessert as part of our meal. Sweets, soft drinks and snacking are our enemy – not a portion of delicious home made pudding.

I routinely reduce the sugar in my recipes and many include fresh fruits. I know exactly what ingredients are included when I bake myself and I can control portion size.

Don't therefore be afraid of eating pudding – remember though not to eat it as a snack!!

I adore the way puddings and desserts particularly reflect the seasons. For example, I would not serve a steamed treacle sponge on a hot summers day nor would I offer a slice of summer pudding when there is snow on the ground even though these days soft fruits are available all year round.

I have so many favourite recipes – from the traditional to the very contemporary. I will weave in tips as I go to ensure success every time.

Fruit Pudding

SERVES 4-6 PEOPLE
(FROM LEFT OVER SCONES)

I hate food waste and when I can create something out of left overs I am very happy. This is a great little pudding a cross between a sponge and a crumble and will make excellent use of day old scones.

Ingredients

- 2-3 day old sweet scones blitzed in a food processor (yielding 125g crumbs)
- 1 lemon
- 1 egg
- 20g caster sugar
- 100g crème fraiche
- 300g apples (or any fruit including frozen fruit) plus 1-2 tsp sugar

USE: DISH SIZE 9 INCHES X 6 INCHES X 2 INCHES DEEP (24CM X 16CM X 5CM) – BAKE 180 DEGREES C FOR 30 MINUTES

Method

1. Simply place the crumbed scones in a roomy mixing bowl then add the finely grated zest and juice of 1 lemon.

2. Separate the egg and place the white in a separate clean bowl. Add the yolk to the crumbs then fold in the crème fraiche.

3. Whisk the egg white to soft peaks and add the sugar and whisk until quite thick.

4. Fold the meringue into the crumb mix until everything is well combined.

5. Slice apples into the base of a deep oven proof dish and sprinkle over a little sugar. Spoon over the scone mix and cover all of the fruit with the back of a spoon then bake for 30 minutes.

6. Serve warm with ice cream, custard or cream.

Hot Puddings

The British pudding is something to be celebrated yet it is sad to see that many restaurant menus fail to include a traditional pudding on their menu and as a result some are in danger of becoming forgotten foods. Mention to anyone of my vintage the words Treacle Sponge (dates back to 1615), Jam Roly Poly (dates back to the 1800s), Queen of Puddings (first documented 1699), Eve's pudding (known from 1824) or Apple Charlotte (referenced 1796) and eyes light up and a smile appears on a face as we remember our childhood and these treats that were part of our everyday staple.

I adore these hot puddings – they are comfort food at its best. They are economical to make and whilst many of these creations involved "steaming" – I have a method that will allow you to steam your beloved pudding with no steamy windows, no pan boiling dry and no special equipment required.

Nancy's Top Tip
Steaming without a steamer
The recipes that follow will all include this method.

You will need a large casserole pan with a well fitting lid. A trivet needs to be in the bottom of the pan so that your pudding basin doesn't sit directly on the base otherwise it could crack and also the sponge inside will not cook evenly. If you don't have a trivet - then use an upturned metal plate, a metal pastry ring or cutters. (I have even used a metal teapot stand in the base of my pan.)

Place then your prepared pudding in its basin onto the trivet and pour boiling water so that it comes about one third up the sides of the basin. Place the lid on the pan then place on the hob and bring to the boil. Simmer for just 20 minutes.

During this time preheat the oven to 100 degrees (c) – fan. After the 20 minute simmer, don't be tempted to take the lid off the pan but transfer it straight away into the preheated oven and allow it to continue to "steam" slowly and peacefully for the time given in the following recipes. No runny windows, no danger of the pan boiling dry and no need to go out and buy a steamer!

Steamed Treacle Sponge

MAKES 6 INDIVIDUAL PUDDINGS

A real winter warmer and I don't know anyone who doesn't love this delicious pudding. Recipe will also make one large 2 lb pudding and the steaming time will need to increase to 3 hours.

Ingredients

- 125g soft margarine or butter
- 125g caster sugar
- 2 eggs
- 125g self raising flour
- 1 tsp vanilla extract
- 4 tbsp golden syrup plus extra to heat for pouring if desired.

USE: 6 X 6 FL OZ (175ML) MINI PUDDING BASINS BRUSHED WITH LINING PASTE OR FOR ONE LARGE FAMILY PUDDING A 2LB PUDDING BASIN BRUSHED WITH LINING PASTE.

PREHEAT THE OVEN TO: 100 °C (FAN)

Method

1. In a roomy mixing bowl whisk together the margarine/butter and sugar until light and fluffy then add the eggs one at a time then the vanilla and finally fold in the flour.
2. Place 1 dsp golden syrup into the bottom of each tin.
3. Divide the mixture between the 6 prepared tins then cover with baking parchment, making a pleat in the centre of the paper to allow for expansion. Tie to secure with a piece of string.
4. In a large casserole pan place a trivet into the base then pop in the puddings. Add sufficient boiling water to just come to about 1/3rd way up the tins. Put on a

lid then pop onto the hob, bring to the boil and simmer for 20 minutes. Preheat the oven to 100 degrees c. At the end of the simmering time immediately transfer the casserole into the oven and cook for one and a half hours.

5. Take from the pan, cut the string and remove the paper. Invert into a dessert bowl and pour over more warmed golden syrup if desired plus custard.

6. These puddings also freeze well. I freeze them uncooked then allow to defrost for about 6 hours in the fridge before cooking as above.

Nancy's Top Tips

Ring the changes in flavour

Orange Drizzle Cake - Use a large orange in place of the lemon and make the cake in exactly the same way.

♥

What if I don't have the right size tin

This recipe will make an 8 inch round cake or 7 inch square cake which can then be finished off with the crunchy glaze. *The Ready Reckoner* in the book will give many options for adapting recipes to fit the size of tin you possess.

Let Me Show You...
Watch My 'Recipe' Video
SCAN HERE

Jam Roly Poly

SERVES 6

This is a beautiful winter warmer pudding, inexpensive, nostalgic and adored by children and adults! A good family pudding. Historically this type of pudding was called a Shirt Sleeve Pudding as it was secured in a shirt sleeve for cooking. In my recipe I have added lemon for extra flavour – the taste of this pudding is fabulous.

Ingredients

- 200g self raising flour
- 1 tbsp caster sugar
- 100g vegetable suet
- pinch salt
- finely grated zest of 1 lemon
- 140ml milk and juice of the lemon
- 4 tbsp raspberry jam

THIS PUDDING BAKES IN THE OVEN IN A BAIN MARIE. YOU WILL NEED A ROASTING TIN AND TRIVET (OR ROASTING DRIP TRAY) TO RAISE THE PUDDING FROM THE WATER IN THE BASE OF THE TIN.

PREHEAT THE OVEN TO: 180 °C (FAN)

Method

1. Start by grating the zest from the lemon into a roomy mixing bowl. Squeeze the juice from the lemon into a measuring jug then add the 140ml whole milk. As it stands, the milk will thicken and start to look curdled – that is absolutely fine.

2. Into the mixing bowl containing the lemon zest add the self raising flour, sugar, salt and suet. Stir with a knife then gradually add the thickened milk. You will probably need all of the liquid but keep a little back just in case.

3. Bring the dough together with the hands. The consistency needs to be a little sticky but not so wet

that it sticks all over the hands but certainly not hard and dry that it is crumbly and falling apart.

4. I find the dough easy to roll between two sheets of plastic. You need to roll a rectangle about 18cm (7inches) x 30cm (11 inches). The rectangle needs to be neat so don't be afraid, after peeling off one side of the plastic to trim with a pizza cutter and use the trimmings to patch up where required. When you are satisfied with your finished rectangle spread with the raspberry jam, allowing a 5cm margin on all four sides.

5. Using the bottom sheet of plastic as an aid roll the dough from one short end to the other short end.

6. The roll then needs to be transferred into a greased (use lining paste for this) "roly poly" tin or alternatively rolled loosely in non stick baking parchment then enclosed in a rolled parcel of aluminium foil, sealing securely at both ends (in the style of a Christmas Cracker) The parcel needs to be fairly roomy to allow for expansion during cooking yet securely fastened so that water droplets cannot penetrate. Seal the ends well and make sure the join of the foil is uppermost.

7. When ready to cook preheat the oven to 180 degrees c and place a medium sized oblong casserole pan or deep roasting tray in the oven to preheat at the same time. You will need a trivet or drip tray in the casserole pan or roasting tin. Have a full kettle of water which has just boiled. When the oven has reached temperature, take the roasting tray/ casserole and trivet and place the pudding parcel or roly poly tin on the trivet and add the boiling water so that it fills the roasting tin/ casserole to about half way. The pudding should be about one third submerged in the water.

8. Cook for one hour then leave to stand for about five minutes before unwrapping or turning out of the tin.

9. Slice and serve hot with custard.

Let Me Show You...
Watch My 'Recipe' Video
SCAN HERE

Bread & Butter Pudding

SERVES 6-8

Classic Bread and Butter pudding is super tasty and I have been making it for years and my family always ask whether it is on the menu.

Ingredients

- 6 slices of thick white bread from a large loaf crusts removed (old bread is best)
- 50g butter
- finely grated zest of one lemon
- 3 eggs
- 280ml whole milk
- 80ml double cream
- 50g sugar
- 40g mixed fruit and peel
- 1 tsp mixed spice
- 1 tbsp demerera sugar to sprinkle over

I USE AN ENAMEL PIE DISH AND MINE MEASURES 10 IN X 8 IN X 1 INCH (26CM X 20CM X 2.5CM) DEEP. YOU WILL ALSO NEED A ROASTING TIN LARGE ENOUGH TO HOLD THE PUDDING TIN.

PREHEAT THE OVEN TO: 190 °C (FAN)

Method

1. Start by well buttering your pie dish or simply brush with lining paste then set aside. In a small bowl sprinkle the spice and sugar over the fruit and give a good stir.

2. Butter the bread on one side then cut into squares.

3. Place the first layer of bread- butter side down into the pudding tin. Sprinkle over one third of the fruit and sugar mix and a good grating of lemon zest. Layer over more buttered bread

fruit, sugar and lemon zest then finishing with a layer of bread, butter side down.

4. In a large jug beat the eggs together then add the milk and cream and give a good stir.

5. Pour the mixture over the bread, allowing it to run down between cracks and crevices. Push your bread down into the liquid making sure the surface bread gets a coating.

6. Preheat the oven to 190 degrees c (fan) and bring a large kettle of water to the boil.

7. Place your pudding into the roasting tin then pour boiling water into the roasting tin allowing it to come about half way up the pudding dish. Sprinkle over the demerera sugar then bake for 30-35 minutes until the pudding is risen and golden brown.

8. Take from the water bath and serve warm with cream, ice-cream or custard. The pudding will be deliciously light, tasty, wholesome with a crunchy top!!

Nancy's Top Tips

This pudding works beautifully using my left over brioche. If you decide to use it omit the butter in the recipe.

♥

This pudding can be prepared ahead of time and kept in the fridge covered. In fact the pudding is much improved if the egg and milk mix is allowed to soak into the bread for at least an hour before baking.

♥

Do use a Bain Marie (placing the pudding in the roasting tin with boiling water). Your pudding will be much better for it with no burning around the edges.

Let Me Show You...
Watch My 'Recipe' Video
SCAN HERE

Nancy's Christmas Pudding

This delicious traditional Christmas pudding is sufficient to fill a large 2lb pudding basin or 2 x 1lb. I bought small foil pudding containers with lids and there is sufficient for three! I like to give them as presents.

Once cooked it will keep for a very long time – in fact if you make two you can have one this Christmas and one next Christmas!

I have added a bit of a twist this year and included glace Morello cherries and cardamom seeds which provide some extra flavour.

It is a tradition that on Stir up Sunday (the last Sunday before advent) we make the pudding. Each family member gives the pudding a stir, closes their eyes and makes a wish!

Ingredients

DRY INGREDIENTS:

- 50g self raising flour
- 100g vegetable or beef suet
- 120g fresh wholemeal breadcrumbs
- 1tsp ground mixed spice
- ¼ tsp ground mace
- ½ tsp ground cinnamon
- 5 cardamom pods (split and the seeds crushed)
- 125g dark muscavado sugar

FRUITS AND NUTS:

- 500g mixed dried fruit and peel
- 1 bramley apple – grated (no need to peel, core etc.)
- zests and juices of 1 orange and 1 lemon
- 100g glace morello cherries washed, dried and cut into quarters
- 25g mixed chopped nuts lightly roasted in a dry frying pan

LIQUIDS:

- 2 eggs and 1 egg yolk (beaten)
- 170ml stout or real ale
- 2 tbsp cointreau or brandy

Nancy's Top Tips

Roasting nuts and seeds enhances their flavour but take care because they can easily burn.

Use a dry frying pan and heat the nuts gently, swirling them around to roast them evenly.
Once they have taken on a good colour, a pale golden brown then turn them out onto a cold plate.
Don't be tempted to simply turn off the heat and leave them in the pan – the residual heat from the pan will burn them.

Method

The main drawback with making your own traditional Christmas Pudding is that it has to steam over a pan of boiling water for some 6 to 8 hours!

Apart from the obvious time involved, the fact that you have to keep an eye on things so that the pan doesn't boil dry not to mention the condensation dripping from the windows is reason enough not to make your own.

However, I have here a solution.

We will steam the pudding overnight or for 10 hours in a pan of simmering water in a very low oven. It is clean, convenient and it looks after itself. Alternatively, if you have a slow cooker you can preheat it for an hour, pour in boiling water from the kettle, place your wrapped pudding inside, cover with the lid and slow cook for 10 hours.

1. Start the morning before and mix all dry ingredients together in a very large mixing bowl. Then add all the fruits. The apple I didn't peel but washed then grated straight into the bowl until I got down to the core. Discard the core.

2. Mix everything well then incorporate the liquids. Give everything a good stir - the mixture will be quite sloppy and drop easily from a spoon. Cover the bowl and set aside.

3. Following an eight hour soak the mixture will be thick and

wholesome and now it is time to give a good stir and prepare for cooking.

4. Lightly grease a 2lb pudding basin with butter or brush with lining paste then invite everyone to have a stir before spooning the mix into the basin and smoothing with the back of a spoon. Cover the basin with a sheet of greaseproof paper making a centre pleat to allow for any expansion then tie off with string. Cover then with a sheet of kitchen foil securing it around the rim of the basin.

5. Use a large casserole / stew pan with a trivet in the bottom (if you haven't a trivet try a metal plate turned upside down – I have even used a number of even thickness metal cutters as a trivet). Place the pudding on top then pour in boiling water so that it comes about 1/3rd of the way up the basin. Cover the casserole pan with a lid.

6. Place the pan on the hob and bring the water to a boil then turn down and simmer for 20 minutes before transferring the casserole to the oven preheated to 100 degrees centigrade.

7. Steam in the oven for 10 hours or overnight. I usually put mine in the oven at 10pm and bring it out at 8am the next morning.

8. Alternatively, if you have an electric slow cooker – preheat it for an hour on high then stand the pudding inside and pour in boiling water from the kettle until it comes 1/3rd way up the pudding basin. Cover with the lid and cook for 10 hours.

9. Leave to cool completely then remove the paper and foil. Place a clean piece of paper and string over the pudding – wrap in foil and leave in a cool dark place until Christmas Day.

10. The pudding can be reheated by steaming for 2 hours the same way, i.e. place in a casserole with boiling water. Alternatively reheat in the microwave. Microwave for 5 minutes – leave for 10 minutes then microwave again for 3 minutes. Remove the greaseproof paper and turn out onto a plate and serve with rum sauce or thick cream.

Let Me Show You...
Watch My 'Recipe' Video
SCAN HERE

Eve's Pudding

SERVES 4-6 PEOPLE

Eve's pudding is a British classic made traditionally as a sponge over apples. My version has a few twists, is naturally gluten free, inexpensive yet very tasty and delicious hot or cold.

Ingredients

- 450g Baking apples or any apples you can get hold of. Even a handful of wrinkled apples from the fruit bowl will be delicious. They need to be peeled, cored and sliced thinly.
- 2-4 tbsp Caster sugar depending on the tartness of the apples being used. Baking apples will need 4 tbsp whereas dessert apples will need only 2 tbsp.

FOR THE GLUTEN FREE SPONGE:
- 50g granulated sugar
- 125g soft margarine or butter
- 125g caster sugar
- 2 eggs
- 125g ground almonds (or for a much more economical option use ground rice)
- ½ tsp almond extract
- to scatter over - 1 tbsp flaked almonds

USE: A DEEP PUDDING TIN OR GRATIN DISH - MINE MEASURES 23CM (9 INCHES) X 15CM (5 INCHES) X 5CM (2 INCHES) DEEP, BUTTERED OR BRUSHED WITH LINING PASTE.

PREHEAT THE OVEN TO: 170 °C (FAN)

Method

1. Start by making the gluten free sponge. Place all the ingredients into a large mixing bowl then mix together with an electric hand whisk until well combined. The mixture needs to be fairly thick – bit like mashed potato – not thin and runny.

2. Peel the apples then slice them thinly into the prepared pudding tin. Sprinkle over the sugar then immediately (before the apples start to go brown) spoon the pudding mixture over the top. Spread the mix over the apples using a fork or the back of a spoon then sprinkle over the flaked almonds.

3. Bake in the oven for 50 minutes exactly.

4. Serve warm with custard or cream. Any leftovers are delicious cold and this pudding will keep for four days in the fridge.

Nancy's Top Tip

My Pudding is over browning!

If your pudding starts to over brown before the end of the cooking time, don't be fooled into thinking it is baked through. Instead, turn the oven from the fan to the conventional cooking setting then place a piece of foil with a hole in the centre (the hole about the size of a cup) over the pudding. This will allow the centre to complete its baking and the edges will not brown any further – the foil will see to that. Conventional cooking will stop any air blowing around which could dislodge your foil.

Let Me Show You...
Watch My 'Recipe' Video
SCAN HERE

Apple Charlotte

SERVES 4-6 PEOPLE

A delightful, inexpensive almost forgotten delicious British pudding to serve warm with custard! A great way to use up left over bread.

Ingredients

- 25g butter
- 500g cooking apples (trimmed weight)
- zest and juice of 1 lemon and 1 tbsp water
- 1/4 freshly grated nutmeg
- 1 tsp sugar
- 1 tbsp apricot jam
- 1 egg yolk
- 80g butter melted
- 5-6 large slices white bread with the crusts removed

USE: A 1LB PUDDING BASIN.

PREHEAT THE OVEN TO: 200 °C (FAN)

Method

1. Start by cooking the apples as they need to be cold before assembling the pudding.

2. In a medium sized saucepan melt the 25g butter then add the lemon zest and juice. I peel the apples then simply cut slices from the apple down to the core. Add the thin apple slices to the melted butter and lemon, stirring well between each apple. The lemon juice will prevent any discoloration. Add the water then bring to a simmer, add a lid and cook until the apple has turned pulpy and very soft. Take from the heat, stir well and add the apricot jam and sugar. When cool stir in the

nutmeg and egg yolk. Taste and check for sweetness - you may need no further sugar.

3. Take the pudding basin and roll the slices of bread gently with a rolling pin to flatten slightly then slice in two from corner to corner. You will have triangular slices of bread. Try the slices in the basin for size – fitting with the pointed ends of the bread at the bottom of the basin. Once you are happy with the number you are going to need - take from the basin and dip each one in the melted butter then place back into the basin - butter side facing the basin. Save one slice of bread to be used for the top. Brush the inside of the bread with a little butter.

4. Pile the cooled apple filling into the basin lined with the bread then place a circle of bread on the top of the filling, sealing the top securely by folding over any overhanging pieces of triangle bread. Place a saucer or loose bottom from a cake tin on the top then weigh down with a 1 Kg weight. Pop into the fridge to chill for at least an hour.

5. When ready to bake preheat the oven to 200 degrees c and pop the pudding into the oven and bake for 25 minutes. Keep the plate and the weight on the pudding during baking then after 25 minutes remove the plate and the weight and allow to bake for a further 10 minutes so that the top browns.

6. Take from the oven and invert onto a plate, admire its beauty then cut into slices and serve warm with custard, cream or ice cream.

Let Me Show You...
Watch My 'Recipe' Video
SCAN HERE

Queen of Puddings

SERVES 6-8 PEOPLE

This is my take on the classic Queen of Puddings dating back to 1699. For me the pudding in its original form is a little too sweet so I have toned it down with a quick jam which is lower in sugar. This is a fabulous, low cost family pudding and can be made using any seasonal fruit.

Ingredients

BOTTOM LAYER:

- 300ml milk
- 300ml single cream
- juice and zest of 1 lemon
- 1 tsp vanilla extract
- 25g caster sugar
- 15g butter
- 130g fresh white breadcrumbs
- 2 egg yolks

JAM LAYER:

- 300g fresh fruit (I used chopped apple and blackberries)
- 25g caster sugar

MERINGUE TOPPING:

- 2 egg whites
- 125g caster sugar
- ½ tsp cream of tartar

USE: A PIE DISH – MINE IS 10 INCHES (25CM) IN DIAMETER AND APPROX. 2 INCHES (4CM) DEEP (PYREX)

PREHEAT THE OVEN TO: 180 °C (FAN)

Method

1. Start making the jam by putting the fruit and sugar in a medium saucepan and stir over a medium heat until all the sugar is dissolved. Turn up the heat and boil for 15-20 minutes until the jam is thick. Leave to cool completely.

2. Generously butter the pie dish (or use lining paste) and put to one side. Bring the milk and cream to the boil then add the zest, juice,

vanilla, caster sugar, butter and breadcrumbs and stir thoroughly. I sometimes blitz my mixture with a stick blender if there are any lumpy bread pieces. Leave to stand and cool for about 15 minutes then whisk in the egg yolks. Transfer to the pie dish then bake in the oven at 180 degrees for 25 minutes until set. Turn the oven down to 150 degrees.

3. Take the pudding dish from the oven and allow to cool. Once the jam is cooled and the custard is cooled then you can start to assemble the pudding.

4. To make the meringue, place the two egg whites in a roomy, spotlessly clean bowl then whisk until the whites are white and frothy. Add the sugar a tablespoon at a time and whisk well between each addition. Incorporate the cream of tartar during this process. The meringue will be shiny and standing in stiff peaks.

5. Spread the jam over the set custard then pile the meringue over the jam, making sure you cover it right up to the edges of the dish. Swirl the top then pop into the cooled oven and bake for 45 minutes until the meringue is crispy and pale golden on the top.

6. Can be eaten hot or cold.

Nancy's Top Tips

Rhubarb and ginger work beautifully as a fresh jam.

Use 300g Fresh rhubarb cut into chunks, 1 piece of stem ginger in syrup cut into tiny dice and 1 tbsp syrup from the ginger. Pile the lot into a foil parcel and cook for 20-30 minutes in the oven until tender then mash with a fork. Alternatively, cook on the hob over a low heat with a lid, stirring regularly about 15 minutes until tender - taking care not to burn.

Let Me Show You...
Watch My 'Recipe' Video
SCAN HERE

Last Minute Christmas Puddings

MAKES 8

These are a lighter version of traditional Christmas pudding and I actually prefer them. Alternatively these puddings are superb in January and will use up any leftover mincemeat. Can be made Gluten free too!

Ingredients

- 300g mincemeat
- 75g soft margarine or butter
- 75g caster sugar
- 2 eggs
- 1 tbsp black treacle
- 75g ground almonds
- 100g self raising flour or gluten free flour
- ½ tsp mixed spice
- ½ tsp ground cardamom
- 100g eating apple grated (one small apple – use peel also)
- zest and juice of 1 orange and 1 lemon

USE: 8 MINI PUDDING TINS 6 FL OZ (175ML) BRUSHED WITH LINING PASTE

PREHEAT THE OVEN TO: 180 °C (FAN)

Method

1. Cream together the margarine/butter and sugar until light and fluffy then add the eggs one at a time whisking well between each addition. Fold in the flour, sifted with the spices then add all the other ingredients.

2. Divide the mixture evenly between the tins then bake at 180 degrees fan for 20-25 minutes until risen and dark golden in colour.

3. These can be served with a brandy sauce or custard.

4. These puddings freeze very well and can be thawed and reheated in the microwave.

Fruit Crumble

SERVES 6 PEOPLE

I have decided to include my crumble recipe because it is one of those fantastic "go to" puddings. Freeze crumble mix then scatter over your choice of fruit (frozen or fresh) and you have a quick wholesome pudding – delicious with custard

I like my crumble to have real crunchiness and bite and I have found that by adding a little milk to the mix, and giving it a stir creates little chunks of crunch. This crumble is easy, deliciously crunchy and inexpensive.

Ingredients

FOR THE CRUMBLE:

- 170g self raising flour
- 90g butter (at room temperature)
- ½ tsp ground nutmeg (or use cinnamon, mixed spice or ginger if you make rhubarb)
- 40g demerera sugar
- 40g porridge oats
- 2 tbsp whole milk

APPLE & BLACKBERRY:

- 300g cooking apples (trimmed weight) – peeled, cored and cut into slices
- 100g blackberries (I used frozen)
- 2-3 dsp caster sugar

USE: AN OVENPROOF DISH – MINE MEASURES 9 INCHES X 6 INCHES X 2INCHES (23CM X 15CM X 6CM)

PREHEAT THE OVEN TO: 180 °C (FAN)

Method

1. In a roomy mixing bowl place the flour, spice and butter then rub in by hand until the mixture resembles breadcrumbs. Stir through the oats and sugar then spoon over the milk. Use a knife to stir the mixture around and you will see lumps will form as the mixture starts to stick together because of the addition of the milk. Pop the bowl into the fridge until you prepare the fruit.

2. Preheat the oven to 180 degrees c (fan)

3. Peel, core and slice the apples into the dish, scatter the blackberries around amongst the apple then sprinkle over the sugar. You may want to add a little cinnamon or nutmeg if you really love it.

4. Take the crumble mix from the fridge and use a large spoon to carefully cover the fruit. Don't be tempted to push the crumble down over the fruit.

5. Transfer to the oven and bake for 30 minutes until the crumble is dark golden in colour.

6. Serve with custard, cream or ice cream.

Nancy's Top Tip

For a quick hot pudding in around 30 minutes try doubling or trebling this mix and transfer the crumble to a freezer bag and store in the freezer. It remains free flowing and when you come home and need a quick handy pudding - place fresh or frozen fruit in the bottom of your ovenproof dish add a sprinkle of sugar, spoon over your frozen crumble then straight into the oven for 30 minutes.

Let Me Show You...

Watch My 'Recipe' Video
SCAN HERE

Rice Pudding

SERVES 6-8 PEOPLE

I love a rice pudding and I used to always make it in the oven but often found it to be either too dry as it had baked for too long or a bit sloppy with gritty rice when I had tried to rush it along. I now make it on the hob, leave it to stand then reheat and I find the results perfect every time.

Ingredients

- 30g butter
- 150g pudding rice or short grain rice (washed in cold water in a sieve and left to drain)
- 50g sugar
- 1 litre whole milk
- 1 tsp vanilla extract
- 1 tsp grated nutmeg
- 400ml evaporated milk (1 tin)

Method

1. So simple. In a large saucepan place all the ingredients then set over a low heat and stir well until the butter and sugar have dissolved.

2. Bring to a very gentle simmer then turn to the lowest power setting and allow it to just tick over, stirring from time to time so that it doesn't burn on the bottom and so that the rice doesn't clump together. Try to stir about every five minutes or so.

3. Allow to cook for about half an hour, stirring regularly until the rice is al dente and almost cooked through.

4. Take from the heat, place a lid on and leave to cool.

5. When cool the rice should be thick, creamy and fully cooked. Give a good stir and a taste. To serve either reheat in the pan or microwave in individual bowls.

Nancy's Top Tips

Rub the base of your pan with the recipe's butter to help avoid the milk burning on the bottom.
Better still a non stick pan will work well as long as you don't have your heat too high.

♥

If you cook on a gas hob place an upturned metal pie plate over the smallest burner on the lowest flame. Once your rice pudding is simmering gently, pop the pan onto the upturned metal plate. This will diffuse the heat and your pudding will cook perfectly without burning.

Let Me Show You...
Watch My 'Recipe' Video
SCAN HERE

Meringue Crown

SERVES 8-10 PEOPLE

With a crispy outside, soft light centre and adorned with fruit jewels of the season this meringue crown is my elevated pavlova!

Ingredients

FOR THE CROWN:

- 3 egg whites
- 150g caster sugar
- 1 tsp cornflour

FOR THE FILLING:

- 300g double cream
- selection of seasonal fruits

USE: A BAKING SHEET AND A SHEET OF BAKING PARCHMENT.

PREHEAT THE OVEN TO: 180 °C (FAN)

Method

1. Make sure your bowl and whisk are completely grease free otherwise your egg whites will not whisk up to their full potential.

2. In a large roomy mixing bowl or the bowl of a table top mixer – place the egg whites.

3. In a separate bowl place the caster sugar and mix with the cornflour. If you have the time pass the two through a sieve to ensure you have no lumps.

4. Whisk the egg whites until they are white and foamy and starting to form into soft peaks then add the sugar/cornflour mix one tablespoon at a time and whisk for about one minute between each spoonful. Finally, you will have a stiff, shiny, thick and luscious meringue.

5. Take the baking sheet and piece of baking parchment and with a marker pen or dark pencil draw a 20cm circle onto the paper. I use the loose bottom from a cake tin as a template. Turn the paper over so that the ink/pencil is not in contact

with the meringue then start to stack the meringue. You may find it useful to secure the paper onto the sheet with a blob of meringue before you start.

6. Keeping within the line of your circle start to smooth the meringue top and sides. I found this meringue bakes without cracks if the meringue is piped onto the paper in circles. There are then fewer air pockets. Use an angled palette knife or bench scraper to smooth the top and sides then you can use the back of a teaspoon or your palette knife to make ridges in the walls of your meringue.

7. When you are happy with the finished design pop into the oven and immediately reduce the temperature down to 120 degrees c (fan) and bake for two and a quarter hours. When the baking time is over, turn off the oven and open the oven door, wedging it open with a wooden spoon and leave the meringue in there overnight to completely dry out.

8. When ready to fill peel the cooled meringue crown from the paper and place onto your display plate then fill with fresh cream and a selection of seasonal fruits.

Let Me Show You...
Watch My 'Recipe' Video
SCAN HERE

Meringue Mishaps

TIP: No Soft Peaks

The initial problem could be that your meringue refuses to whisk up and that is because there is grease present in the bowl or on your whisk. Always make sure your equipment is super clean. Also, egg whites will whip up quicker and to their full potential if they are at room temperature.

♥

TIP: My meringue was very hard and almost biscuit like but I wanted it crisp on the outside and fluffy in the centre

Try adding a little cornflour - I use it often when making meringue because it helps to bind the mixture and achieve a soft centre and a crispy outside.

Meringue actually dries out in the oven rather than bakes and a very hard meringue may have been in the oven for too long. Bake for half an hour less next time- also take a look at the amount of sugar used in the recipe. I usually work on 50g sugar per egg white. Any more than that will produce a hard meringue which is perfect for meringue garnishes like "kisses" but not for a crown or pavlova.

♥

TIP: My baked meringues have little brown beads on them

The little brown beads on meringues have appeared because some of the sugar has been undissolved during the whisking and mixing. Use caster sugar as it is fine and add just one tablespoon of sugar at a time to ensure it has been well incorporated before moving on.

TIP: My meringue cracked

There will be a couple of reasons for this. Whipping up the egg white on too high a speed too quickly can cause problems because large unstable air bubbles form which later collapse causing cracks. Always start beating the whites on a low speed until they become frothy. If your recipe calls for lemon juice, vinegar or cream of tartar add this before the sugar. These little acidic additions strengthen the proteins in the egg white making for a more stable meringue.
Add then the sugar one tablespoon at a time, whisking well between each addition. The meringue will become smooth, thick and glossy. Too much mixing will cause the meringue to collapse and separate so stop mixing when your meringue peaks are shiny and stiff.

A meringue can crack because it cooled down too quickly so to avoid this at the end of the cooking time turn off the oven then wedge the door open with a wooden spoon. The meringue will cool very slowly and prevent cracking.

♥

TIP: My baked meringues have little brown beads on them

The little brown beads on meringues have appeared because some of the sugar has been undissolved during the whisking and mixing. Use caster sugar as it is fine and add just one tablespoon of sugar at a time to ensure it has been well incorporated before moving on.

♥

TIP: Can I make meringue ahead?

Meringue is great as a "get ahead" dessert and once made and kept in a tin it will keep for up to one week.

TIP: My little meringue kisses were perfect when they came out of the oven but now they've gone soft!

Meringue suffers terribly if the atmosphere is humid. In fact I remember reading an old French recipe book that suggested refraining from meringue making if the weather outside was wet! That said, bear in mind that any dampness will fill find its way very quickly to your meringue and make it sticky and soft. The best thing to do is to pop them into an airtight box or tin until ready to use.

Even better – pop your gorgeous crisp pavlova, kisses or shapes in a tin or bag then throw in a Silica sachet (yes – that's right! One of those little bags that was found in the bottom of your handbag when you bought it). Silica gel absorbs any moisture and will keep your meringue perfectly crispy until you are ready to fill and decorate.

♥

TIP: Is it possible to reduce the amount of sugar used in meringues?

Here is a half sugar meringue which works very well and worth a try if you are working on reducing your sugar intake but still want to enjoy a treat.

Half Sugar Almond Meringues

MAKES 6 MERINGUE NESTS

Battling to reduce the sugar content in my recipes and after various experiments I have developed this great little meringue containing half the sugar of standard recipes whilst maintaining a good structure, crispy on the outside and soft on the inside.

Ingredients

- 2 egg whites
- 60g icing sugar
- 15g cornflour
- 20g flaked almonds
- ¼ tsp almond extract (optional)

PREHEAT THE OVEN TO: 125 °C (FAN)

Method

1. Your bowl and whisks need to be completely clean and free from grease otherwise your egg whites will not whisk up to their full potential.

2. Start by toasting the flaked almonds in a dry frying pan over a medium heat until just turning golden brown. Immediately turn the nuts out of the pan onto a plate otherwise they will continue to cook and may burn. Once cool blitz to a fine crumb using a food processor or coffee grinder. Set aside.

3. Place the icing sugar and cornflour together, stir then pass through a sieve to make sure there are no lumps.

4. In a clean roomy bowl place the egg whites and whisk on a low speed to start with then increase as the whites thicken. Whisk until the whites stand in stiff peaks. Adding just a tablespoon at a time start to incorporate the icing sugar and cornflour

mix – whisking well between each addition. Once all the sugar mix has been included finally fold in the nut crumb – just briefly – don't whisk it in otherwise you risk collapsing the meringue.

5. Take a baking sheet lined with reusable baking parchment and either spoon or pipe the meringue mix – you will have enough for 6 small meringue nests. Transfer to the oven and bake for 30 minutes. Turn off the oven but leave the meringues inside – leave overnight.

6. The next day peel from the parchment and these meringues will keep in a tin for up to two weeks. Fill with cream, crème patissiere, seasonal fruits and a dusting of icing sugar.

Let Me Show You...
Watch My 'Recipe' Video
SCAN HERE

Meringue Cake

I have called this a Meringue cake but it is in fact a sublime dessert that is a real showstopper. This is a great recipe for the summer and as with any meringue this bake can also be gluten free.

Ingredients

FOR THE MERINGUE:

- 30g flaked almonds
- 4 egg whites
- 200g caster sugar
- 1 tsp cornflour

FOR THE LEMON CURD:

- 75g caster sugar
- 50g butter
- 4 egg yolks
- zest and juice of one lemon

TO COMPLETE THE FILLING:

- 300ml double cream
- 125g fresh berries

USE: 2 X 7INCH (18CM) CAKE TINS FULLY LINED WITH PAPER (BOTTOM AND SIDES)

PREHEAT THE OVEN TO: 125 °C (FAN)

Method

1. Start by toasting the flaked almonds. I heat a dry frying pan then lay the nuts on in a single layer then just as they start to colour give them a shake before transferring them to a cold plate. Do not be tempted to let them cool in the pan as they will carry on toasting and may burn. When the nuts have cooled blitz them briefly to a rough ground mix. You can alternatively use ground almonds but I think more flavour is gained from the method explained.

TO MAKE THE MERINGUE...

1. Whisk the egg whites in a clean grease free bowl until they have formed soft peaks.

2. Start to add the sugar one tablespoon at a time, whisking well between each addition. Don't be tempted to rush – the whisking should take about 15 minutes. The meringue will be stiff and shiny. With the final spoon of sugar add the cornflour.

3. Finally, fold in the crushed toasted almonds.

4. I have found that by piping the meringue into the tins air pockets are avoided so take the time to do this for a better result.

5. Place the two tins in the oven and allow to bake for one and a half hours. At the end of the cooking time turn off the oven and open the oven door very slightly, I wedge mine open with a wooden spoon.

6. Leave the meringues to cool completely in the oven. I leave them overnight.

7. The next day lift the meringues out of the tins by the papers then remove the papers from sides and base. If you want to get ahead the meringue cakes will freeze perfectly and you can fill and decorate later. Alternatively place them in a tin and they will keep for 4 days.

TO MAKE THE LEMON CURD...

1. In a small saucepan (off the heat) mix the egg yolks then add the sugar and mix well.

2. Add then the finely grated zest and juice and finally the butter.

3. Place over a low heat, stirring continually until the butter melts. The curd will then start to thicken and when you see the first bubble appear take off the heat, give a really good beating then transfer to a bowl to cool.

TO ASSEMBLE THE MERINGUE CAKE...

1. In a large mixing bowl whisk the double cream to soft peaks. Loosen the cold lemon curd with a little cream, give it a good mix then pour the lemon curd mix into the whipped cream – folding just enough to incorporate but leaving some lemon ripples.

2. Divide the mixture – use one half to sandwich the cake together along with a few berries then pile the rest onto the top and decorate with the rest of the fruits.

Summer Lemon & Elderflower Cheesecake

SERVES 10-12

A fantastic dessert for the summer which, with a little thought about decoration, can really impress your friends. It is easy to make and can be made ahead of time – up to two days before. Fresh, seasonal and colourful fruits, a smooth lemon filling, thin base and a topping of elderflower jelly makes for sheer elegance!

Ingredients

FOR THE BASE:

- 110g digestive biscuits (about 9 biscuits)
- 50g butter
- ½ tsp chinese five spice

FOR THE CURD:

- 2 eggs
- 75g caster sugar
- 50g butter
- zest and juice of 1 lemon

FOR THE GLAZE:

- 2 gelatine leaves soaked in cold water
- 4 tbsp elderflower cordial
- 140ml cold water
- tiny amount of lemon yellow food colour

FOR THE FILLING:

- selection of colourful fruits – strawberries, raspberries, blueberries, melon, etc..
- 500g mascarpone cheese (at room temperature)
- 170ml whole milk
- 180g icing sugar
- 4 gelatine leaves (soaked for at least 10 minutes in cold water)
- zest and juice of 1 large lemon (or 2 small)
- the lemon curd

FOR DECORATION:

- mixed seasonal fruits

USE: A 9 INCH (23CM) LOOSE BOTTOMED SPRING FORM TIN AND I REMOVE THE METAL BASE AND REPLACE IT WITH A THIN CAKE BOARD OF THE SAME SIZE. MAKES FOR EASY RELEASE AND PROFESSIONAL PRESENTATION.

Method

START BY MIXING THE BASE...

1. Crush the biscuits in a large freezer bag using a rolling pin (or pop them into a food processor and blitz to a crumb) then place in a small saucepan containing the butter which has been melted over a low heat.

2. Add the five spice then stir well to combine.

3. Transfer the buttery crumb into the base of the prepared tin and press down firmly using the back of a spoon or small angled palette knife.

4. Chill for about an hour.

5. Soak the 4 gelatine leaves in cold water for at least 10 minutes.

TO MAKE THE LEMON CURD...

1. Place the eggs in a small saucepan and beat together then add all of the other ingredients.

2. Set over a low heat and stir until the butter has dissolved. Turn up the heat slightly, still stirring all the time and then when the curd starts to thicken, remove from the heat and give it a really good stir with a wooden spoon or whisk to make sure it is smooth and silky.

3. Take the 4 gelatine leaves from the water and drop into the curd whilst it is still hot but not boiling.

4. Stir them through until dissolved.

5. Leave the whole lot in the pan and set aside.

Nancy's Top Tip

If you decide to decorate the sides of your cheesecake with fruits it is advisable to line the sides of the tin with a strip of acetate. The acetate will hug the sides of the tin and the fruits will stick to it and stay in place. Decorate the sides with your fruits then pop it all back into the fridge whilst you prepare the filling.

1. In a large bowl whisk the mascarpone cheese with the sifted icing sugar until smooth then gradually whisk in the milk a little at a time. Add then the lemon juice and zests and stir well. Pour in then the lemon curd and gelatine from the pan and whisk the whole lot together.

2. Take the chilled cheesecake base from the fridge and pour the filling over, smooth over the top then pop back into the fridge to set for at least 3 hours.

3. Whilst the cheesecake is setting the jelly top can be made. Simply soak the two gelatine leaves for at least 10 minutes in cold water. Place the cold water and elderflower cordial in a small saucepan and heat gently – do not boil. It is worth tasting the mixture to make sure it is flavoursome enough, adding a little more cordial if required. It needs to be slightly stronger than a drink would be.

4. Add the drained gelatine leaves to the warm liquid and stir until dissolved and the mixture is completely clear.

5. Add then the tiniest amount of lemon yellow food colour to tint the jelly then transfer to the fridge in a microwave jug and leave to set.

6. When the cheesecake and jelly have set – take the jelly from the fridge and pop into the microwave for just 10 seconds at a time, stirring between each session. Dissolve the jelly just sufficient for it to have turned back to liquid and be just luke warm and not hot.

7. Take the cheesecake from the fridge and spoon over the jelly – sufficient to cover the filling. You may not need all of the jelly – you just want a light glaze to cover. Pop back into the fridge to set for about 2 hours.

8. About 2-3 hours before serving decorate with more fresh fruits. I like to take my cheesecake from the fridge about an hour before serving to take the chill off and release the lovely fruity flavours.

Let Me Show You...
Watch My 'Recipe' Video
SCAN HERE

Nancy's Top Tips

TIP: Easy Out Cheesecake

A cake board fitted into the bottom of the cake tin in place of the metal base) will give you a perfect easy-out cheesecake that can be taken straight to the table.

TIP: Working with Gelatine

Some people I know are fearful of working with gelatine but once a few basic rules are understood it is a great ingredient to use in cold desserts. First and foremost gelatine doesn't like extreme temperatures – bit like ourselves really ! It will fail if it is brought to the boil and it will fail if it is frozen and that's it ! Bear those two things in mind and your gelatine will set.

TIP: Powder or Leaf?

I use both but tend to choose leaf gelatine because of its ease of use and I just know that when calculating recipes 1 leaf will set 100ml liquid. If you prefer powdered gelatine then 1 tbsp powder (usually 1 sachet) will equal 3 sheets. There are vegetarian options for gelatine on the market which work extremely well.

TIP: My cheesecake, mousse or dessert had little shards of gelatine in it

This will have happened because the gelatine wasn't fully dissolved before it was added to the cold mixture. Gelatine leaf needs to be softened in cold water for at least ten minutes but then it must be dissolved using heat before stirring through a cold mixture. I tend to drain my soaked gelatine leaves into a small pan and then put over the gentlest heat for a few seconds (do not boil) until you see those wobbly leaves completely dissolve and a clear liquid appear. At this stage your gelatine can be safely poured and quickly mixed into your main liquid.

Pina Colada Cocktail Dessert

This recipe will yield 8 individual desserts in moulds measuring 3 inches (8cm) wide x 2 inches (5cm) deep which I line with acetate strip. Alternatively you can make one full sized cheesecake in a 9 inch (23cm) loose bottomed cake tin.

These little no bake desserts are absolutely delicious, light and can easily be made gluten free if you use gluten free biscuits.

They can be made ahead and decorated just before serving – they will last four days in the fridge.

Ingredients

FOR THE COCONUT CREAM:

- 400g tin coconut milk refrigerated overnight upside down
- 30g coconut milk powder (don't worry if you haven't got this)
- 120ml double cream
- 2 eggs
- 120g caster sugar
- 75ml rum (dark or white rum)
- 5 ½ gelatine leaves soaked in cold water
- fresh fruit to decorate and chocolate shards

FOR THE BISCUIT BASE:

- 170g digestive biscuits
- 70g butter
- half a nutmeg finely grated

Method

TO MAKE THE BASE...

1. Melt the butter in a small saucepan then crush the biscuits either in a freezer bag with a rolling pin or blitz in a food processor then add the grated nutmeg.

2. Add the crumbs to the melted butter, mix well.

3. Then divide between the lined moulds which have been first placed on a baking sheet. I like to cover the bases with individual pieces of baking parchment, so that I can slide a knife underneath and move them easily. The moulds are metal rings with no bottoms.

4. Chill for at least half an hour.

TO MAKE THE COCONUT FILLING...

1. Over a pan of simmering water whisk together the eggs and the sugar until the mixture is pale, light and doubled in volume – by this time the eggs will be cooked through.

2. Take off the heat and set aside.

3. Take the tin of coconut milk and carefully open with a tin opener and pour off the water which will have risen to the top of the tin as the coconut milk set in the fridge.

4. Turn out the coconut milk in a separate bowl and whisk with the coconut milk powder until smooth.

5. Add in the double cream and whisk until thick.

6. Gradually add the egg/sugar mix and finally the rum. Taste the mixture and add more rum if desired.

7. Dissolve the gelatine in the warm pan after pouring away the warm water which was used under the eggs/sugar and when the gelatine has dissolved, whisk this into the coconut cream.

1. I then transfer the mix to a jug and carefully fill the chilled moulds.

2. Leave to set in the fridge for three hours or overnight.

3. Make up the pineapple jelly then leave to cool before pouring a thin layer over each set dessert. Leave the jelly to set for about four hours then remove from the moulds directly onto a serving plate and remove the acetate then decorate with a selection of fresh fruit, pineapple, chocolate or berries.

Nancy's Top Tip

Pina colada is of course a delicious Caribbean cocktail flavoured with coconut, rum and pineapple and these are the flavours in this recipe. Pineapple is reluctant to set with gelatine as does kiwi and papaya so it is necessary to buy jelly and make up a half pint.

Let Me Show You...
Watch My 'Recipe' Video
SCAN HERE

Raspberry & White Chocolate Bundt

SERVES 6-8 PEOPLE

This is a real stunner.

A delicious light dessert which can be served any time of the year as I have used frozen berries throughout. Almond fat-less sponge supporting a white chocolate panacotta then topped with a berry filled jelly.

It can be dressed up to look irresistible and then served at any dinner party or family gathering.

Ingredients

FOR THE JELLY:

- 250ml fresh fruit puree (I used a mix of raspberries and strawberries from the freezer, thawed and passed through a sieve)
- 300ml simple syrup (200ml water, 120g sugar, strip of lemon zest and 2.5cm vanilla pod – boiled together for 2-3 minutes then left to cool)
- 5 leaves gelatine (soaked in cold water for 10 minutes)
- 200g frozen raspberries

Nancy's Top Tip

If you really want to speed up this dessert instead of making your own jelly make up 1 pint strawberry or raspberry packet jelly to use along with the frozen raspberries.

FOR THE PANACOTTA:

- 200ml double cream
- 120ml milk
- 100g white chocolate
- 1 tsp vanilla extract
- 50g sugar
- 2 gelatine leaves

FOR THE ALMOND SPONGE:

- 2 eggs
- 50g caster sugar
- 50g plain flour (or gluten free flour) for gf dessert
- ½ tsp almond extract
- 1 tbsp flaked almonds (opt.)

YOU WILL NEED: A 9 INCH (22CM) BUNDT TIN

Method

1. Start by making a template for the sponge. Using the bundt tin draw a circle on a piece of baking paper and mark the hole in the middle also.

2. Cut out the shape as this will be used later when cutting the sponge.

TO MAKE THE JELLY...

1. Sieve any seeds from the fruit puree then pop into a jug. Once you have made your simple syrup and whilst it is still warm drop the gelatine leaves (drained of their soaking water) and stir well until dissolved. Mix together the fruit puree and simple syrup containing the gelatine and mix well.

2. Place half of the fruit in the bottom of the tin and pour over half of the jelly. Place in the fridge to set for 2 hours.

3. Leave the rest of the jelly at room temperature. Fruit will always float in jelly so if you want a whole berry on the presentation of your dessert simply chill your tin then lay a whole frozen berry around the base (this will of course be the top when turned out).

4. Set in place with just 1 tsp liquid jelly then pop into the fridge for 20 minutes until set.

5. You can then add the remainder of the half of the fruit and pour on the rest of the half pint jelly and your presentation berry will be secure at the bottom of the tin and will not float.

TO MAKE THE PANNA COTTA...

1. Break the chocolate into a bowl then put the gelatine in a bowl of cold water to soak.

2. Bring the milk, cream and sugar to a gentle simmer then pour it over the broken chocolate then add the softened gelatine.

3. Stir until the chocolate melts and the gelatine is dissolved. I then pass the whole mix through a sieve as there can be chocolate solids left behind.

4. Leave to cool at room temperature (don't put it in the fridge at this stage otherwise it will set.

5. When the jelly has set remove it from the fridge and pour over the panna cotta. The whole lot can now be transferred to the fridge for at least two hours to firm up completely.

6. Layer the rest of the frozen berries over the panna cotta and pour on the other half of the jelly.

7. Leave to set in the fridge for a further two hours. If the second half of the jelly in its jug has set simply pop it into the microwave in 15 second bursts until it turns to liquid but is not hot. If it is hot allow it to cool down otherwise it will melt your panna cotta as it is poured over.

TO MAKE THE FAT-LESS SPONGE...

1. Whisk together the eggs and caster sugar until doubled in size and the whisk leaves a trail.

2. Then add the almond extract and fold in the flour. Spread onto greaseproof paper or reusable baking parchment making sure the sponge is larger than the paper template made earlier.

3. Scatter over the flaked almonds then bake for 8-10 minutes at 180 degrees.

4. Leave to cool then using the template cut out the shape of the savarin mould. Carefully peel your baked sponge from the paper before cutting out – its easier that way.

5. When the jelly has set lay the sponge over the top almond side uppermost then turn out onto a serving plate.

6. Decorate with fresh fruit, mint leaves, chocolate curls etc.. if you wish.

Nancy's Top Tips

Spoon the jelly over the panna cotta until you have an even layer. Don't be tempted to pour it over as the weight of the jelly may penetrate the panna cotta and you will breach the surface.

♥

Fruit will automatically float in the jelly so if you want to be able to see fruit at the top of your finished dessert simply place a few presentation berries at the bottom of the tin then spoon over a little jelly to help keep them in place... Pop in the fridge for about 20 minutes to set. Take from the fridge and top up with the rest of the half of the jelly.

♥

To easily turn out your set jelly, briefly place the chilled bundt tin into a bowl of hot water – just about 30 seconds. Your jelly will then release easily.

♥

Gelatine will refuse to set if it is boiled or frozen so don't be tempted to speed things up by placing in the freezer.

Let Me Show You...
Watch My 'Recipe' Video
SCAN HERE

Chocolate and Orange Delice

SERVES 8-10 PEOPLE

Beautifully rich, dark, decadent and delicious – a treasure for chocolate lovers and easily adapts to gluten free too!

This "top end" patisserie comprises a praline base then a tangy orange layer topped off and decorated with dark, deep chocolate. The chocolate sets and no gelatine in sight.

Ingredients

FOR THE BASE:

- 40g whole hazelnuts
- 40g caster sugar
- 40g shreddies or gluten free cereal

FOR THE ORANGE LAYER:

- 3 tbsp marmalade and the finely grated zest of 1 orange

FOR THE CHOCOLATE:

- 140ml whole milk
- 300ml double cream
- 3 eggs
- 360g dark chocolate broken into pieces
- 1 tsp instant espresso coffee
- ¼ tsp ground star anise or chinese five spice (optional)
- ½ tsp vanilla paste

USE: AN 8 INCH (18CM) SQUARE LOOSE BOTTOMED CAKE TIN. LINE THE SIDES WITH PAPER OR ACETATE STRIP

Nancy's Top Tip

TIP: For easy cutting pop the delice into the freezer for an hour and your portions will be incredibly neat and clean.

Method

1. Start by making the praline. In a dry frying pan gently roast the hazelnuts until they have taken on a golden colour.

2. In a medium sized saucepan place the sugar and just 1 tbsp cold water and heat gently. Do not be tempted to fiddle with the sugar – leave it to gradually dissolve only gently moving the pan from side to side.

3. Once the sugar has dissolved then turn up the heat and allow the syrup to take on the colour of pale yellow then drop in the nuts. Swirl the pan around gently and allow the nuts and syrup to darken to the colour of golden syrup.

4. Immediately turn the mixture out onto a baking sheet covered in baking parchment or foil and allow to go completely cold. Leaving the mixture in the pan will cause your praline to burn and taste very bitter.

5. In the bowl of a food processor with the blade attached roughly blitz the Shreddies (or chosen cereal if you have chosen to make a gluten free dessert) until they have formed a rough crumb.

6. Transfer to a bowl.

7. Break the nutty caramel into pieces then blitz this in the food processor continually until the praline has formed a thick paste.

8. Transfer this paste to the bowl with the Shreddies and mix together. Transfer this mix to the baking tin and spread over the base, pressing down firmly and evenly. Transfer to the fridge and allow to chill for an hour.

9. Mix the marmalade with the orange zest then spread this over the firm base – pop back into the fridge.

10. Place the milk and cream into a medium saucepan and bring to the boil.

11. In a separate large bowl beat the eggs then take the recently boiled milk/cream and pour this over them in a thin steady stream whisking all the time The heat from the liquid will cook the eggs. Once all has been mixed add the chocolate, coffee, vanilla and spice (if using) and stir slowly until the chocolate has completely dissolved and the mixture is thick, dark and smooth.

12. Take the tin from the fridge

and pour on the chocolate then pop back into the fridge and allow to set for 6 hours or better overnight. As this dessert doesn't contain gelatine it will freeze very well.

13. Cut into tidy portions and serve! I like to serve this delice lightly chilled.

14. Decorate as desired but I think something simple is all that is required. Even just a dusting of cocoa powder as shown. The pattern was created simply by laying cocktail sticks over before dusting with the powder.

Let Me Show You...
Watch My 'Recipe' Video
SCAN HERE

Crème Caramel

This is a traditional dessert but one that people tell me they cannot get right and indeed I had many unsatisfactory results myself to begin with. This is a great dessert for entertaining as it has to be made at least 24 hours before it is served. These crèmes will in fact keep well in the fridge for 3-4 days.

Ingredients

FOR THE CUSTARD:

- 550ml whole milk
- 100g sugar
- ½ vanilla pod or 1 tsp vanilla paste
- 3 eggs
- 3 egg yolks

FOR THE CARAMEL:

- 50ml water
- 150g caster sugar

USE: 6 RAMEKIN DISHES 3.5 INCHES WIDE X 2 INCHES DEEP (9CM WIDE X 5CM) AND A SMALL PAN WITHOUT A NON STICK COATING IS PREFERABLE BECAUSE YOU NEED TO BE ABLE TO SEE THE SUGAR CHANGE COLOUR. A NON STICK PAN WITH A BLACK INTERIOR WILL PROVE DIFFICULT.

PREHEAT THE OVEN TO: 130 °C (FAN)

Method

FOR THE CARAMEL:

1. Put the water and sugar in a pan and allow the sugar to dissolve over a low heat. Don't be tempted to mess with it. Do not stir or introduce any forks, spoons etc. as any grease whatsoever will cause the sugar to crystallise. I tend to swirl the pan from side to side gently to help the sugar to dissolve.

2. Once all is dissolved and you have a clear liquid in the pan then you can increase the heat and allow the sugar to boil.

3. Once all the water has evaporated the sugar will start to colour. When the sugar has the colour of golden syrup take it off the heat and divide between the six ramekin dishes then set aside.

FOR THE CUSTARD:

1. Split the vanilla pod in half lengthways, scrape out the seeds and place them into the milk. Bring the milk to simmering point then remove from the heat and allow to infuse a short time whilst you mix the eggs and sugar. If you are using vanilla paste simple add this to the milk at the outset.

2. In a large mixing bowl mix the eggs and egg yolks with the sugar. Slowly pour the vanilla milk over and mix thoroughly using a whisk.

3. I now transfer the mix to a large jug but first pass the custard through a sieve which removes any egg solids and disperses any bubbles.

4. Divide the milk/egg mix between the ramekins then place them on a piece of kitchen paper in the bottom of a roasting tin. The kitchen paper prevents the bowls from sliding around in the tin.

5. Fill the roasting tin with tap hot water so that it comes just below the level of the custard in the ramekin.

6. Cook at 150 degrees for 30 minutes.

7. The custards should still have a tremble when you take them from the oven.

8. Remove immediately from the baking tin and water and allow to cool.

9. When cold, lay the ramekins side by side on the fridge shelf and lay over a beeswax wrap or flat plate. Leave them to chill for 24 hours.

10. When ready to serve - slide a knife around the custard then invert onto a dish or serving plate. The caramel sauce will surround your lovely crème. Serve as they are or with a little fresh fruit garnish on the side.

Let Me Show You...
Watch My 'Recipe' Video
SCAN HERE

Nancy's Top Tip

TIP: My Crème Caramels tasted delicious but most of the caramel was left in the ramekin

It is unlikely you will remove every trace of caramel when you invert your dessert but the more there is the better. Take your caramels from the fridge and gently run a knife around the side of the custard to loosen it then leave them to come to room temperature before serving. The caramel will run more freely from the ramekin if it is not chilled.

♥

TIP: My Crème Caramels had little bubbles in the custard

This happened to me so many times and I followed so many recipes to try and get them right. Every photograph in every book looked perfect but mine had bubbles ! After many attempts and different experiments I finally discovered that boiling water in the roasting tin was too hot for the custard which caused the bubbles to form. I now use hot water from the tap and this is gentle enough to cook the custard perfectly.

♥

TIP: Don't throw away your egg whites

You have needed 3 egg yolks for this recipe which leaves three egg whites. Pop them into a plastic container with a lid (I save yoghurt and cream cartons for this), mark clearly then freeze. These egg whites defrosted and used for a number of recipes in this book, Coconut and Passion fruit angel cakes Meringue crown as well as Italian Meringue and Swiss Meringue Buttercreams (Desserts & puddings).

Crème Brûlée

A classic dessert which it is said has its origins in France, Spain and there are those who believe it was invented in England at Trinity College, Cambridge and was known as Burnt Cream.   Whoever invented this beauty is applauded – it is one of my favourite desserts. Smooth creamy custard topped off with a thin caramel crunch. This one is easy, great for entertaining because you can get ahead the day before and it looks amazing when presented with just a few fresh berries. Gluten free too!

Ingredients

FOR THE CUSTARD:

- 300ml double cream
- 300ml milk
- 4 egg yolks
- 1 vanilla pod (seeds scraped) or 1 tsp vanilla extract
- 1 tsp cornflour
- 30g caster sugar

FOR THE CRACKING CARAMEL TOP :

- 1 tsp demerera sugar for each pudding and cooks blow torch for finishing

USE: I HAVE SOME PERFECT LITTLE DISHES, NOT RAMEKINS – THEY ARE WIDER AND MORE SHALLOW. THEIR MEASUREMENTS ARE 4 ½ INCHES WIDE X 1 INCH DEEP (12CM X 3CM). THE FRENCH SERVE CRÈME BRÛLÉE IN SUCH A DISH. THIS RECIPE WILL MAKE 4. YOU CAN ALSO USE 4 RAMEKINS – 3 INCHES IN DIAMETER (7.5CM)

Method

1. Place the cream, milk and vanilla pod and seeds (or extract) in a medium saucepan and bring to the boil slowly.

2. Place the egg yolks, sugar and cornflour in a medium bowl and stir thoroughly

3. Slowly pour the hot cream over the egg mix, stirring all the time then transfer the whole lot back into the pan and over a low heat.

4. Stir continually until the custard thickens then divide between the ramekin dishes. Allow to cool then pop into the fridge and leave for at least six hours and preferably overnight

5. When ready to serve sprinkle 1 tsp demerera sugar over each pudding and tilt from side to side to spread it out.. Take then a cooks blow torch and caramelise the top until the surface is golden brown and crunchy. This caramel will stay crisp for about one hour.

Nancy's Top Tip

I would love to make this dessert but I do not have a blowtorch

1. Try instead placing 125g sugar (caster or granulated) in a clean small saucepan and set over a low heat. Do not be tempted to fiddle with the sugar, no stirring. The most you should do is gently swirl the pan from side to side to enable even dissolve of the sugar. Slowly the sugar will start to melt and will then turn from a clear liquid to a colour the shade of golden syrup

2. Take the pan off the heat, keep your pan swirling around then pour 1-2 tbsp over each chilled crème and quickly swirl it around to make sure it runs to the edges of the custard before it quickly sets. You need to be swift so do just one at a time. Leave for a few seconds for the caramel to set and take on its classic hard top that can be tapped and broken up.

3. This caramel will stay crunchy for around two hours but then will start to suffer from the humidity and turn sticky even though it will still taste good!

Let Me Show You...
Watch My 'Recipe' Video
SCAN HERE

Citrus Posset with Blueberries

Possets are steeped in history – William Shakespeare even gives the good old posset a mention in Hamlet, yet back then a posset was a dessert or drink made from curdled milk enriched with sugar and alcohol. It was often used for medicinal purposes and it is mentioned in the Journals of the House of Lords that King Charles I was given a posset drink from his physician. Nowadays presented as a dessert this little beauty is much under rated. No cornflour, eggs or gelatine required to set this traditional English delight.

Ingredients

- 350ml double cream
- 100ml single cream
- 130g granulated sugar
- 1 lemon, 1 lime and 1 orange – finely grated zests and 90ml juice

USE: I USE 6 X 4 FL OZ (120ML) GLASS TUMBLERS.

Method

1. Start by heating the cream, sugar and zests in a medium saucepan. Keep the juice separate for the time being.

2. Heat on a low temperature to start, stirring constantly until the sugar is dissolved. Turn up the heat and bring to a boil then reduce the heat and simmer, stirring regularly for 10 minutes exactly. The cream mixture should be thick and bubbling – my grandson said it looked like frog spawn. The mixture needs to have reduced by one third.

3. Take from the heat, stir in the juice then transfer to a cold bowl and leave for 20-30 minutes to cool and a skin will form.

4. Take a fine mesh sieve and push the cooled mixture (and skin) through then transfer to the serving tumblers and leave to go completely cold. Cover and chill for three hours or overnight.

5. Take from the fridge about an hour before serving, decorate with blueberries and some lemon zests.

6. These possets will keep for 3-4 days in the fridge.

Let Me Show You...
Watch My 'Recipe' Video
SCAN HERE

Ice Cream
VANILLA AND PASSION FRUIT

MAKES 2 PINTS (1 LITRE)

My section on cold desserts just has to include ice cream. There are so many ice creams on the market that you may think it is not worth making it yourself especially if it involves having to invest in an ice cream maker – and I tend to agree. However, there will be times when maybe you find yourself with a surplus of egg yolks, or you have looked and been alarmed when reading the list of ingredients on your ice cream tub and like so many foods prepared at home, the taste of home-made ice cream has absolutely no comparison. It is delicious! I have included just a few recipes and the good news is – no ice cream maker is required...

Most of us adore vanilla ice cream and home made ice cream is the best. This recipe of mine is ultra simple, tastes delicious and is inexpensive. If you have an ice-cream machine then the results are smooth and luscious but if not I can explain how to get a very good result.

Ingredients

FOR VANILLA FLAVOUR:

- 400ml tin of evaporated milk chilled overnight in the fridge
- large clean bowl chilled in the fridge for an hour
- 2 eggs
- 50g caster sugar
- 1.5 tsp vanilla extract (or if you want to make your ice-cream really special - half a vanilla pod, seeds scraped)

Method

1. Bring a small pan of water to the boil then turn off the heat.

2. In one mixing bowl whisk the eggs, sugar and vanilla together. Place over the pan of boiled water and whisk continually until the mixture thickens, turns pale in colour and when the whisks are lifted out they leave a ribbon trail on the mixture. Whisking over the hot water will ensure the eggs are cooked.

3. Take the bowl off the heat and set aside.

4. Take the chilled bowl from the fridge and pour into it the chilled evaporated milk. With the same whisks, whip up the evaporated milk until thick and doubled in volume. Again the whisks will leave a ribbon trail in the mixture as they are lifted out.

5. Stir the two mixes together then transfer to an ice-cream machine and churn until thick, smooth and iced. Either transfer to a plastic tub and place in the freezer or eat at once! If frozen hard leave to ripen in the fridge for about half an hour to an hour before serving.

NO ICE CREAM MACHINE:

1. If you do not have an ice cream machine you can achieve good results by following the process below.

2. Transfer your whipped up mixture into a roomy plastic bowl (maybe an old save and washed out ice cream tub) which has a lid. Transfer to the freezer and leave for 1.5 hours.

3. Take from the freezer and whisk either by hand or with your electric whisk. This breaks down any ice particles that may be forming and incorporates some air into your mixture. Place back into the freezer.

4. After another hour repeat as above. Your ice cream should be setting and by giving this final whisk you should have a light delicious vanilla ice cream. This home made ice cream will set very hard so remember to take it out of the freezer and pop it into the fridge about an hour before serving to allow it to ripen and make easier to scoop.

MAKES 800ML – SERVES 12

Ingredients

FOR PASSION FRUIT FLAVOUR:

- 8 passion fruits (yielding 150ml juice)
- 20ml passion fruit liqueur
- 250ml condensed milk
- 300ml double cream

Method

1. Start by juicing the passion fruits and set aside 150ml juice.

2. In a large bowl place the condensed milk, fruit juice and cream and simply whisk until thickened. Transfer to a plastic tub with a lid to freeze or alternatively fill silicone moulds and freeze until required.

3. Take from the freezer half an hour before required and pop the tub or moulds into the fridge to ripen. This ice cream is unbelievably good!

Nancy's Top Tip
How to Juice a Passion Fruit

Cut each fruit in half, scoop out the seeds then either push through a metal sieve with a metal spoon or alternatively pop the fruit pulp into the goblet of a food processor along with the alcohol (passion fruit liqueur) and blitz for a minute.
The juice will then pour through the sieve easily.

Let Me Show You...
Watch My 'Recipe' Video
SCAN HERE

Ice Cream

NO CHURN RASPBERRY RIPPLE

Super easy to make and no ice cream maker required. Children and adults adore it and remember to ripen it in the fridge for about an hour before serving.

Ingredients

- 2 eggs separated
- 120g caster sugar
- 300ml double cream
- 1 tbsp lemon juice
- 400g fresh raspberries blitzed to a pulp then passed through a sieve
- few drops of vanilla extract

USE: YOU WILL NEED THREE ROOMY MIXING BOWLS AND AN ELECTRIC HAND WHISK.

Nancy's Top Tip

I decided to reduce down my raspberry puree to a fairly thick sauce (200g sauce) about the consistency of tomato ketchup. Simply place in a small saucepan and boil rapidly for about 6 minutes. Turn out into a cold bowl and allow to cool completely.

Method

1. In the first bowl whisk the egg whites with half of the sugar using clean whisks until the whites have increased in size and formed stiff peaks.

2. Move on to the second bowl and place this over a pan of hot water. Add the two egg yolks and the remainder of the sugar plus the vanilla. Whisk continually until the mixture has doubled in size and has taken on a pale straw colour.

3. Remove from the pan of water and set aside.

4. Move on then to the third bowl and whisk the double cream to very soft peaks – be careful you don't want to over whip the cream at this stage.

5. Fold the egg whites into the egg yolk/sugar mix, then add the double cream and lemon juice. Make sure all is well combined then finally briefly fold in the thickened raspberry puree – giving just a few turns. We want a ripple effect, not a pink ice cream.

6. Transfer to 2 x 1 litre plastic pots, place lids on and put into the freezer for at least four hours.

7. Take from the freezer and place in the fridge to ripen about an hour before serving.

Let Me Show You...
Watch My 'Recipe' Video
SCAN HERE

Arctic Bundt

LEMON AND RASPBERRY

SERVES 14-16 PEOPLE

I couldn't close this chapter without including this showstopper dessert which has many advantages. It can be made ahead – weeks ahead in fact! Children and adults adore it and it is easy to make, not expensive and looks very impressive.

Ingredients

FOR THE SPONGE:

- 250g soft margarine or butter
- 250g caster sugar
- 5 egg yolks
- 150ml whole milk plus the juice of 1 lemon
- 250g self raising flour
- finely grated zest of 1 lemon
- 5 egg whites
- 1 tsp cream of tartar

FOR THE ICE CREAM:

- 200ml double cream - chilled
- 200ml condensed milk - chilled
- 100g frozen raspberries

TO DECORATE:

- selection of fresh berries (I used strawberries and blueberries)
- icing sugar for dusting

USE: YOU WILL NEED A 10 CUP BUNDT TIN APPROXIMATE 9 INCHES (22CM) DIAMETER

PREHEAT THE OVEN TO: 170 °C (FAN)

Using my lining paste will guarantee your bundt will leave the tin with ease. When you decide to start to make this dessert place a roomy mixing bowl in the fridge and this will be referred to later.

Nancy's Top Tip

TIP: If you don't eat the whole dessert in one sitting, whilst still firm, as you would with ice cream – pop it back into the freezer for later.

Method

TO MAKE THE SPONGE:

1. Preheat the oven to 170 degrees fan.

2. In a measuring jug place the whole milk and then after zesting the lemon into a mixing bowl add the juice to the milk and set aside to thicken.

3. In the large mixing bowl containing the zest then add the margarine or butter and sugar then whisk well until light and fluffy.

4. Add the five egg yolks one at a time whisking well between each addition.

5. Fold in the sifted self raising flour and once well combined then add the thickened milk a little at a time until all is well incorporated.

6. In a separate clean bowl with clean whisks, mix together the egg whites and the cream of tartar then whisk vigorously until the whites have become thick, shiny and standing in soft peaks.

7. Fold the whites into the mixture one very large spoonful at a time then transfer the whole lot into the prepared bundt tin. Bake for 40-45 minutes until the top is dark golden in colour and firm to the touch.

8. Remove from the oven and stand on a cooling rack for 5-10 minutes until cool enough to handle then turn out and allow to cool completely.

9. Once completely cold take a bread knife and slice off the bottom 1 inch (2cm) of the bundt. Use a basin that fits the bundt comfortably then cover and flip the whole lot over so that the cake is contained within the basin and you can remove the recently sliced lid.

10. Remove the lid and set aside.

11. With a sharp vegetable knife cut a trough out of the remaining sponge and this will be filled with ice cream.

12. Children love these offcuts!

TO MAKE THE ICE CREAM:

1. Take the chilled mixing bowl from the fridge and pour in the double cream and condensed milk which are both well chilled.

2. With an electric hand whisk mix together at high speed until the mixture becomes very thick. Fold in the frozen raspberries – I find the finish much more effective if the raspberries have been broken into frozen crumbs but that is up to you.

3. Spoon the ice cream mixture into the cake trough, replace the lid then pop into the freezer for at least 6 hours but preferably overnight.

4. The next day take the basin from the freezer and turn out onto a cake board or presentation plate (that will fit back into your freezer). If the bundt seems stuck in the basin do not worry.

5. Place warm towels around the outside of the basin and in no time the bundt will release.

6. Return the bundt to the freezer until 2 hours before you want to serve it.

7. When ready to prepare your dessert. Take from the freezer and fill the central cavity with a selection of fresh berries. Pop the whole lot into the fridge and allow to "ripen" for two hours. When ready to serve take from the fridge, dust all over with icing sugar, slice and enjoy!

Let Me Show You...
Watch My 'Recipe' Video
SCAN HERE

Home
Time

Home Time

PRESERVING & GROWING OUR OWN FOOD

This book is by no means a gardening book but for those people wanting to try just a little "home growing" – here are a few ideas...

CONTINUAL SALAD LEAVES, MICRO HERBS, CRESSES AND GARNISHES

A packet of mixed salad leaves and/or herbs has so many uses. Sprinkle into a tray of potting compost every three weeks or so through the summer months and you will be rewarded with a regular supply of leaves. "Cut and Come Again" salad leaves are available – use them when they are tiny as micro herbs to garnish the most delicate of bakes or dishes, grow them to full size for salads and cooking and when you have finished your tray the chickens will nibble at the rest or leave them out for the wild birds before then tossing the whatever is left into the compost bin to be recycled.

MARROWFAT PEAS

If you just want to grow pea shoots for garnishing there is absolutely no need to purchase pea seeds that will be grown into full crops. A handful of marrowfat peas placed in a pot of compost will germinate and you will be rewarded with perfect little pea shoots to decorate your risotto or salad.

PERENNIAL HERBS

Whatever the size of your garden and in fact even if you only have space for a few pots I urge you to invest in a few perennial herbs. Herbs add so much flavour and if you can put your hand on fresh herbs even better. Don't be worried about using dried herbs by the way – I use them a lot during the winter months.

If you are thinking of investing in just a few herbs that will be available all the year round and need little or no care, can be grown in a pot and will save you pounds in the long run as you become self sufficient and don't need to call on the supermarket for a bag – try these.

Rosemary – woody plant with fragrant evergreen needle like leaves and edible (often blue) flowers in the spring. Delicious in so many recipes including pork, lamb, chicken, roasted with vegetables and I use it with cranberries dusted in icing sugar as to decorate my chocolate tart at Christmas and they add a little interest as leafy decorations on my carrot cake.

SAGE

The leaves are greyish green and soft and velvety to the touch and again have so many uses. I use it chopped in my sausage meat for sausage rolls, pork pies and a really favourite is chopped up really small along with chives and stirred through fresh mashed potato.

MINT

A pot of fresh mint is a must. Nothing beats the smell of home grown new potatoes being boiled with a sprig of fresh mint. Use chopped in salad dressings and try very finely chopped mint leaves in a chocolate traybake.

THYME

This small bushy plant and thyme's tiny leaves will provide tiny edible lilac coloured flowers in the spring. Use the flowers as a garnish or stir into butter to give a lemony flavour to foods. Thyme leaves can be used all year round with roast meats, chicken, roast vegetables, soups, stews and is a favourite with duck. Lemon cakes and puddings enhanced with a little thyme are always a favourite in my house.

This is just a start. There are so many herbs and aromatics to choose from and once you have these available at your fingertips you will want to have more.

PRESERVING

When growing your own food it is inevitable there will be gluts and far too much to be able to eat whilst the season lasts. Historically of course preserving, pickling, jamming, smoking and curing were carried out to a whole range of foods in order to store produce that would feed us during the dreary winter months.

The necessity to preserve food is no longer so pressing but for me the pleasure still remains. Home made jam spread on a freshly baked scone can present a memory of cream teas in sunny June even though it may be a dreary foggy November day. My home made 'end of season' Chutney served with cold meats at Christmas always reminds me of my greenhouse packed with fresh tomatoes in August.

Anyone who cares about the food that they eat and have put the effort into growing it will want to savour every last berry or bean – and preserving does just that. Once you have made your own jam, pickles, bottled fruits or chutney and tasted real flavour you will realise that bought equivalents are often overly sweet and lack any real substance.

I have many recipes to hand but here are a few of my favourites...

Strawberry Jam

MAKES 5-6 JARS

Strawberry jam home made is more than delicious! It is afternoon tea, cream tea, Victoria sandwich cake, fresh bread - fabulous.

Making a delicious jam is not difficult and if you grow your own strawberries and when strawberries are plentiful what better solution than to preserve them for the months to come.

The main problem with soft fruits is that they can soon be destroyed by over stirring, boiling and handling. So firstly I do not wash the fruits and I pick them when the weather is dry. We don't want any extra moisture going on as there is plenty contained within the fruits.

Ingredients

- 2 kg fresh strawberries
- 1 kg granulated sugar
- finely grated zest and juice of 1 lemon

USE: A PRESERVING PAN AND I LIKE TO RUB BUTTER ON THE BASE OF THE PAN TO PREVENT STICKING.
PREHEAT THE OVEN TO: 100 °C (FAN)

Nancy's Top Tip

When cooking with fruit and sugar a scum will probably form during the cooking. To disperse this when your jam is ready simply add a knob of butter, stir and it will disappear.

Method

1. Place two or three saucers or tea plates in the freezer.

2. Heat your jars (to sterilize them) without their lids in a warm oven (100 degrees) when you start to make your jam.

3. The night before you want to make your jam - remove the hull (the green leaves and little core) from your strawberries and place in the pan. Finely grate over the lemon zest and add the juice. Sprinkle over the sugar then leave until the next day.

4. When you return to your pan the sugar will have started to dissolve around the fruit. Place over a low heat and gently stir from time to time until all of the sugar has melted. Wait until the grittiness of the sugar has disappeared - you can feel this with a wooden spoon on the base of the pan. Turn up the heat and bring the pan to a fast boil. Time the boiling period and cook for twenty minutes then remove it from the heat.

5. Take one of your saucers from the freezer and take a tablespoon of your jam from the pan and place onto the freezing cold plate. Pop the plate and the jam into the fridge for 2-3 minutes

6. Take out the plate, then push the jam from one side with your finger. If it is still liquid and the track made by your finger immediately fills with jam then boil for another five minutes and repeat. If however, when you push the jam it wrinkles and has formed a thin skin and your finger leaves a trail then it is cooked perfectly and will set when it is cold.

7. Take your warm jars from the oven and fill with the hot jam. The heating of the jars not only sterilizes them it prevents them from cracking when the hot jam is poured in.

8. Seal the jars immediately and leave to cool.

Let Me Show You...
Watch My 'Recipe' Video
SCAN HERE

Sugar Free 'Freezer Jam'

MAKES 3 JARS

This is simply fantastic. Summer strawberries, fresh in flavour to be enjoyed all the year round. I have used honey as a sweetener. As there is no boiling of sugar this jam is thinner in consistency than standard jam but tastes amazing. Serve with breakfast, alongside desserts, on ice cream, rice pudding – lots of options!

Ingredients

- 450g fresh strawberries – leaves and hull removed
- finely grated zests and juice of 1 lemon and 1 orange
- 45g honey
- 1 tsp vanilla paste
- 1 tsp ground cinnamon

Method

1. Place the strawberries in a roomy bowl then use a potato masher to break them down. I then finish off with a hand blender but don't blend down to a pulp – you still want some good strawberry lumps.

2. In a small saucepan place the lemon and orange zests, honey, fruit juice and 200g of the strawberry pulp.

3. Place over a moderate heat, stirring all the time then bring to a fast boil and bubble away for 3 minutes stirring from time to time. The mixture will thicken considerably, make sure it doesn't burn!

4. Take off the heat and add to the remainder of the strawberries in the bowl.

5. Stir in the vanilla and cinnamon then transfer to three clean jars with screw top lids or plastic containers if you prefer.

6. Do not fill to the top of the jar – allow some headroom as the jam will expand as it freezes.

7. This jam will freeze for one year. When ready to use, take from the freezer, thaw overnight in the fridge and then it will keep for at least a week.

Let Me Show You...
Watch My 'Recipe' Video
SCAN HERE

Redcurrant Jelly

THIS SMALL AMOUNT WILL MAKE ABOUT TWO JARS BUT OF COURSE YOU CAN DOUBLE OR TRIPLE IF YOU HAVE SUFFICIENT FRUIT.

If you grow your own redcurrants (and I urge you to do so) - one little bush will yield pounds and pounds if looked after properly. Home made redcurrant jelly is far superior to any shop bought version and I use it in all sorts of recipes especially at Christmas time. It is delicious served with cheese, cold meats and I add a spoonful to savoury pie fillings, stews, casseroles and a spoonful stirred into an over-salted gravy or sauce provides an instant rescue.

Ingredients

- 900g redcurrants – stalks and all.
- granulated sugar (see method for quantity)

Method

1. Place the berries in a large casserole or preserving pan. Turn the heat onto low and let the fruits break down. As the cooking progresses I use a potato masher to help burst the berries. Bring to a boil then turn off the heat and transfer the hot puree to a jelly bag.

2. A jelly bag is a fine nylon bag and can be purchased for a few pounds with its own stand. The bag is attached to the stand and the whole lot is suspended over a large pan or jug. Fruit puree is poured into the bag and the juice allowed to drip through slowly. The puree is left overnight undisturbed. If you squeeze the bag to try and rush things along, you will not get a clear jelly.

3. The next day whatever volume of fruit juice you

have produced you then use the same weight in granulated sugar.

4. For this recipe I had a yield of 200ml fruit juice which I poured into a clean saucepan to which I then added 200g granulated sugar.

5. Dissolve the sugar over a low heat then when all is dissolved, turn up the heat and allow the jelly to reach a fast boil. Boil for 1 minute only.

6. Turn off the heat.

7. You will have a scum over the jelly but drop a knob of butter into the pan, stir and this will disappear.

8. Quickly transfer the jelly into two hot clean jars before it sets.

9. Place the lids on the jars and store until required.

Let Me Show You...
Watch My 'Recipe' Video
SCAN HERE

Seville Orange Marmalade

MAKES 5-6 JARS

Allow four hours for marmalade making. The first time I made it I started early evening and then couldn't go to bed because I was waiting for it to reach a set! Seville oranges are in season in January and early February – that's the only time you can buy them so I make enough for the whole year. This recipe is reduced to make a batch of 5-6 jars. The house will be filled with a lovely orange smell but if it is particularly cold outside your windows will steam up – try and choose a windy day and then the condensation will not be so bad. I am lucky enough to have an outside hob for frying fish and I am afraid the marmalade is done outside too.

Ingredients

- 1 kg Seville Oranges
- 1 lemon
- 2 litres water
- 2 kg granulated sugar

- 6 x 1lb glass jars with screw tops

USE: A VERY LARGE SAUCEPAN AND A MUSLIN SQUARE TO HOLD THE PITH AND PIPS. IF YOU DON'T HAVE A MUSLIN SQUARE USE A BRAND NEW DISHCLOTH AND CUT OPEN ONE END (THEY ARE DOUBLE THICKNESS).

Method

1. Start by juicing the fruits. I have a juice attachment on my food processor but if not squeeze out as much juice as possible and put into the pan containing 2 litres water.

2. Next, with a teaspoon, scrape out the pith and pips from the fruit and place into the pocket of the dishcloth. It is important to keep these scraps because they contain the pectin which will go on to set the marmalade. You will be left with a bag of pips and pith so tie up with string and tie onto the handle of the pan and allow it to sit in the water.

3. Next, take all the orange and lemon fruit shells and cut into thin strips. This can seem tiresome but the thinner the strips, the lovelier the marmalade with be.

4. Transfer the fruit strips into the pan then set over a high heat, bring to the boil then turn the heat down and simmer for 2 hours – yes 2 hours! The pan should have a very gently simmer only.

5. At the end of the cooking time check to make sure the strips of peel are tender and soft. In the meantime put the sugar in a large mixing bowl and place in a low oven at 100 degrees to warm it through – this will prevent the marmalade being cooled down too much when the sugar is added.

6. After the two hours – the first thing to do is remove the muslin bag, place in a bowl and allow to cool down slightly. I wear a pair of rubber gloves and carefully squeeze the bag firstly between two large plates and then between my hands to extract the lovely gooey pectin. This pectin mix needs to be dropped into the pan with the now tender orange peel. Keep going until you cannot extract any more then discard the cloth bag.

7. Carefully add the warmed sugar to the pan and stir over a gentle heat until completely dissolved. At this point I then place 2 tea plates in the freezer and my clean jars into the warm oven that had the sugar.

8. Bring the oranges and sugar up to a fast boil and keep it there for about 20 minutes. If you have a sugar thermometer the marmalade has reached its correct temperature at 104 degrees centigrade. If you don't have one then take your plate from the freezer and put a spoonful of the marmalade onto it. Wait a minute then push the cooled liquid from one end with your finger. If it crinkles then the marmalade is done – if it is still liquid then give it another 10 minutes boiling then try again with the other clean chilled plate.

9. When the marmalade is done – take off the heat and leave to stand for 20 minutes. This is important as the mix starts to thicken and then when placed in the jars the rind will not float to the top.

10. Take the warm jars from the oven and I use a Pyrex jug to pour from the pan to the jar. Place the tops on whilst still hot.

Let Me Show You...
Watch My 'Recipe' Video
SCAN HERE

End of Season Chutney

MAKES 8-10 JARS

I actually call this my 'end of season' chutney. It makes excellent use of all of my leftover tomatoes; green, red and yellow at different stages of ripeness. I have a few windfall apples in there plus onions, dried fruit and garlic. So often chutney is brown, but I make this one with granulated sugar and distilled white vinegar which results in a chutney that is colourful and vibrant... Autumn in a jar!

If you decide to make this chutney, give yourself a good few hours as it needs to simmer away gently for three and a half hours! But it's worth it.

Ingredients

FOR THE CHUTNEY:

- 1 kg tomatoes, all sizes and colours
- 1 kg apples - eating or cooking
- 1 kg onions
- 6 cloves garlic
- 200g ready to eat apricots - chopped small
- 200g golden sultanas
- 500g granulated sugar
- 1 tbsp salt
- 1.5 litres distilled white vinegar

FOR THE PASTE:

- 1.5 tsp ground allspice
- 1 tsp ground coriander
- 1/2 tsp chilli powder
- 1 tsp ground ginger
- 1 tsp ground cinnamon
- 1 tbsp turmeric
- 1 tbsp mustard seed

USE: A PRESERVING PAN OR LARGE CASSEROLE.

Nancy's Top Tip

Butter the bottom of your pan before starting to prevent chutney burning on the bottom and prevent a scum forming whilst cooking.

Method

1. Prepping this chutney will be speedy if you have a food processor.

2. Start by making the paste. Mix all the paste ingredients together with vinegar taken from the measured amount for the chutney until you have a smooth mixture about the consistency of single cream. Set aside.

3. Cut the large tomatoes into quarters and small ones in half then chop roughly in your processor with the blade attached. Transfer to the preserving pan.

4. Peel the onions, cut into quarters and chop roughly - transfer to the pan. Chop the garlic too.

5. Add the sugar, dried fruit, salt, paste and vinegar and give everything a good stir.

6. Finishing with the apples simply cut into quarters, slice out the core, cut the quarters in half and chop them in the processor too. Transfer them to the pan and stir well in. Note: I leave the apples until the last because I don't want them to brown.

7. Bring your pan to the boil then turn down and leave on a steady simmer for three and a half hours, stirring from time to time. If you feel your chutney is sticking to the base of the pan then turn the heat down a touch.

8. The chutney is cooked sufficiently when the vinegar is almost cooked off, the chutney is thick and your wooden spoon leaves a brief trail in the mix when stirred.

9. Turn off the heat and leave to cool a little then transfer to warm sterilised jars and place a lid on immediately. Label the jars when cold.

Let Me Show You...
Watch My 'Recipe' Video
SCAN HERE

Pickled Onions

If you have grown your own shallots or indeed find them cheap in the shops – try making your own pickled onions!

I give below two recipes – one easy and quick and the other traditional recipe which is still easy but not as quick.

Ingredients

EASY RECIPE:
MAKES 4 JARS

- 1 kg shallots
- 1 litre malt vinegar or white vinegar
- 25g pickling spice

Method

EASY RECIPE:

1. Place the shallots into a roomy bowl, pour over hot water and leave for five minutes then peel.
2. Place the peeled onions into jars, sprinkle over the pickling spice then pour over the vinegar making sure the onions are covered, pop on a screw top and leave for 2 months before eating.
3. These quick pickles will last 3-4 months.

Ingredients

TRADITIONAL RECIPE:
MAKES 4 JARS

- 1 kg shallots
- 1 litre white vinegar (or malt vinegar)
- 25g pickling spice

FOR THE BRINE:

- 120g table salt
- 1 litre cold water

Method

TRADITIONAL RECIPE:

1. Place the shallots in a roomy bowl, pour over hot water and leave for five minutes then peel. Put the salt into another bowl, pour over the water then pop the peeled shallots into the brine

2. Cover with a plate to make sure all the onions are submerged then leave until the next day.

3. In a saucepan place the pickling spice and add the vinegar. Bring to a fast boil and cook for 3 minutes then take off the heat and allow to cool completely.

4. Strain the onions from the brine and dry on tea towels then pack into four jars.

5. Pour the cold spiced vinegar over the onions and divide the spices left behind between the jars.

6. Cover with a screw top and keep a month before eating. These pickled onions will keep for a year.

Let Me Show You...
Watch My 'Recipe' Video
SCAN HERE

Fresh Tomato Sauce

YIELDS 1.5KG TOMATO SAUCE

If you grow your own tomatoes and the middle of August you have a glut – make a batch of this delicious, thick tasty sauce which then is frozen in clean 300ml plastic cream or yoghurt containers and frozen. This is then used as a base for pizzas, bolognese, lasagne, moussaka or any recipes that calls for a tin of tomatoes.

Ingredients

- 2 kg fresh tomatoes
- 3 tbsp olive oil or rapeseed oil
- 2 onions chopped
- 4 cloves garlic chopped
- 1 ½ tbsp mixed herbs
- 100ml red wine (optional)
- salt and pepper
- 2 tbsp sugar

Method

1. Start by skinning the tomatoes which may seem tedious with so many tomatoes, but it is worth it because the skins are tough and unpleasant.

2. Slit each tomato at its base with a sharp knife. Do this twice making a cross.

3. Place the tomatoes in a large bowl then pour boiling water over. Leave for about 2-3 minutes then pour off the water.

4. Starting at the base of the tomato where you have made the cross, carefully peel off the skins. They should come off easily especially if the tomatoes are really ripe.

5. In a very large casserole pan, heat the oil then add the chopped onion and fry gently for about 10 minutes until they have softened.

6. Add the herbs, sugar and garlic and stir well before adding first the red wine, salt and pepper and finally the tomatoes. I tend to cut the tomatoes in half.

7. Turn up the heat and bring everything to a bubble then turn down the heat maintaining a gentle simmer and leave uncovered for one and a half hours. Stir occasionally.

8. If you would like a really smooth passata then give a quick blitz with a stick blender. Taste for seasoning – you should have a very thick sauce.

9. Leave to cool in the pan then freeze in containers as above.

Hints and Tips

FOR A SUSTAINABLE HOUSEHOLD

When I consider the number of labour saving machines and appliances there are now, compared to fifty years ago I am surprised I don't have more time on my hands. No longer do women find themselves spending all day Monday on the washing, hand making bread, pastry and clothing. We now enjoy a whole range of equipment which speed things up.

Modern living is however starting to take its toll – our over use of single use plastics, harmful chemicals and a general 'throw away' culture is now proving to be creating problems of global warming, pollution of our planet and a non sustainable use of raw materials.

Since the 1st January 2019 I stopped using cling film which for me was one of those single use plastics that is proving to be a real problem in our waterways as it breaks down into tiny particles which then are eaten by fish and wildlife and absorbed into all manner of things – even our drinking water!

This chapter is dedicated to introducing a number of alternatives to single use plastic, some natural cleaning alternatives for even the toughest of stains and a few hints and tips that make everyday life that much cleaner and simpler.

Nancy

Let Me Show You...
Watch My 'Upcycling' Video
SCAN HERE

CLING FILM

I was certainly the 'cling film queen' – I loved it and used metres of it. Wrapping of sandwiches, vegetables, cheese, pastry for resting, bread for proving, bowls of hot and cold food – you name it, it probably had cling film wrapped around it. I then realised I needed to change, after all – I can actually remember the days when cling film didn't exist so all I needed to do was go back in time. Greaseproof paper is very good as an alternative until I discovered the beeswax wrap!

Beeswax wraps are now hitting the market at an alarming rate. They are pieces of cotton fabric, usually in various sizes and patterns which have been coated both sides with beeswax and can be used to wrap food, sandwiches, cheese etc. The heat from the hands holds the wrap in place and your food is covered securely and can be stored in the fridge, keep your sandwiches fresh and to cover pots of food etc.. They can be washed between use and be used again and again.

They can be expensive – retailing in some places for around £5 each... Unless – you make your own for as little as 70p!

All you need to do is buy a packet of Beeswax pellets – mine cost about £4 and I bought them online. Don't be tempted to use candle wax – candles contain petroleum.

1. Heat the oven to 180 degrees. Choose your cotton fabric then cut into various sizes using pinking shears. The pinking gives an attractive finish to your wrap and will prevent fraying. I had some gingham cotton fabric in red and green and these made great little wraps.

2. Make one wrap at a time. Lay the cotton flat in the base of a lipped baking tin then scatter a handful of beeswax pellets over. Don't worry about how many you should use because any surplus will run off the fabric. Pop the tin, beeswax and fabric into the oven for 1-2 minutes.

3. Take it out of the oven and the wax will have melted – it will look like oil and will have soaked into your cotton. With gloved hands or using two pairs of tongs lift the fabric by two corners and allow surplus wax to run off. Continue to hold the fabric

above the tin for a minute or two and very quickly the fabric will cool down and the wax will set. That's it – you have your very own beeswax wrap.

4. Set aside and continue to make your other wraps using the same method, adding further wax pellets as necessary.

Any wax left in the base of your tin after making your wraps should be left to set and then scraped off using a metal scraper then popped back into the bag to use for later. Don't be tempted to pour liquid wax down the sink – you will block it.

TO REFRESH YOUR BEESWAX WRAPS

With regular use, your wraps will develop fold lines, the beeswax may start to feel gritty and your wrap may look a little careworn.

Don't be tempted to throw it away. Simply lay your wraps, one at a time on a lipped baking tray and pop into a preheated over at 180 degrees for just 1 minute.. The wax will melt. You can take your wrap by two corners (with gloves on), lift it up and you will see it is well coated in beeswax once more. The creases have disappeared and they look like new.

Let Me Show You...
Watch My 'Reuseable Wrap Tip' Video
SCAN HERE

CLEAN YOUR IRON INSIDE AND OUTSIDE

If you live in a hard water area like me then your steam iron will get a build up of limescale if you use tap water (which I do) rather than distilled water.

Your steam iron jets will start to splutter and at worst will spit out brown water which can stain your best silk blouse! My iron holds 250ml water so I make up a solution of one half water and the other half lemon juice and pour that into the iron. Have to hand an old towel, folded up on the draining board. Turn the iron on at the mains then when it has come to temperature turn it plate side down onto the folded towel. It will splutter and the solution will spit out. Turn the iron off at the mains and leave your iron plate face down on the towel overnight.

The next day drain the solution out of iron, there may be brown stains on your towel. Rinse the iron in a few changes using clean water then fill, switch on and use the old towel again to absorb the steam. The steam jets of your iron will now be clean and free flowing.

In the olden days (as my children describe them) and before the introduction of man-made-polyesters and nylon an iron that was too hot would scorch a brown stain on cotton. These days an iron slightly too hot will just shrivel up and wither the finest polyester blouse or shirt. The remains stick to the plate of the iron and the garment is ruined. What to do about the iron? The plate has black plastic stuck to it!!

It can be rescued and returned to its former glory. You will need a wooden spatula or spoon (not plastic) then turn the iron on at the mains and once hot turn it off. Then, using the wooden tool gently rub away at the burnt on plastic. Whilst the iron is warm the plastic will just rub off onto the spatula. If it becomes stubborn after a short while, simply turn the iron on again, allow to heat up, turn off and repeat.

Once all the plastic has been rubbed off you will probably be left with brown staining to the plate. Make sure the iron is switched off, unplugged and cold. Mix a solution of baking powder and lemon juice and rub this over the cold iron plate. If any of the paste gets into the steam jets, gently lower the plate into warm water whilst the paste is still wet and rinse off any remaining. Don't submerge your iron in water, just gently lower the plate so that it is just touching the water, enough to rinse away any paste.

Dry the plate thoroughly – job done!

Let Me Show You...
Watch My 'Clean Iron Tip' Video
SCAN HERE

HOW TO CLEAN A DECANTER OR VASE

Are you puzzled as to how to clean a narrow necked glass decanter or vase without resorting to sterilising liquid or bleach? Wine decanters can be very badly stained at the base where residue has dried and flower vases often go brown at the base for the same reason.

All you need to do is place a few tablespoons of sand in the base and cover it with warm water, 2 tbsp lemon juice or vinegar and then swirl away. Keep shaking and swirling, leave to soak overnight then repeat. Discard and rinse away the sand and your glass vessel will be sparkling and clean. No harmful chemicals used at all.

TAKING CARE OF YOUR WASHING MACHINE

The automatic washing machine is now part of life – long gone are the days of twin tubs, wringers and mangles and Monday washday. The washing machine is so often taken for granted then the day it starts to misbehave has us in a flat panic! Regular care will ensure your washing machine continues to perform well all of its natural life. I was told when I bought my last one that five years is maximum life I could expect yet, (fingers crossed) it is still going strong at seven years even though it is used most days, deals with the dirtiest working clothes and has to operate in a hard water area.

My regular maintenance is simple. I use washing soda every single wash unless I am doing one of those 30 minute quick refresh cycles. I believe it doesn't really have time to dissolve so I don't bother. I add about a cupful in the detergent drawer every wash. Washing soda is inexpensive, around £1 for a kilogram bag and it softens the water, works on grease and grime and prevents limescale build up. If you have ever encountered grey streaks on your clean white sheets this is due to soap scum trapped in the seal around the washing machine door being dislodged as you pull your sheets out of the washer. Regular use of washing soda will prevent this soap scum.

When you pull out the detergent drawer of your machine you may be alarmed at the build up of black mould and slime. This is due to liquid detergent and in particular fabric softener being left in the dispenser. My washing machine was a disgrace. I took out the detergent dispenser and gave it a soak in hot water and washing soda. All that mould and unused fabric detergent just lifted off and the plastic drawer was as good as new. When I looked inside the drawer hole the problem was just as bad. I took an old toothbrush along with a cup of white vinegar and started to scrub away at the filth. After some minutes the whole lot was gleaming and white once again! I decided this would not happen again – so, I have dispensed with bought fabric conditioner. When I looked on the bottle the synthetic chemicals contained in there alarmed me so I decided to make my own environmentally friendly alternative.

TO MAKE 500ML NATURAL FABRIC CONDITIONER

- 200ml white vinegar (cuts through detergent)
- 200ml water
- 15 ml vegetable glycerine (for softening)
- 15 drops lemon oil (for perfume)

Place all the ingredients in a bottle (I used a plastic vinegar bottle) and give a shake. Then use 50-100 ml per cycle. My washing routine now is as follows :-

1. Cup of washing soda in the detergent drawer
2. Natural fabric conditioner in the conditioner compartment
3. Liquid detergent is poured into the lid of the bottle of detergent (as a measure) and the whole lot (lid and detergent) put with the clothes in the machine.
4. Result: Well cared for washing machine, no soap scum, no filth whatsoever in the detergent drawer and clean stain free laundry.

LAUNDRY

COLLARS AND CUFFS

I remember clearly when my children were at school. Each day they wore a clean white shirt and at the end of each day they were always grubby around the collar and cuffs. Rather than an overnight soak or the need to buy special stain removing sprays just drizzle a line of washing up liquid straight from the bottle along the line of the dirt then rub it in and leave for a minute or two. Pop it into the washing machine and your shirts will be returned to their former glory.

FLUFFY TOWELS

I am old enough to remember using terry towelling nappies for my babies and it was every mother's pride and joy to see a line of super white fluffy nappies blowing on the line in the sunshine. When the weather was cold and windy the nappies were their softest and fluffiest but not so soft and fluffy when the weather was still and hot – they baked dry on the line.
Of course, the same applies to towels and so this is what you need to do...

Take your towels from the washing machine and take them outside and if the weather is windy and cold all will be fine. Peg them on the line. If the conditions are not then you will need to do a full workout.

Take one end of the towel and hold both corners then give that towel the biggest shake for a minute or two. Take then the other end of the towel and do the same. Your vigorous shake will loosen the pile and your towels will dry soft and fluffy whatever the weather.

I do realise so many readers do not dry their laundry outside due to lack of space or no garden but I would still routinely give them a good shake however you dry them.

NATURAL STAIN REMOVAL

With so many products on the market that will "do the job" of removing the worst stains, we tend to ignore the fact that there are cheaper, safer and 'eco-friendly' solutions sitting there on our cupboard shelf.

BLOOD STAINS

Blood stains are probably the most stubborn to remove and if not treated correctly they will become permanent stains on your sheets, clothing or towels. If you have an old blood stain that has been washed and didn't come off, you may have it forever.

Fresh blood spills should be plunged straight into cold water and left to soak until the blood has lifted from the fabric. Any residual mark should just be rubbed with salt then popped into the washing machine on a cool wash with detergent.

Dried in blood stains can be more problematic and these will "fix" on a hot wash if not treated beforehand. Rinse the dried stain under the cold tap or dampen with cold water then sprinkle ordinary table salt over the stain. Give the salt a rub into the blood stain and leave for 30 minutes. You will see the blood stain start to pale in colour and dissolve away. Don't rinse the salt off just pop into the washing machine on a 30 degree wash and your stain will remove.

One of my followers messaged me to say that a mattress had become badly stained with blood following a leaking leg wound after an operation. I suggested she make a very strong solution of equal parts salt and water. Dissolve the salt into the water by bringing the water to the boil, stirring in the salt until the solution was clear. Allow it to cool completely then get to work. She messaged me to say it had worked and she was delighted!

GREASE STAINS

I should always wear an apron when working in the kitchen and I so often forget. I have a favourite waistcoat that I have had for years and when frying I noted I had grease spots (lots of them!) down the front. They were so noticeable I just had to get to work to restore my favourite garment to its former glory. A blob of washing up liquid or any dish detergent will dissolve grease readily. I popped a drop over each splash, rubbed it in, left it for 20 minutes then popped the garment into the washing machine.

SWEAT AND DEODORANT MARKS

Coloured shirts particularly can suffer from white stains left from dried sweat and deodorant. The best treatment for this is a solution of baking powder mixed with lemon juice then dab this onto the stain. Leave for just 10-15 minutes before popping into the washing machine.

BIRO AND FELT TIP PENS

Children are probably the main culprits when it comes to stains from pen, biro and felt tip pens. Some permanent markers may be impossible to remove particularly if they have been there a long time. Quick attack on stains is often the best remover. Let us say we have an ink mark on a white school shirt.

1. First of all place an old towel under the stain because you don't want it to transfer to a clean part of the white shirt whilst you are trying to remove it.
2. Start by wetting the stained area with cold water then rub in a paste made from baking powder mixed with lemon juice. I use a finger to rub in circular motions until the mark starts to lift.
3. If the pen or ink is still present then I have found that rubbing a dishwasher tablet over the stain (in the way that you would use a pencil eraser) will gradually lift the mark.
4. Don't rinse but transfer straight into the washing machine for a thorough clean.

LEATHER RESTORER
(USE ON ANY LEATHER GOODS ANY COLOUR)

I have a dark brown, leather sofa. It is many years old now and it always used to be periodically given a service! It suffers from light damage which results in cracking and fading and in the past I have bought leather restoration kits – some retailing for as much as £30 a time. My latest project used my home-made "Nancy's Natural Nurture" and whilst it started as an experiment it has proved to be a beautiful, inexpensive, long lasting treatment for leather.

I started by working on covering up the scratches and marks, so I used a dark brown food colour gel mixed with a little water and worked this into the leather using cotton wool. This solution covered up as I went along. Be sure to test for colour match on a hidden area first before you start and work it well in, so there are no streaks. I allowed this stainer to soak in and dry and then applied my finish.

* 50ml rapeseed or olive oil – to moisturise
* 20ml vegetable glycerine – to soften
* 50 drops of lemon oil – with anti fungal properties to perfume and condition

Put the above ingredients into a screw top jar and give a good shake and then apply with cotton wool. Leather that has become really dry may need 2-3 coats – allow 2 hours between each application. The treatment soaks in and whilst it may look oily and sticky when first applied will soon be absorbed and you will be left with a plush soft leather.

Let Me Show You...
Watch My 'Leather Tip' Video
SCAN HERE

CLEAN SILVER AND BRASS

Many branded cleaners for silver and brass now carry a warning stating 'toxic to aquatic organisms and dangerous to the environment' and whilst many of them have been around for one hundred years, and are very effective I thought I must try a natural alternative.

I have a brass fender around the fireplace which gets very badly tarnished. Mixing a paste of baking powder and lemon juice was enough to clean it! I dabbed the thick paste over the fender and just left it to dry. I then took a dry green pan scourer and gently worked on rubbing at the dry paste and the fender came up a treat. I used a vacuum cleaner to then take up the powder, washed it all over with warm soapy water then polished it dry with a duster. The tarnish isn't quick to reappear either.

Silver needs to be treated with a little more respect because it can easily scratch. Dab the baking powder and lemon juice paste all over and rub with cotton wool to clean. For stubborn tarnish allow the paste to dry on then use a soft cloth to gently rub any stubborn stains. Baking powder just on it's own will clean silver that is not so badly tarnished. A cloth, a little water and baking powder worked into the silver will clean it up as new.

CLEAN COPPER PANS WHILE YOU SLEEP

I have a set of copper pans which will last a life time and they look beautiful when they are clean but once tarnished they can be quite unsightly. I used to buy a very expensive paste which cleaned them up a treat but they need doing regularly if they are to stay sparkling. Once again I worked on a natural cleaning option for copper and this one is fantastic as it will get to work on your tarnished copper while you sleep.

You will need a large plastic bucket or a vessel large enough to accommodate your largest pan. You simply need equal amounts of coca cola and malt vinegar. Submerge the pan and leave overnight. The next day, take from the solution and polish up using a paste made up of baking powder and lemon juice – your pan will be like new!

Repeat the next night with another pan and use the solution over and over again. Although after six pans my solution was starting to loose its umph!

Let Me Show You...
Watch My 'Copper Pans Tip' Video
SCAN HERE

SLOW FLOW SINK

The dreaded soap scum can slow down the flow of your sink, particularly in bathrooms. A cheap and easy remedy, no need to go out and buy branded unblockers, is as follows:-

- 1 cup washing soda (sodium carbonate)
- 200ml boiling water

Place the washing soda in a Pyrex jug then pour over the boiling water and when everything is well dissolved, pour the solution directly down the plug hole of the sink. Put the plug in and leave it overnight. The next day, remove the plug, pour down a kettle of boiling water and your sink will be free flowing again.

CLEANING THE FRIDGE

I find the fridge is easy to keep clean – a regular wipe of the shelves and sides with hot water and dish detergent is enough to keep things fresh. Keep an eye on foodstuffs - ensuring there are no leaks or smells and on a weekly basis that is often all it needs. However, on closer inspection there may be other problems.

HAVE YOU CHECKED THE DOOR SEALS FOR MOULD?

This is a common problem and if not treated will build up and where food storage is concerned – fresh food and mould should be kept well apart. This can be cleaned naturally and easily. I have to confess I had a bad case of fridge mould on my door seals and cleaned this off effectively and beautifully using only natural products. To clean off the surface mould I used a solution of baking powder/bicarbonate of soda and lemon juice mixed to a paste. This removed about three quarters of the offending mould but I was still left with stains. Simple table salt and a damp cloth then whipped through the residual mould and my fridge was sweet and beautiful once more.

Let Me Show You...
Watch My 'Fridge Mould Tip' Video
SCAN HERE

HAVE YOU NOTICED THAT YOUR FRIDGE KEEPS FREEZING UP AT THE BACK?

Most fridges nowadays have automatic defrosting which will only work efficiently if that little drain hole and hose at the base of the fridge is kept free flowing. Any particle of food fixed down into that hole will block it, your fridge will probably start to smell and the back will freeze up because the little hole and drain hose at the back has become blocked.

1. First of all remove the plastic plunger as this may have collected most of the debris. Wash it and set aside.

2. Next you need to get down into that hole to collect the rest of the grey slimy mess. Refrain from using plastic cotton buds. I use a piece of kitchen paper and wrap it around a cocktail stick or metal skewer then get this into the hole and lift out the offending debris.

Keep turning the paper around to find a clean part and keep going until the paper is clean. Replace the cleaned plunger and your fridge will return to proper functioning.

CLEANING THE TEAPOT
(AND TEA STAINS FROM MUGS, CLOTHING, TABLE CLOTHS ETC...)

I am an old fashioned tea drinker! I love my teapot and I prefer tea leaves (which are compostable, while some tea bags contain plastic) – oh - and I adore a china mug!

However, tea contains tannin which gives tea its colour. Tannin is also used as an agent in many dyes, hence the reason that a stain is left in teapots and cups. Don't be tempted to reach for the bleach to clean your teapot or cups. Follow this simple method and your teapot will clean quickly and naturally and no need to soak.

1. Take your teapot and rinse it around in warm water then pour the water out. The inside of the teapot needs to be wet.

2. Next take 2 tbsp baking powder or bicarbonate of soda and drop that into the pot then swirl your pot around so that the baking powder adheres up the sides and down the spout.

3. Take then a tbsp. lemon juice (a jiffy lemon will do) and pop that in. I then get my hands in and agitate that lemon juice and bicarb together and you will see the tannin just lifts off. I use my hands to get into every nook and crannie (down the spout, around the rim at the top and along the moulding at the base).

4. Rinse under warm water then wash in soapy water – job done!

RUST STAINS

Rust stains can appear on carpets often from old furniture which have metal casters. Rust marks can also appear on vintage clothing or curtaining. I had a very badly rust-marked new carpet caused by my dog Wilfred when he was a puppy. He found an old rusty brillo pad (scouring wire wool pad) and brought it inside, tore it to shreds and managed to scatter every speck of rust well into the pale carpet.

My first thoughts were to use the vacuum cleaner to suck up the rust particles but this seemed to make things worse and spread the rust even further. I decided to then make a bowl of solution using equal amounts of salt, lemon juice and white vinegar. I then used a clean damp cloth to dab this solution all over the stain – the carpet was quite damp. Leave the carpet then for four hours. After that time you can use kitchen towel and I found the best method was to lay pieces over the stain and then stand on them. My footprint lifted a heavy brown rusty stain away from the carpet. Keep repeating using clean paper until the rust has lifted completely and the carpet is dry.

STICKY LABELS ON JARS

I hang onto pretty jars and bottles so that I always have them to hand when I am ready to make jams and chutneys. How annoying is it when there are remnants of the previous sticky label that just will not come off. You have soaked the jar, popped it into the dishwasher but still that sticky mark persists.

Rather than reach for smelly solvents – try this.

1. Take 1 tbsp baking powder (bicarbonate of soda) and about 1 tbsp oil (vegetable oil is fine).
2. Dip a cloth into the oil and then into the baking powder then rub this mix onto the sticky label mark.
3. Give it a gentle rub, applying a little more to make sure the whole label is well covered.
4. Leave for 5 minutes then return to the jar – rub again with the cloth and you will feel the sticky label has disappeared.
5. Rinse in warm soapy water and your jar is sparkly and ready to be reused.

Let Me Show You...
Watch My 'Fluffy Towel Tip' Video
SCAN HERE

Let Me Show You...
Watch My 'Shiny Taps Tip' Video
SCAN HERE

Let Me Show You...
Watch My 'Lining Paste Tip' Video
SCAN HERE

Let Me Show You...
Watch My 'Clean Sink' Video
SCAN HERE

Let Me Show You...
Watch My 'Clean Oven Tip' Video
SCAN HERE

P.S...

WHY I DECIDED TO WRITE THIS BOOK...

I was sitting in front of my computer at 5am and already I had 'writer's block'. It's not that there was no story or insufficient data. It's not even that I had to fumble around the keyboard, because I can 'touch type'. I learnt that at school along with Pitman shorthand, where I used to be the fastest in class (120 wpm and I can still do it now).

Isn't it astounding that facts, skills, lessons and experiences gained when we were young, somehow manage to stick in the brain? Whereas things we want to remember which were learnt recently have to be constantly recalled, written down or worse still, get simply forgotten.

So, who is Nancy Birtwhistle? Nancy is 65 years of age and living her life just like everyone else, except that looking back I realise I have done an awful lot and I have been around a long time. Like so many people, I have a circle of family who are extremely important to me. I also have a group of close friends who have been around me for many years. They know who they are, and they also know how each of us can pick up the phone at any time to discuss a whole range of 'people stories' and crisis that affect our day to day struggles, and how to try to put these things right.

My life is rich, however richness for me does not mean money ~ it suggests a wealth of experience and knowledge that has often come about because I have made many mistakes and at times, been very short of cash!

Being short of money makes people extremely resourceful and totally averse to waste, and for some years now we have all been guilty of enjoying our throw away culture ~ the results of which are presenting themselves now as we all battle to save our planet.

I am sometimes asked, "Where did you learn this?" Or, "How do you know that?" Often the answer is that I have just picked things up along the way. I have worked all of my adult life and in the 1970s when I was a young mother, going back to work when there was a child in the family, was not always met with approval. However, with two children under five and being short of cash, I decided to apply for jobs. I regularly met with rejection, even for evening work and for someone with good secretarial qualifications... This nearly drove me nuts!

Finally, I was interviewed by someone who has since gone on to be one of my dear friends ~ Joan. She too had children and held down a responsible job. She gave me the chance of a part-time position and from then on I continued to work. I soon moved from part-time to full-time employment and embarked on a course of study culminating in a University Masters' Degree (at the age of 40) and continued to move up the career ladder until I retired.

By the time I got into my fifth decade my plan was to enjoy some free time. I had worked for over 30 years full time in the National Health Service, so I wanted to enjoy more of my garden, spend time with family and friends and have more holidays. The trouble is that after just six months I was bored. There is only a certain amount of gardening to do before one gets obsessive about every tiny weed which shows its first pair of leaves. Not only that, but grandchildren misbehave when they see you regularly and holidays and travelling for me lost their appeal, when there wasn't the need to escape the daily slog of going to work. Yet I had done it, I had retired!

I would take myself off to the shops during the day when all the young people were at work, consequently I was surrounded by old retired people, with no-one to talk to. I missed the camaraderie, the laughter, chat, moans and groans and even the work! Was I ready for this?

Of course I found plenty of housework tasks to do on most days. The trouble is that an obsessiveness creeps in and once the bathroom has been cleaned ~ I dared anyone to use it! I found Thursdays to be quite a good day, as that became my day and I would do something different to housework and gardening. Maybe a hairdo, a trip to the shops, or simply a pamper day.
I would spend time making myself look the best I possibly could, to then take the dogs out, get soaking wet with rain coming back in a worse state than before I started. However, Thursdays soon morphed into my kitchen days.

I LOVE FOOD. GROWING ~ COOKING ~ BAKING ~ EATING!

I understand how to grow my own food, how to get the best flavour from food, how to cook on a budget and how to feed a family.

MAYBE I AM A MODERN-DAY HOUSEWIFE?!

Having worked full-time I know how hard it is to come home after 5pm with a family waiting to be fed, whilst feeling tired and hungry myself. I know what it is like to be a single mum when payday arrives and after all expenses have been taken off there is very little left, and certainly not enough to pay for a new washing machine which then has to go onto the credit card.

SAVINGS ACCOUNT? WHAT'S THAT?

I understand that buying in bulk saves money but having just enough for essentials makes it impossible to buy in bulk and even if you can, maybe the kitchen is so small there is nowhere to store it.

BACK TO MY THURSDAYS. I STARTED TO BAKE AND COOK...

I had always baked and cooked to feed a family but not with any finesse or style. I had a number of recipes stuck in my head that tended to be churned out on a weekly basis. Thursdays, however, became a day of new things. I had started to watch The Bake Off and my Sister-in-Law suggested I watch it. I had missed Series 1 and 2 but tuned into Series 3 and I loved it, so much so that I decided Thursdays would become 'Technical Challenge Day'. Whatever had been the technical challenge for that week would be my task and I soon realised I was quite good. Having said that, there was no tent or camera, no time constraint and no nerves.

Baking then became an obsession because like anything ~ the more you know ~ the more there is to know. Reading, practising, failing, then succeeding became the norm. Before long, one day just wasn't enough time! I was finding time to bake most days, and no-one ever complained of course as there is always someone willing to take cake, pastry or bread off your hands! Baking had now given me a purpose and the motivation to apply for the show. I filled in and submitted the form by the due date and was shocked, thrilled and excited to be invited for an audition. So audition one was done and then to be invited for a second ~ well that was it...

I was convinced I would be accepted! My bakes were a success and for this audition I had to take bread and scones but shock horror ~ Mr Hollywood told me my bread was under- proved. WHAT?

Devastated but not undeterred, I spent a year practising my bread-making and applied again, this time for Series 5. The rest, you may have heard or probably seen for yourself. I believe the Final was watched by some 13,000,000 viewers in the UK alone and is now watched all over the world thanks to Netflix.

Winning Bake Off changed my life. Instantly I was taken out of retirement. I was meeting people, speaking to large audiences and going into schools and colleges. I was addressing groups of all ages as Bake Off is a family show. I was being interviewed on the TV and Radio and demonstrating at food shows and events and even booked as entertainment on a cruise! I was recognised wherever I went, and I soon realised that I loved an audience!
Unlike boardroom meetings, staff presentations and motivational talks that I gave when I was working ~ this was different. Gone were the glum faces, tired and oppressed by the ever-changing rules, regulations and ways of working which is the norm in the public sector. Instead I could see that my audiences were interested in what I had to say, they were listening. My stories and self-deprecating experiences made people laugh. They had questions ~ lots of questions about problem solving, mistakes and their own disasters and I seemed to have the answers! My motivation then became the sharing of tips, hints, short-cuts and rescues that turn problems into positives.

Since February 2017 social media has become my biggest platform. I have shared every hint, tip, 'how to video' or recipe, every day. I cover a whole range of topics and since then, my followers have asked for a book. Somewhere to go to reference these valuable nuggets. Whether you are a baker, cook, housewife, gardener, young or old, there will be something of interest to you.

That's little potted history about me... Now let's get back to this book!
Housekeeping is probably described as the world's oldest industry and as a word seems a little dated. Having said that, we all do it. Even today with modern technology and labour saving devices, fast living and each member of the household going out to work ~

the house still needs a carer. In any era and at any social level if the house is cared for, then the occupants will also be comfortable, healthy and well catered for too.

Food is fantastic, we all need it and I for one am obsessed by it. I am always thinking about the next meal. Am I cooking from scratch today? Will it be something out of the freezer that I had made in bulk earlier? Will it be a quick omelette or snack? Whatever it is, I always know what will be on the menu each day. The worst scenario is to come home cold, wet and hungry and the fridge hasn't got anything of substance, so it has to be a takeaway or a ready meal! My hope is that this book will help in so many ways. I am going to teach you how to make the best pastry and avoid those pitfalls that so often lead to soggy bottoms and tough crusts. You will find life changing tips to make your baking and cooking experiences much easier and simpler.

I describe in detail the various cake baking methods and slip in a few favourite recipes along the way. A sinking cake and split buttercream will be a thing of the past. Breads and biscuits feature too, with tips to ensure success every time.

There is a number of simple 'pennywise' nutritious meals and I devote time too to those readers whose food allergy or diet can make cooking and baking a little more challenging. I have included great recipes for my gluten free, vegan, fat free and sugar free readers.

Cooking and baking can be a messy business, so I present a number of cleaning tips and short-cuts ~ I even explain how to clean your oven whilst you sleep… You can keep the lid on that jar of elbow grease!

LAST BUT BY NO MEANS LEAST IS OUR ENVIRONMENT...

Since 1st January 2019 I have stopped using single use plastic cling film. I have a number of alternatives to suggest, including great little beeswax wraps that can be made at home. I explain how to make your own environmentally safe cleaners for brass, copper, limescale removal plus how to keep your washing machine clean and sweet by making your own aquatic safe fabric softener.

Those friends who have been following me on social media will know what this book is about because you have been asking for it. I have taken the most popular content and written it up for you.

Please enjoy my work.

Nancy

Acknowledgements

This book has taken some significant time to plan, structure and write. It has seen every emotion in me; frustration, fatigue, fun, fear and now friendship. I adore this book.

There are a number of people I have to thank – without them my thoughts, aspirations and instincts could not have materialised.

My publisher Daisa & Co. They absorbed my ideas and enthusiasm and have skilfully held on to all of those elements when devising and structuring this gorgeous book. This small friendly team have it all – professionalism, expertise and an accessibility which I found invaluable as a first time author.

My agent and friends at Yellow Poppy Media. They have supported, advised and signposted me for the past five years and continue to instil in me the fact that quality counts.

My website and IT support at Codebase Consulting. Patience is required when dealing with me and IT. My raw thoughts and aspirations and the need to be able to incorporate video access, integrate my website and generally make everything work has been done seamlessly.

My photographer Pink Feet Photography who patiently and expertly captured the essence of "what I am" on the cover and pages of this book.

My followers for whom without the continued support, engagement and encouragement I doubt a book would ever have materialised.

My Instagram "bestie" Jonathan Van Ness for taking the time out of his epic schedule and engagements to have a look at my posts every day, offering the best feedback and writing the most amazing Foreword.

My family members and close friends – they are always there for me!

Last but by no means least – him indoors! Tim has that ability to never lose sight of what is important in life. He takes away the stresses, carries the bags, does the washing up, upgrades computers and phones, manages the paperwork - enabling me to do what I do!

Thanks Everyone x

BAKE OFF